IMAGES
of America

BRIDGEPORT

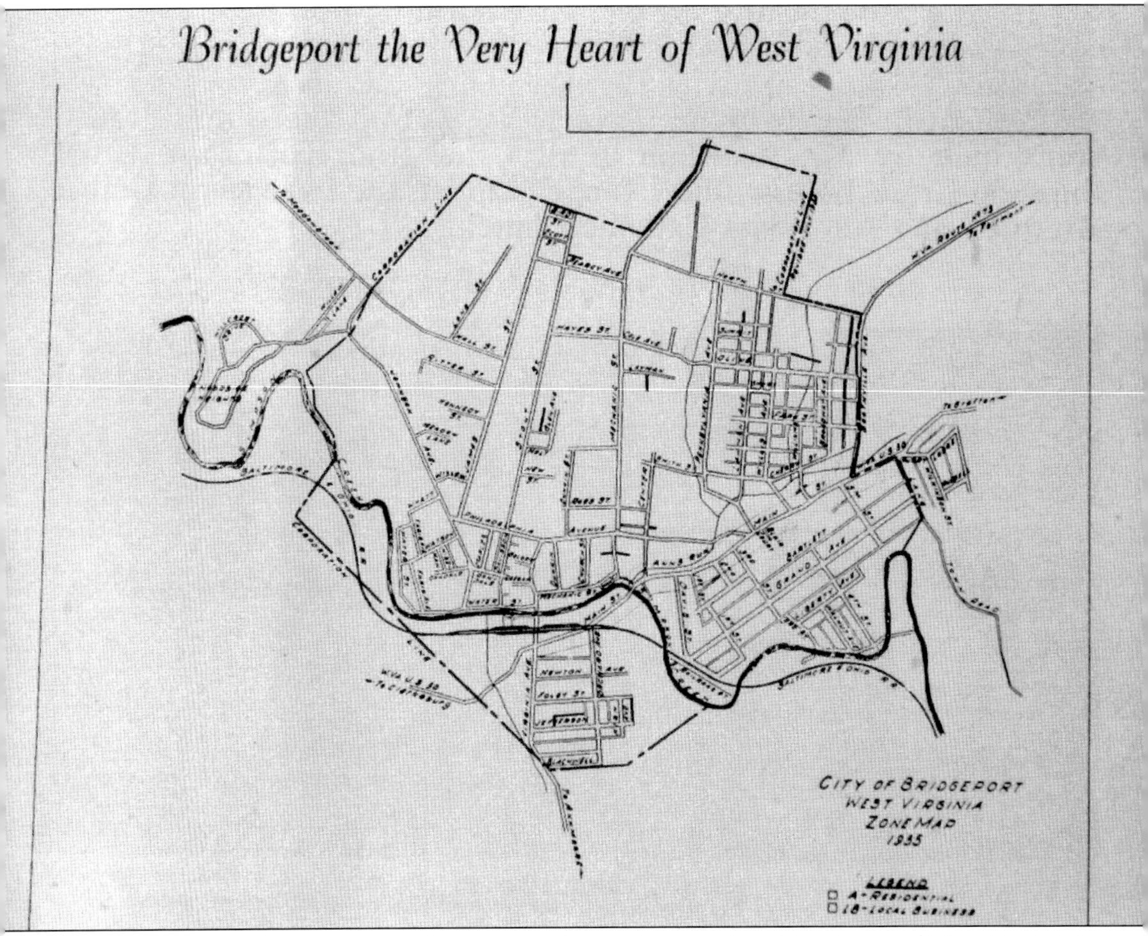

This is a map of the city of Bridgeport—as the words state, "the Very Heart of West Virginia." This map was issued in 1955, about the time the city began its pattern of constant growth and never looked back. (Courtesy of Dick Duez.)

ON THE COVER: The progress of Bridgeport, West Virginia, began from a time such as this, when businessmen moved around on horse-drawn carriages over dirt, mud, and sometimes snow. The following pages will illustrate the forward direction that the city has ceaselessly taken over scores of years to reach where it is today. (Courtesy of Dick Duez.)

IMAGES
of America

BRIDGEPORT

Robert F. Stealey

ARCADIA
PUBLISHING

ISBN 978-0-7385-5302-3

Published by Arcadia Publishing
Charleston, South Carolina

Printed in the United States of America

Library of Congress Catalog Card Number: 2007929906

For all general information contact Arcadia Publishing at:
Telephone 843-853-2070
Fax 843-853-0044
E-mail sales@arcadiapublishing.com
For customer service and orders:
Toll-Free 1-888-313-2665

Visit us on the Internet at www.arcadiapublishing.com

This book is dedicated to my friends, Dick and Norma Duez of Bridgeport, West Virginia, without whose unfailing assistance in every aspect of the book's preparation, it never would have become possible.

Contents

ACKNOWLEDGMENTS

Although I dedicated this book to a fine couple who are longtime residents of Bridgeport, I'd certainly be remiss if I didn't once again mention Dick and Norma Duez and express my most sincere thanks to them for their painstakingly reading over my many lists of images and their proper placement on these pages. Their patience with my late telephone calls and my quizzing their knowledge of Bridgeport people and places, as well as their seemingly endless supply of photographs for use in the book, were much appreciated.

Bob Nichols, formerly of Bridgeport and now residing in Alabama, was quite instrumental in providing some photographs in his collection for inclusion in this book. He once owned the Bell Studio of Photography in Bridgeport.

I also gleaned various items of information from the booklet *Bridgeport: The Town and Its People* by Avis Caynor and *Two Hundred Years in Bridgeport* by Adelaide Pence and her fourth and fifth graders.

Phil Dye of the Bridgeport Fire Department also provided Dick Duez with information about the fire department from past years.

Last but not least, I'm appreciative once again to my wife, Nadine, for putting up with me in my process of compiling images and information for the book.

INTRODUCTION

To some people, Bridgeport has been regarded as a bedroom community of Clarksburg. If that is true, then the bedroom is constantly growing.

In reality, Bridgeport has become one of the most rapidly growing towns or cities in the northern half of West Virginia. U.S. census figures show Bridgeport's population as 7,475 in 2000, another increase.

The center of the city is about five miles east of Clarksburg and around 30 miles south of Morgantown. Interstate 79 passes from north to south on the western fringe of Bridgeport, and the city is at the eastern terminus of the very busy four-lane U.S. 50, also known as Corridor D.

Bridgeport does not have, nor has it ever had, what one might consider a "downtown," yet it has more businesses operating on its Main Street than cities that do have a downtown in north central West Virginia.

The Meadowbrook Mall, which opened its doors in the fall of 1982, is within Bridgeport's corporate limits. Its anchor stores are J. C. Penney, Sears, Elder-Beerman, and Target, with a large food court and a variety of stores.

One of Harrison County's very first strip shopping centers was Valley Hills, which opened in 1962 and remains a busy place today. In addition, there's another shopping center that includes a new Home Depot store, and a short distance away is Holiday Plaza, named for the nearby Holiday Inn.

Bridgeport has a high school, a middle school, and two elementary schools. Bridgeport High School has turned out many students of high scholastic achievement, as well as athletic teams that perennially stand at or near the top of their leagues. Most team photographs have been kept out of the book, so as to avoid favoring one over another.

Numerous professional people have established their practices in Bridgeport, including doctors, lawyers, engineers, and others.

The city boasts exceptional fire and police departments and has a low crime rate, as well as minimal fire loss because of quick response by those departments.

Bridgeport is the birthplace of quite a few well-known individuals, such as Michael Late Benedum, who made his fortune in the oil business, becoming a true wildcatter. With his wealth, he demonstrated his selfless nature by providing money to build a civic center for the city and a new Methodist church, as well as other contributions. He was born in 1869 and passed away in 1959 in Pittsburgh, where he resided in his later years.

Also there was Joseph Johnson, who became governor of the state of Virginia in the 1850s, a decade before West Virginia became a state on its own. He was self-educated but well-educated. He began working for a local farmer, later becoming his manager, and served several government offices before becoming governor in 1851. He was the first and only governor of Virginia to come from west of the Allegheny Mountains.

His brother, William Johnson, and his son, John "J. C." Johnson, owned considerable property throughout Bridgeport in the middle 19th century. The elder Johnson built the two-story brick building at the corner of Main Street and Virginia Avenue in 1840, the year the younger Johnson was born. J. C. Johnson was accused of conspiring with the Confederacy and was jailed in both 1861 and 1862.

There was also Col. Benjamin Wilson, who had been a lieutenant and aide to Lord Dunmore, governor of the Virginia Colony, in his stand against the Shawnee Indians in southern Ohio.

In addition, there was John Davisson, who, with James H. Hurry, operated a mill at a bend in Simpson Creek near the end of Water Street. Hurry sold his interest to Davisson in 1882, and Davisson sold it to Oakdale Milling and Manufacturing Company in 1895. That firm added a planing mill to the saw- and gristmill and operated it until 1916, when it sold the land to S. S. Faris, who abandoned the operation and had the old mill torn down.

Simpson Creek was named for John Simpson, the first white man to appear on its waters and who came across the mountains from eastern Virginia as a trapper of fur-bearing animals. He supposedly lived in a hollow sycamore tree.

The city was incorporated as the Town of Bridgeport by an order of the Harrison County Circuit Court, entered on March 21, 1887, by Thomas J. Stealey, judge of the Fourth Judicial Circuit. The first mayor was Sylvester Wright, and C. C. Riley was recorder.

The first settlers in Bridgeport were John Powers, Andrew Davisson, Joseph Wilkinson, James Anderson, and Thomas Webb.

Many students of West Virginia history have learned that one of the very first churches established west of the Alleghenies the Simpson Creek Baptist Church, organized in 1776 and built of logs near the center of the old Baptist section of the Bridgeport Cemetery.

Historians have reported that the first mill for grinding grain stood near where Center Street enters East Main Street.

The first record of a bridge in Bridgeport was reportedly found in an order made by the county commission on January 18, 1811. A total of $150 was appropriated to build a bridge across Simpson's Creek about a quarter-mile or more above Johnson's Mill, at the location of the present bridge on Virginia Avenue.

The Baltimore and Ohio Railroad served Bridgeport since the first track was laid in 1856, with the original station building used until it was razed by fire in 1929. Trains continue to pass through Bridgeport operated by CSX, formerly Chessie Systems.

Notable industries that have been located in Bridgeport have been Master Glass, later a marble factory; the Bridgeport Pottery Works; Carroll Lumber Company; Sandusky's Grain Mill; and others.

The Bridgeport Stockyards became a well-known landmark at the corner of West Main Street and Virginia Avenue, with livestock sales held every Monday except holidays.

Perhaps the best of Bridgeport's resources have been its people, who put Bridgeport on the map well over a century and a half ago and have kept it there since, contributing to the city's expansion.

One

Business and Industry

Like other cities and towns in West Virginia, Bridgeport has seen some of its longtime businesses and industries close down. But in a modern way with Meadowbrook Mall, there are four anchor stores and numerous smaller shops of different kinds. And with at least three strip shopping centers in Bridgeport, there are even more stores for people to stop, look, and purchase their many household and automotive needs, as well as groceries, medicine, and items that catch the shopper's eye.

The images on the following pages, however, reflect those businesses and industries that in past years formed the foundation for Bridgeport's economy, which has been strong.

In the late 19th or early 20th century, the first mill for grinding grain was completed in what is now mid-town Bridgeport. However, the first mill that historians officially recorded was the Bridgeport (or Johnson) Mill, built by James Anderson in the latter part of the 18th century. The mill, on Simpson Creek in Faris Acres Addition, was later enlarged to accommodate the installation of machinery. It changed hands several times from around 1854 until 1916, when Samuel S. Faris bought the mill property and soon afterward had it demolished. Several other mills were built and sold but eventually torn down.

In 1815, Calvin Waldo opened Bridgeport's first general store. William Johnson led a number of other early Bridgeport merchants, including J. N. Wilkinson, W. C. Fitzhugh, M. E. Kester, J. W. Coffman, and E. N. Coplin. They were joined by others such as John C. Johnson, John Dunkin, and Emanuel Benedum. Taverns were situated along a stage line on the Northwestern Turnpike. The first ones were owned by William Johnson and a man named Tyson. Others were Thomas B. Martin, Elias Lawson, Hamilton Lang, D. D. Wilkinson, and Bing Sandusky. Early farmers were John Dunkin, William Johnson and son J. C. Johnson, Samuel S. Faris, Flavious B. Davisson, and Capt. J. H. Hurry.

One of the key industries has been the Baltimore and Ohio Railroad (B&O). William Johnson built the first railroad in 1855, and the very next year, the very first B&O train stopped in Bridgeport. The B&O has been serving Bridgeport for a century and a half.

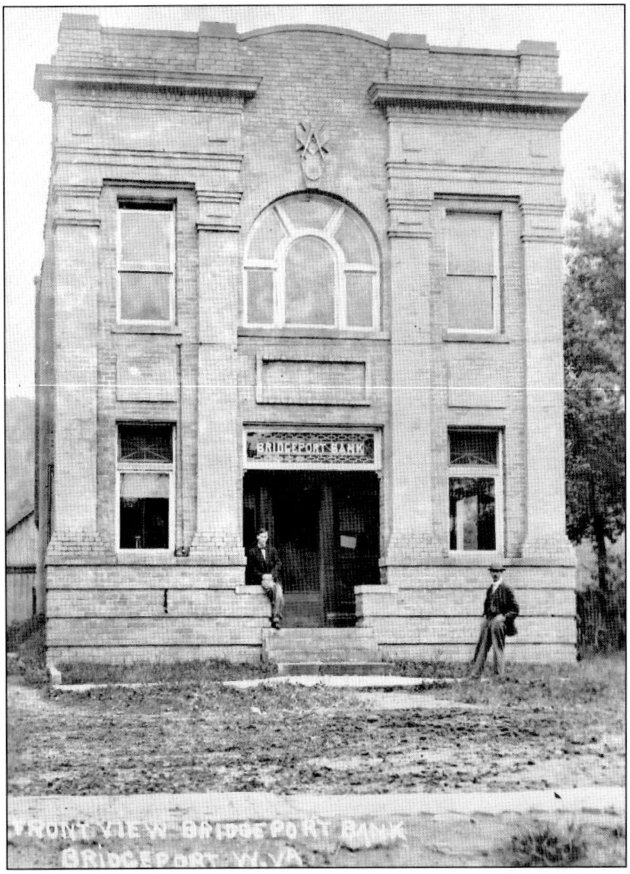

The Bridgeport Bank has always had numerous customers, even in the very early years of the 20th century. Some of them can be seen here, back when Main Street was just dirt and mud. At the close of business on December 30, 1911, the bank's resources totaled $47,161.56. A brick structure was built in 1909. (Courtesy of Dick Duez.)

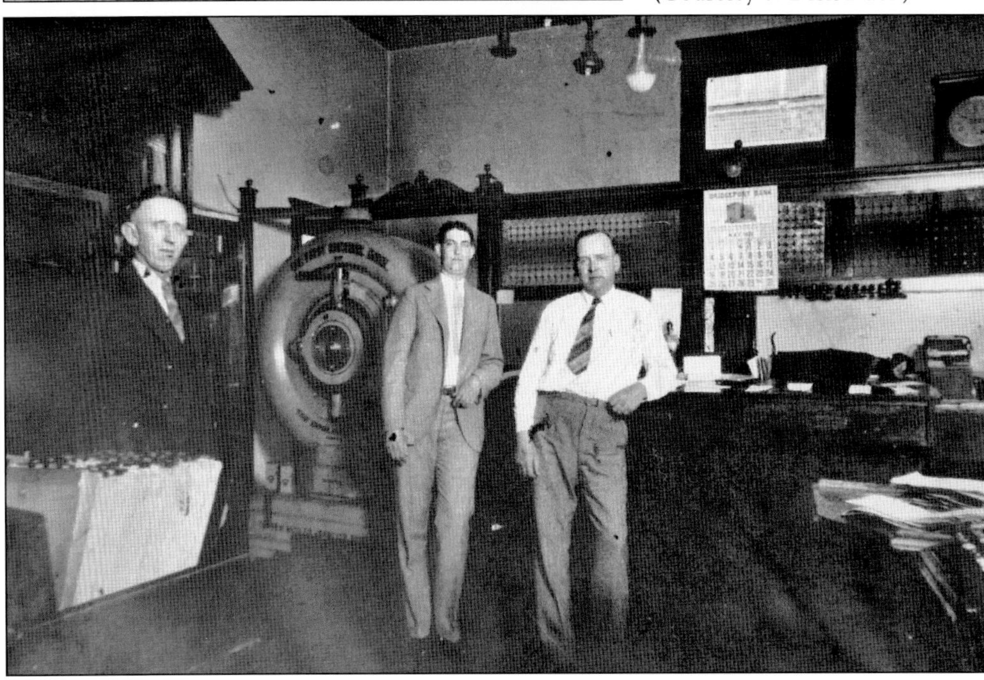

This is the interior of Bridgeport Bank in 1933. From left to right are bank president Jim Johnson with tellers Hornor Jones and Arden Teter. (Courtesy of Dick Duez.)

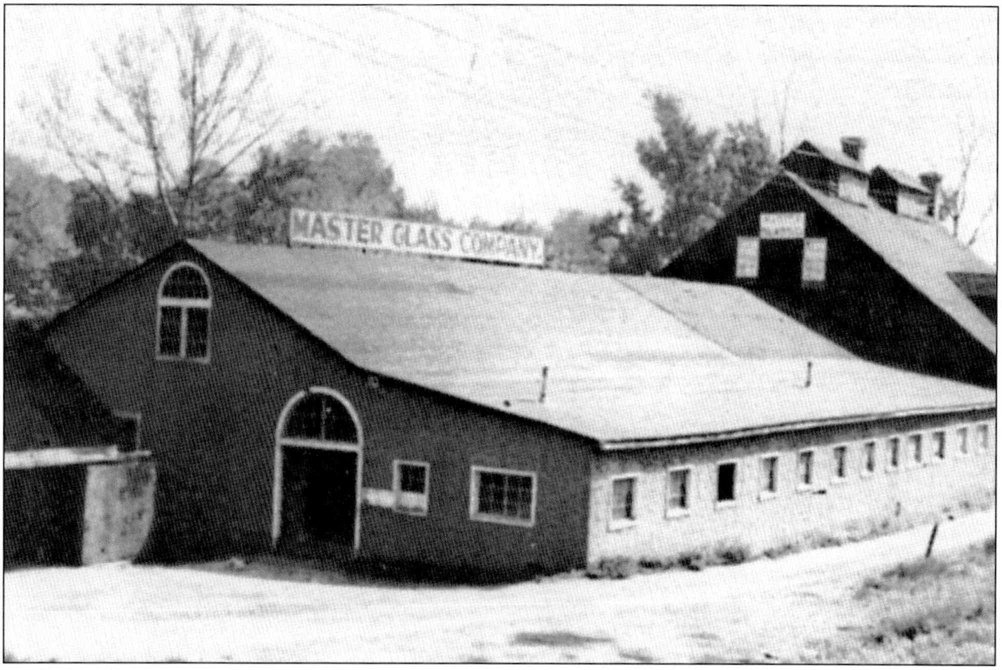

Probably the most prominent industry in Bridgeport in the first half of the 20th century was Master Glass Company, a marble factory established on May 15, 1930, by Clinton Israel. The plant moved from Anmoore to Bridgeport in 1941 and in 1950 took over the assets of the Akro-Agate Marble Company of Clarksburg. (Courtesy of Dick Duez.)

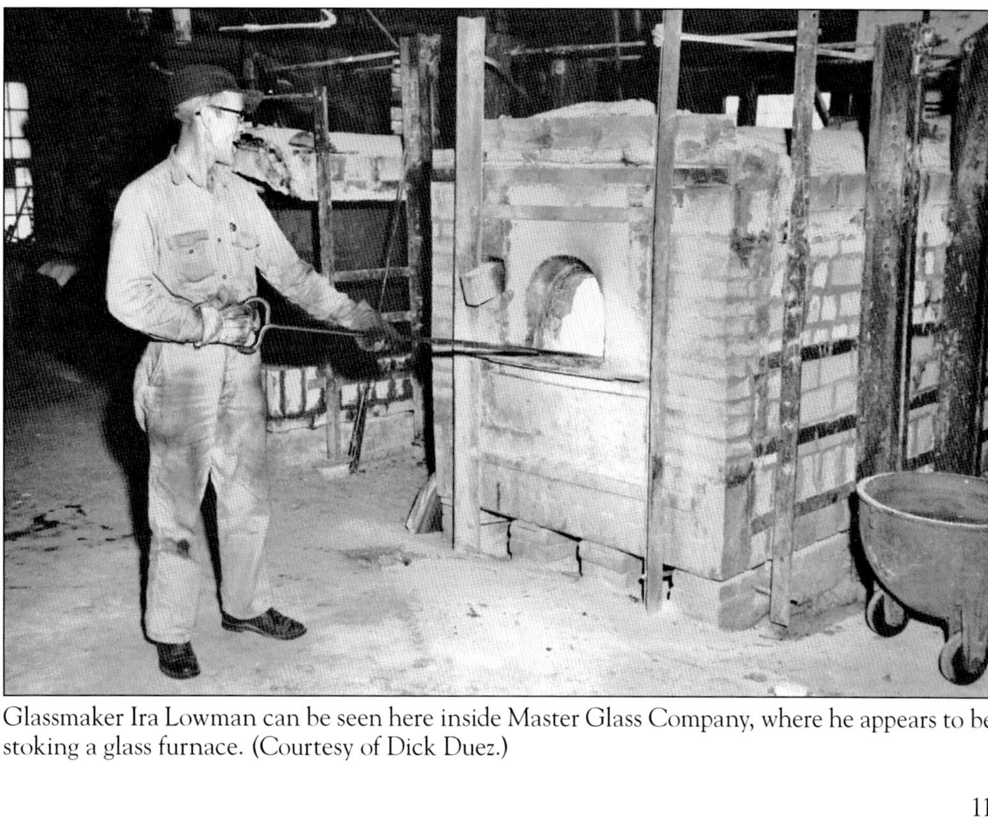

Glassmaker Ira Lowman can be seen here inside Master Glass Company, where he appears to be stoking a glass furnace. (Courtesy of Dick Duez.)

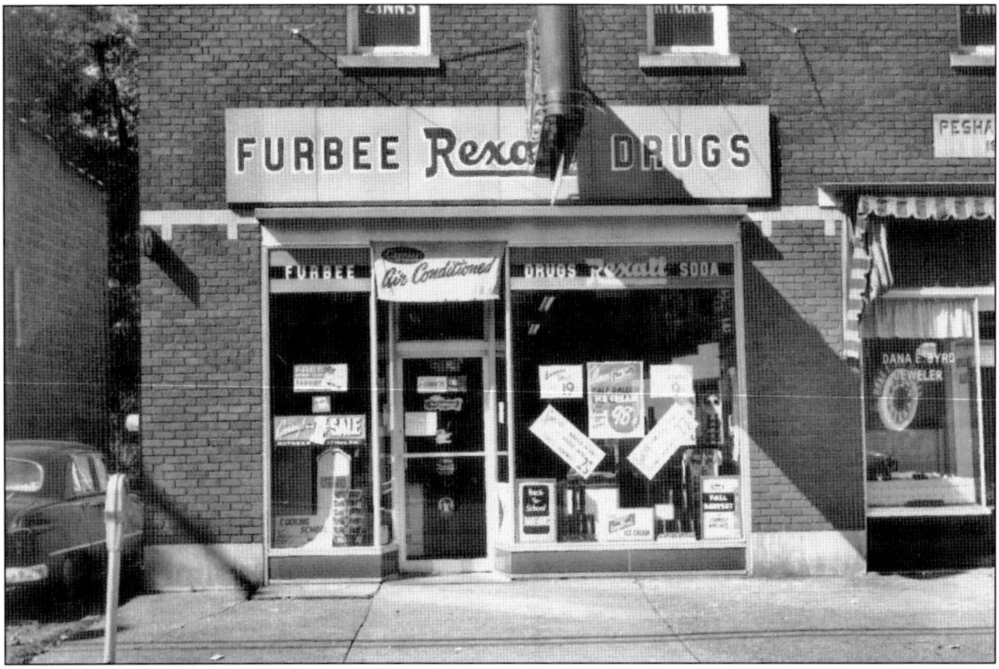

Before it moved to Valley Hills Shopping Center in Bridgeport, Furbee's Rexall Drug Store was located on West Main Street in the city. (Courtesy of Dick Duez.)

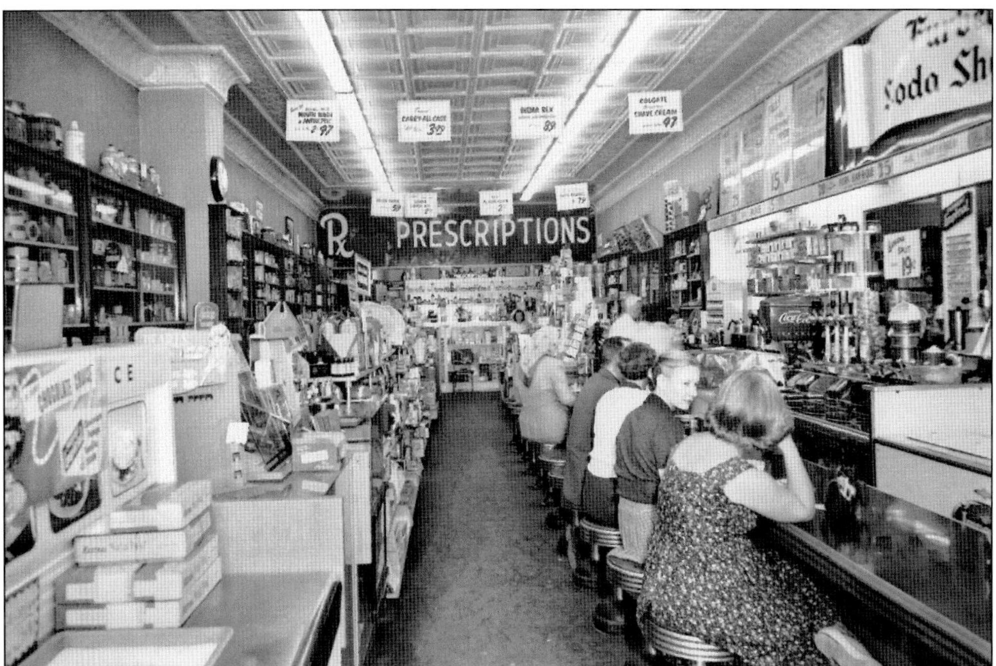

This long view of the inside of Furbee's Rexall Drug Store shows the prescription counter in back, a soda fountain in front, and aisles of merchandise in between. The photograph was taken about 1961. (Courtesy of Dick Duez.)

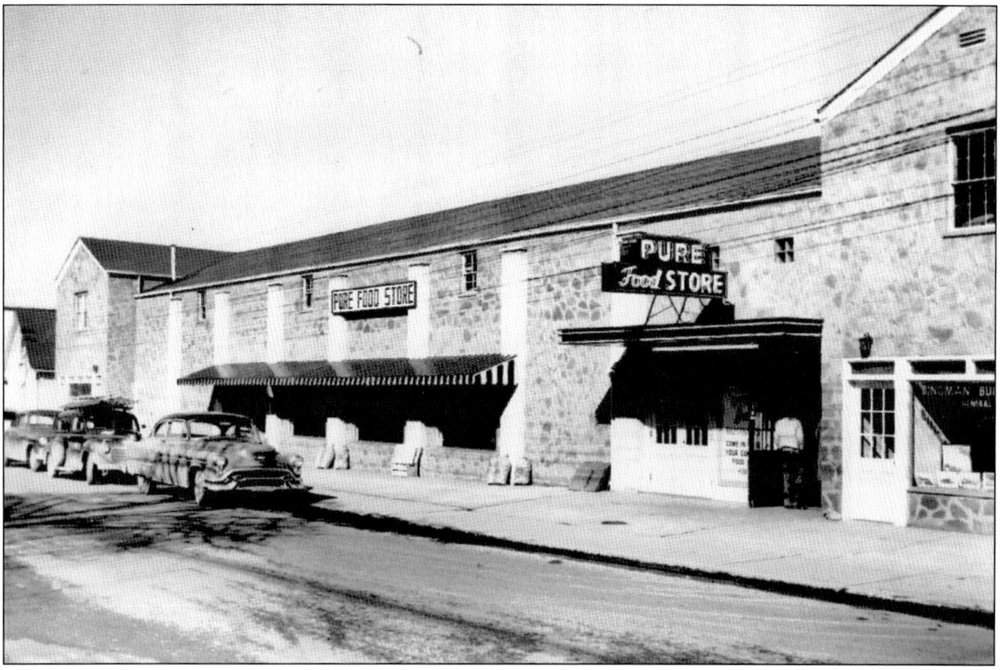

The Pure Food Store had considerable traffic from shoppers picking up their week's groceries or perhaps just a few odds and ends. It opened in the late 1950s and was located on East Main Street. The Pierce Theater occupied to site in the late 1940s and early 1950s. Shahady's Antique Shop is located there today. (Courtesy of Dick Duez.)

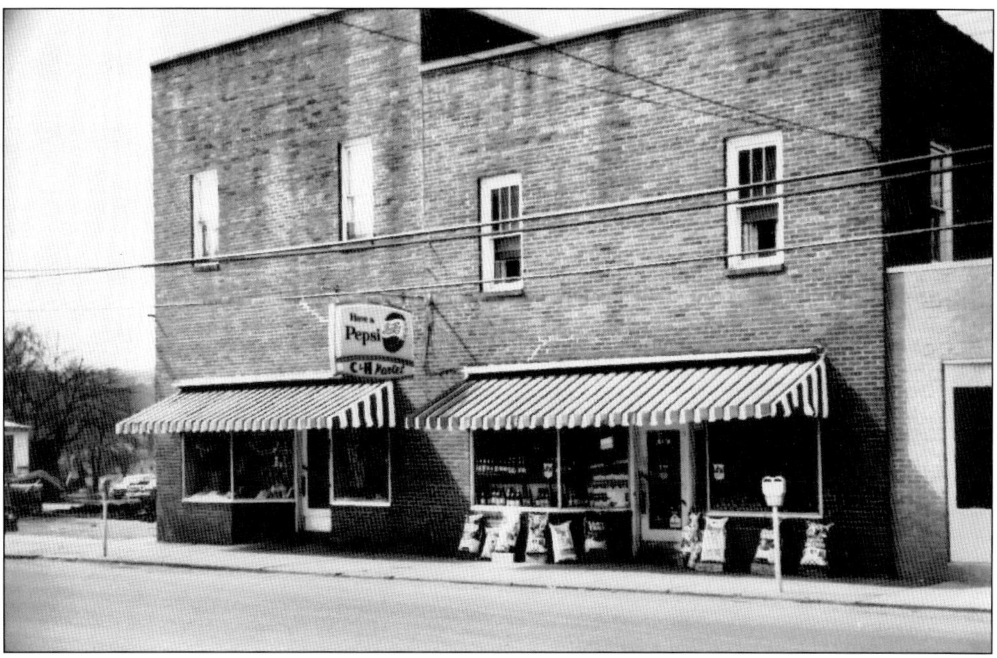

The C&H Market on Main Street, photographed in 1962, was across from the Bridgeport Bank. (Courtesy of Dick Duez.)

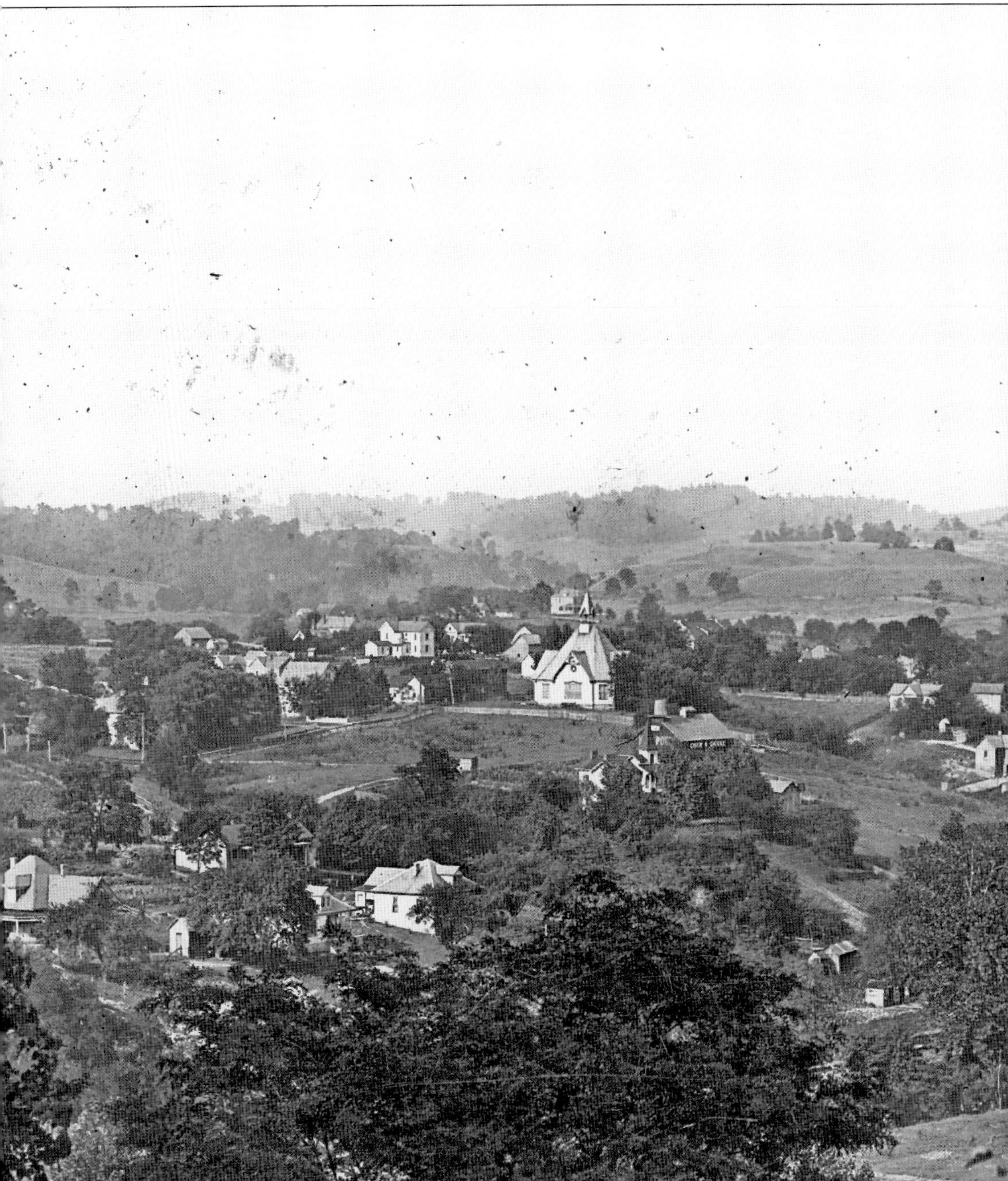

This bird's-eye panorama shows Bridgeport in 1912. It was photographed from behind what is now the Ace Hardware store, looking east and showing businesses along the B&O line. (Courtesy

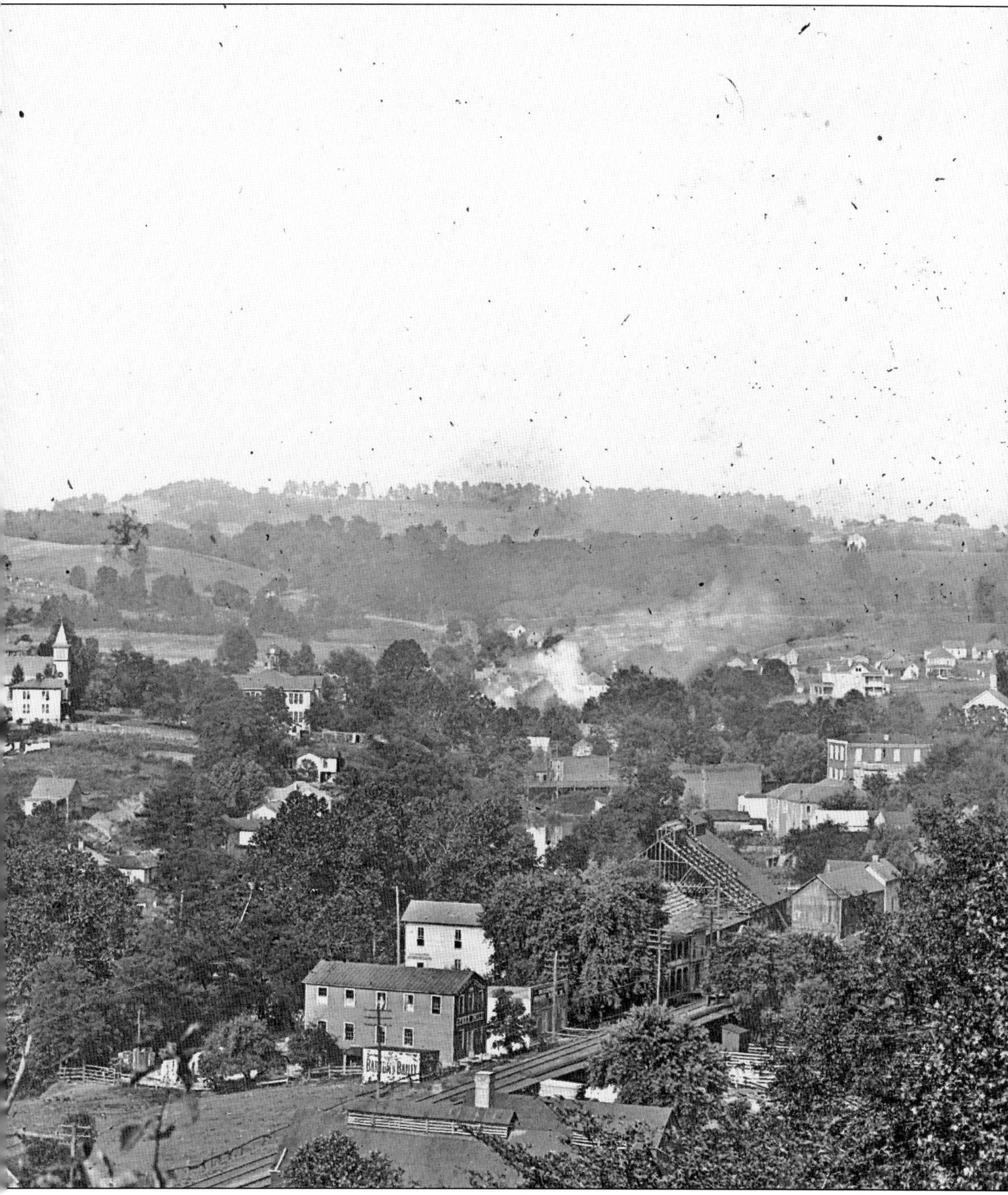

of Roger Hardy.)

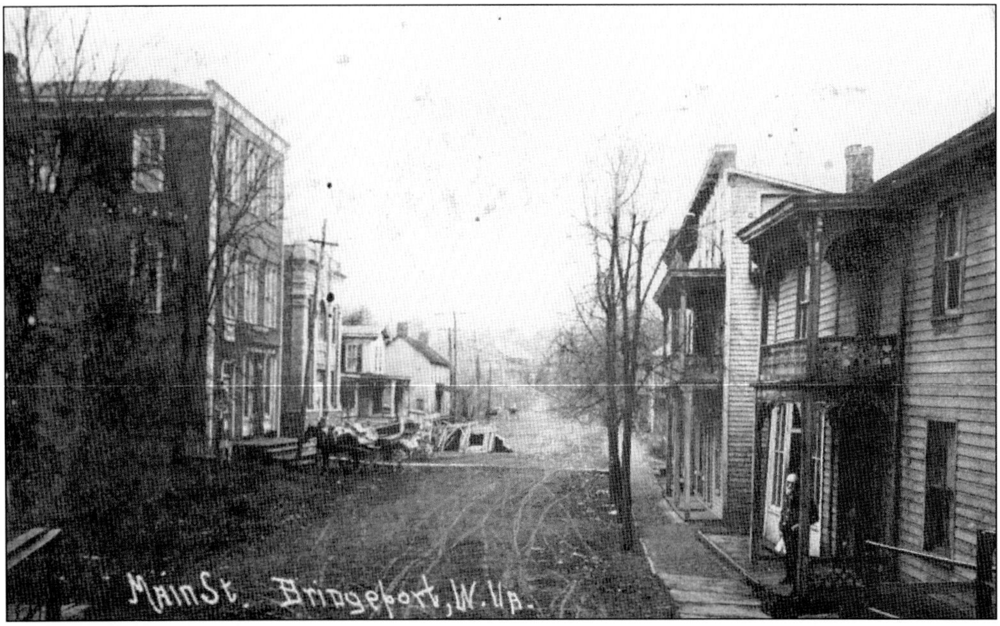

This view, looking west from the iron bridge over Simpson Creek in Bridgeport, shows the Fitzhugh Building and the newly constructed Bridgeport Bank. Remains of the office of Dr. William Late's, removed because of the building's demolition to make way for the Bridgeport Bank, can be seen in the middle of Main Street. (Courtesy of Dick Duez.)

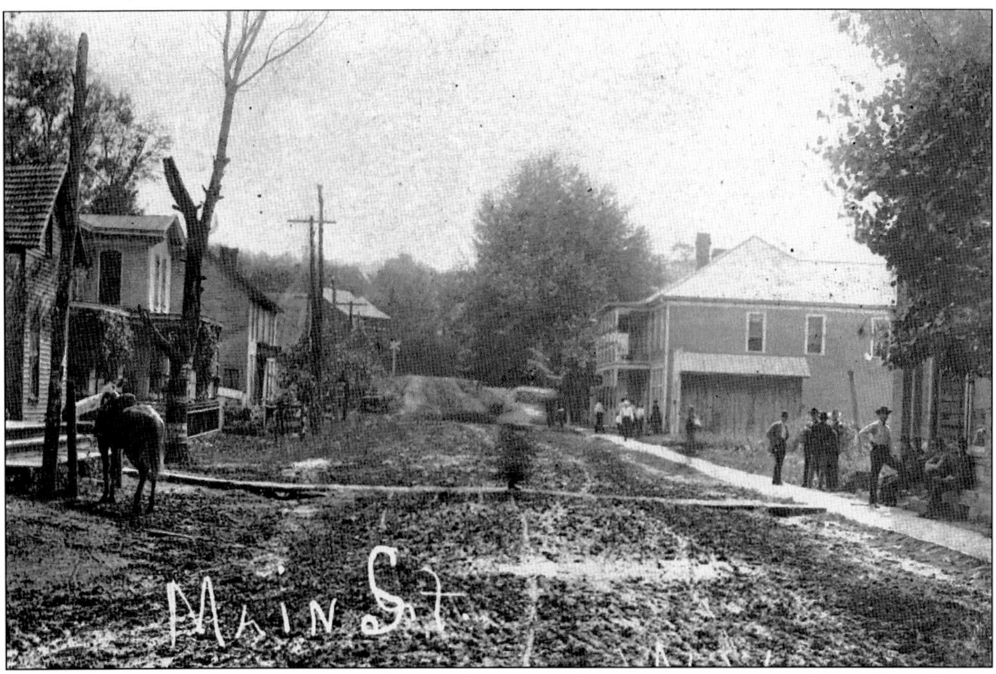

The Kester Hotel is in plain view at right in this view of Main Street. On the left is the office of Dr. William Late, beyond the Fitzhugh Building. (Courtesy of Rose Davis.)

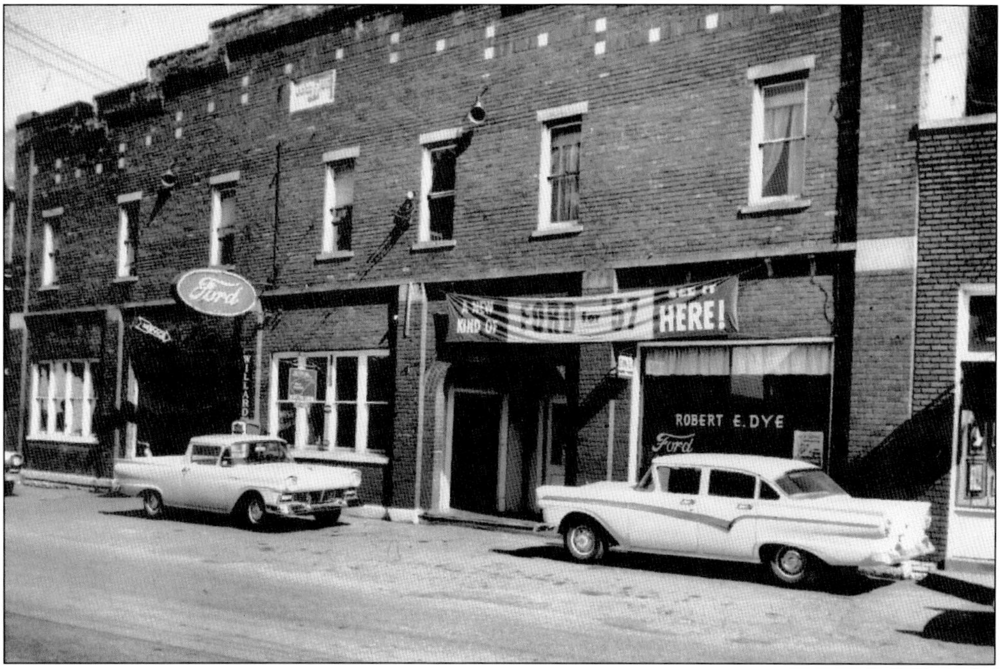

The Ford garage, photographed in 1957, was owned by Robert Dye in the John Utt Building on the south side of East Main Street. The building is currently occupied by the Barewood Refinishing Company, owned by Jerry Pomeroy. (Courtesy of Dick Duez.)

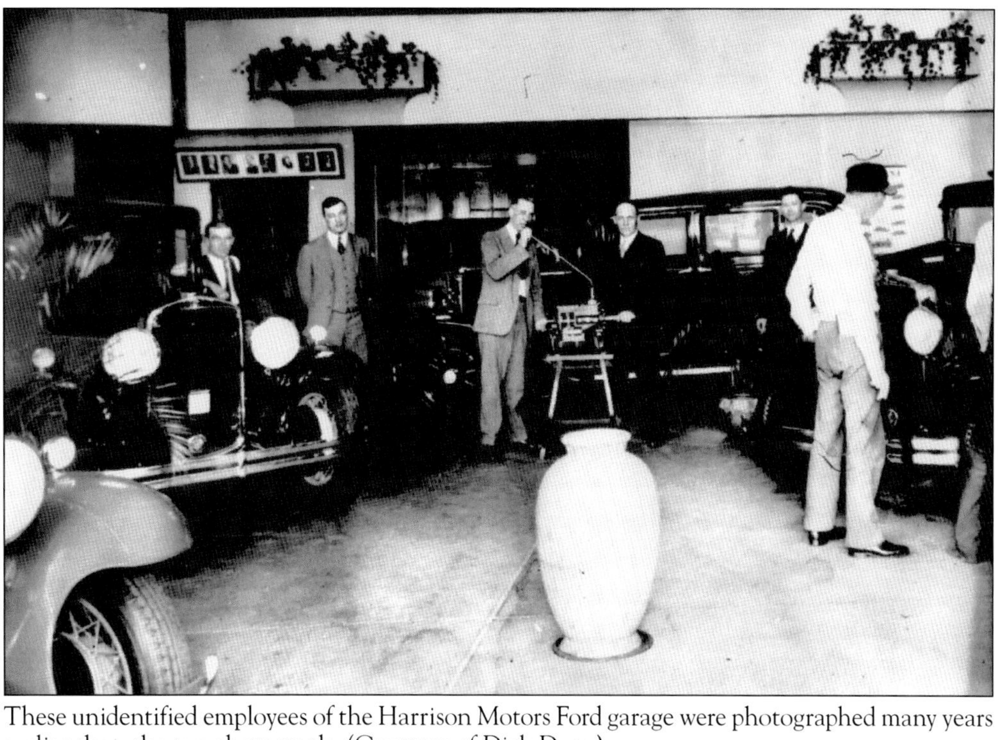

These unidentified employees of the Harrison Motors Ford garage were photographed many years earlier than the top photograph. (Courtesy of Dick Duez.)

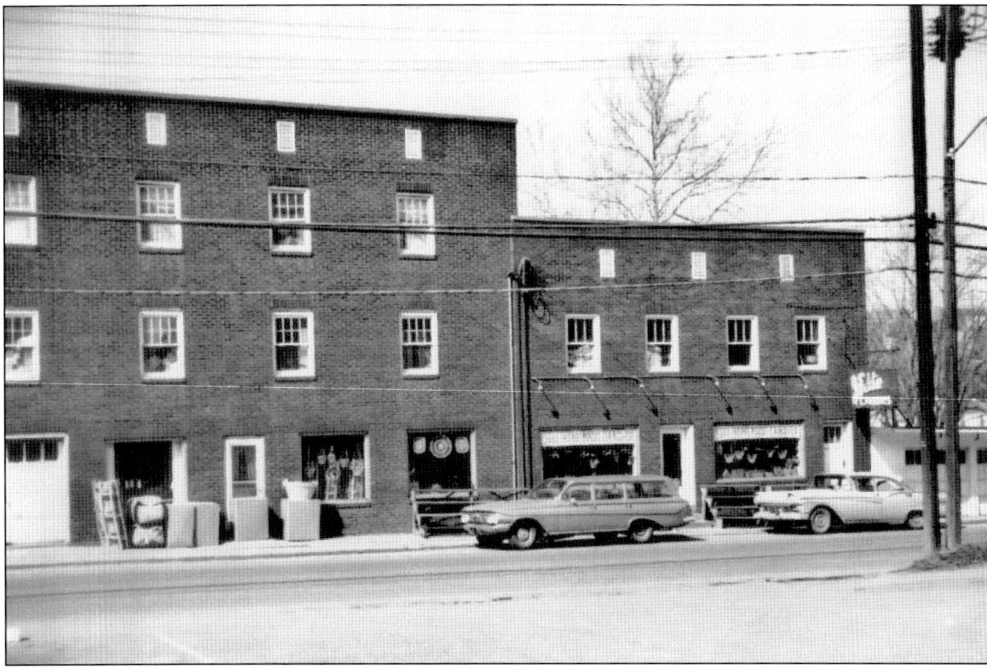

Folks with a sweet tooth certainly enjoyed the wares of J. Eddie's Candies on West Main Street, shown here in 1961. An adjoining basket shop is just to the left. The building and business were owned by J. Eddie Sheets. (Courtesy of Dick Duez.)

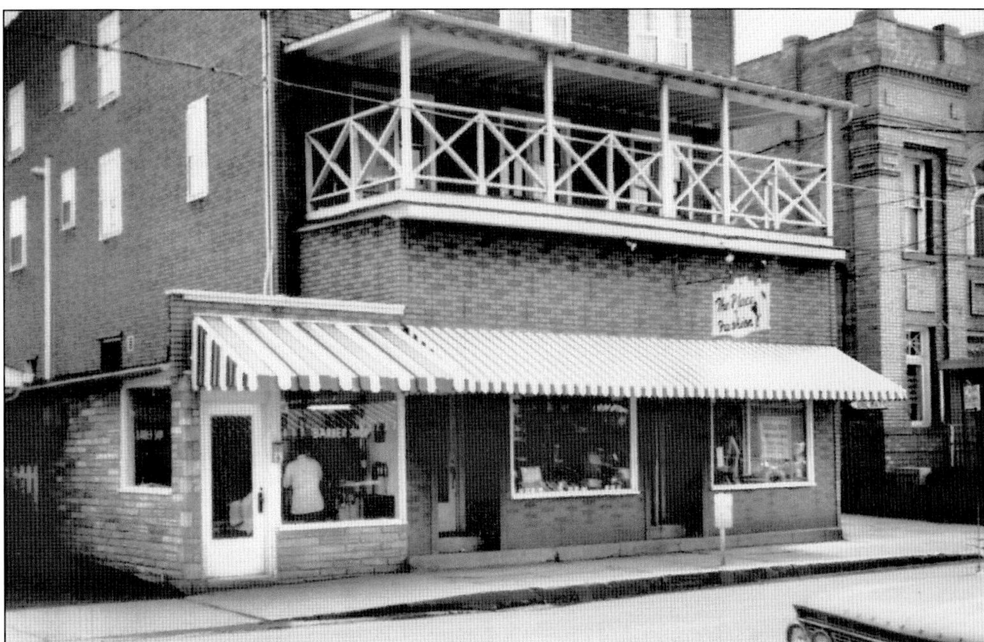

The Place of Fashion, a woman's clothing store, was open for business in the early part of the 1960s in the city's mid-town. Bridgeport Bank is at the right. (Courtesy of Dick Duez.)

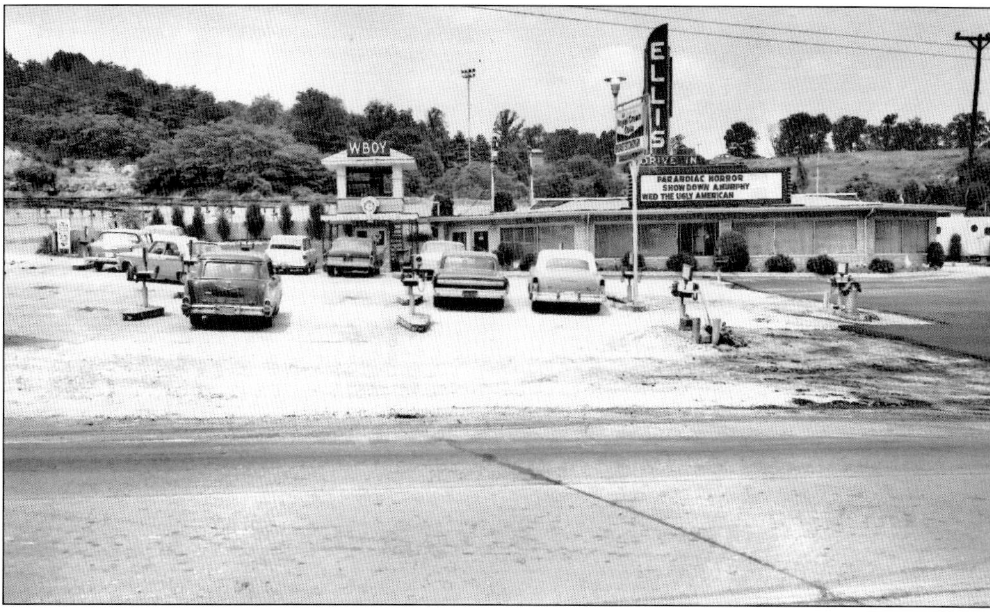

The Ellis Drive-in Theater and Restaurant then west of Bridgeport on U.S. 50, was truly one of Harrison County's most popular places to go at night. The restaurant would later become the Brothers Four Supper Club. (Courtesy of Dick Duez.)

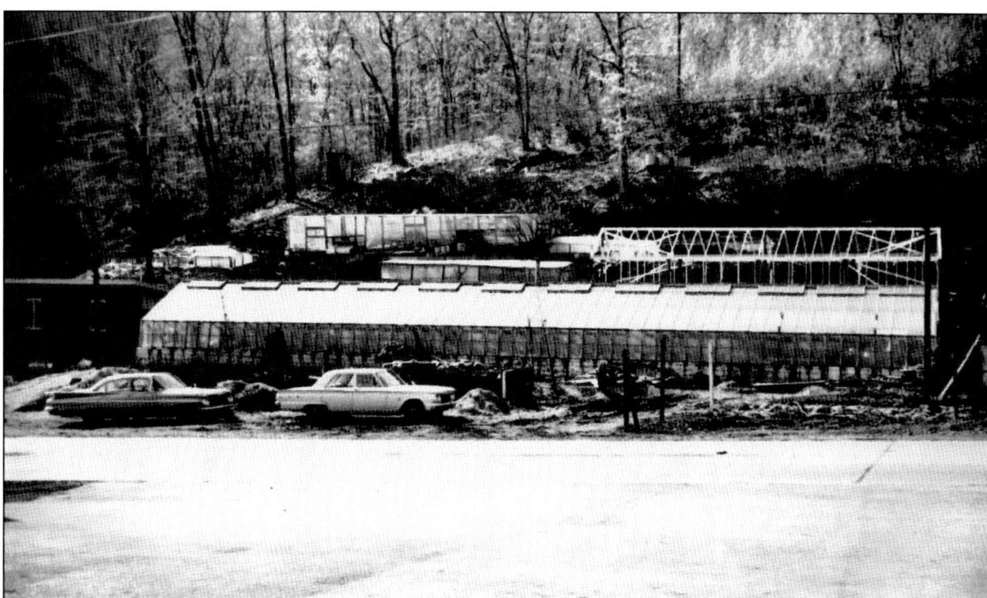

Louis Curry was the owner of this greenhouse, which was located across from Twin Oaks Restaurant in the 1960s and 1970s. (Courtesy of Dick Duez.)

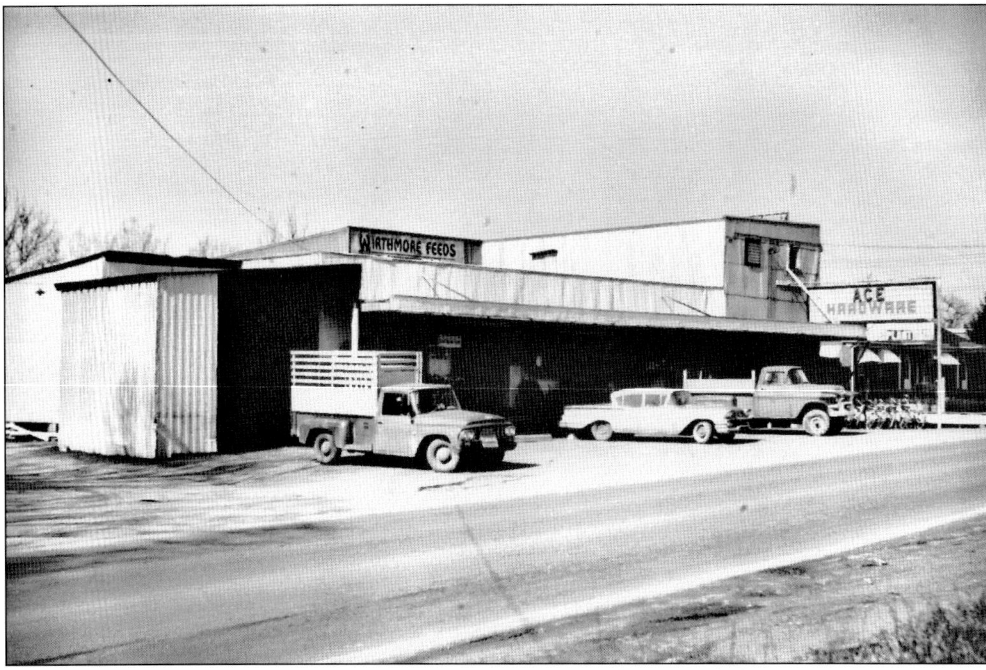

Ace Hardware, which has stood at 414 West Main Street (Route 50) for many years, is among the foremost hardware businesses in Harrison County. The store also deals in giftware, toys, and other useful household needs. (Courtesy of Dick Duez.)

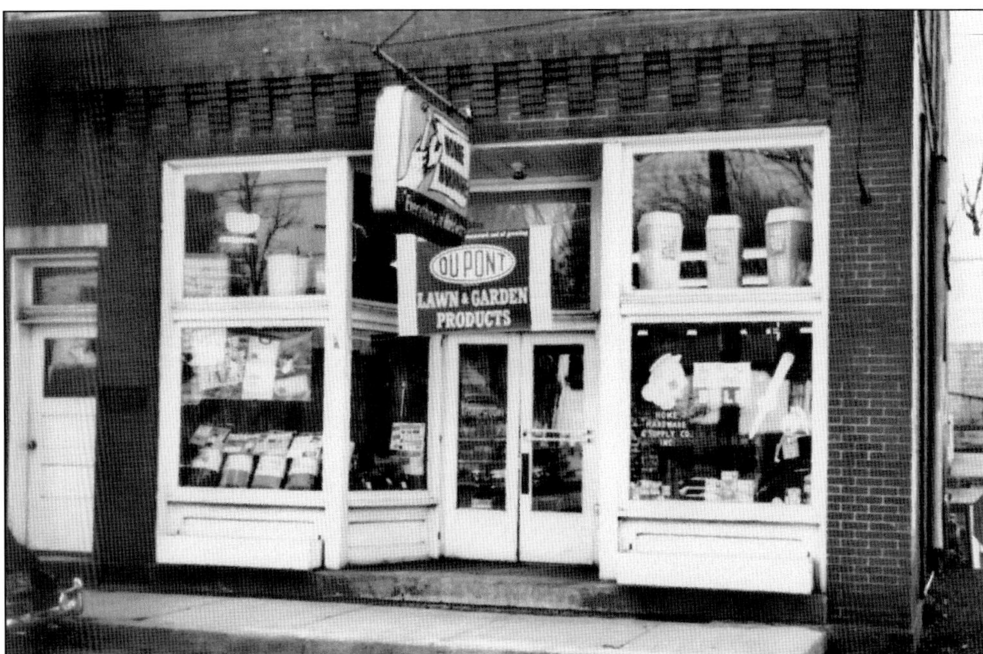

Home Hardware and Supply Company, which was located at 101 East Main Street, was another popular mid-town business in Bridgeport and a supporter of the cause of this growing city. (Courtesy of Dick Duez.)

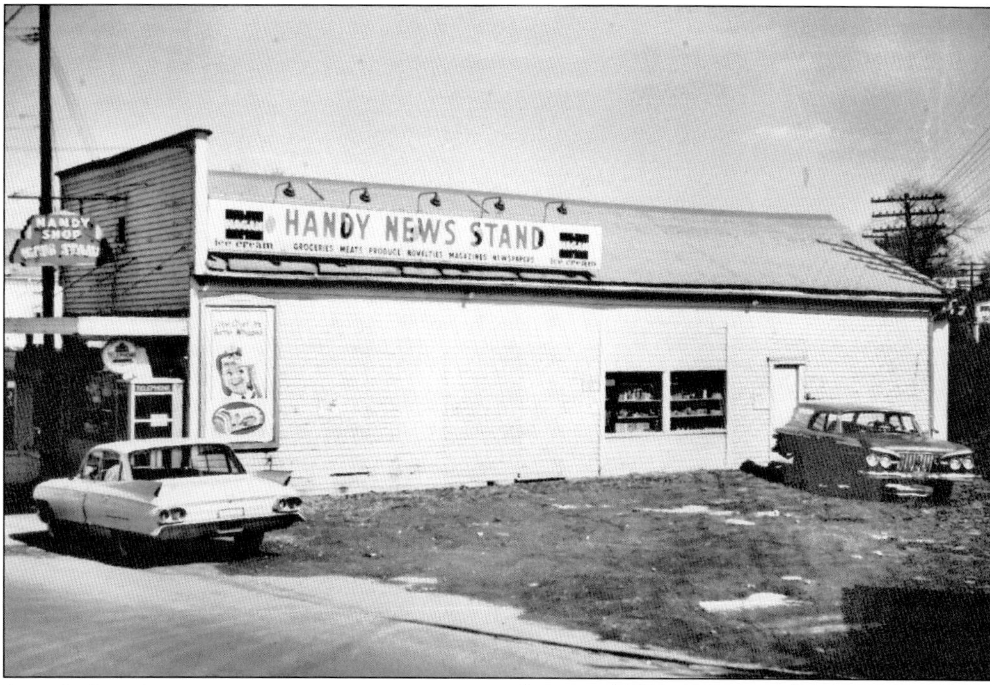

Long before there were convenience stores in north central West Virginia, there was the Handy Store, which was a very short distance east of the B&O crossing on West Main Street. The Chevrolet dealership was previously located here. (Courtesy of Dick Duez.)

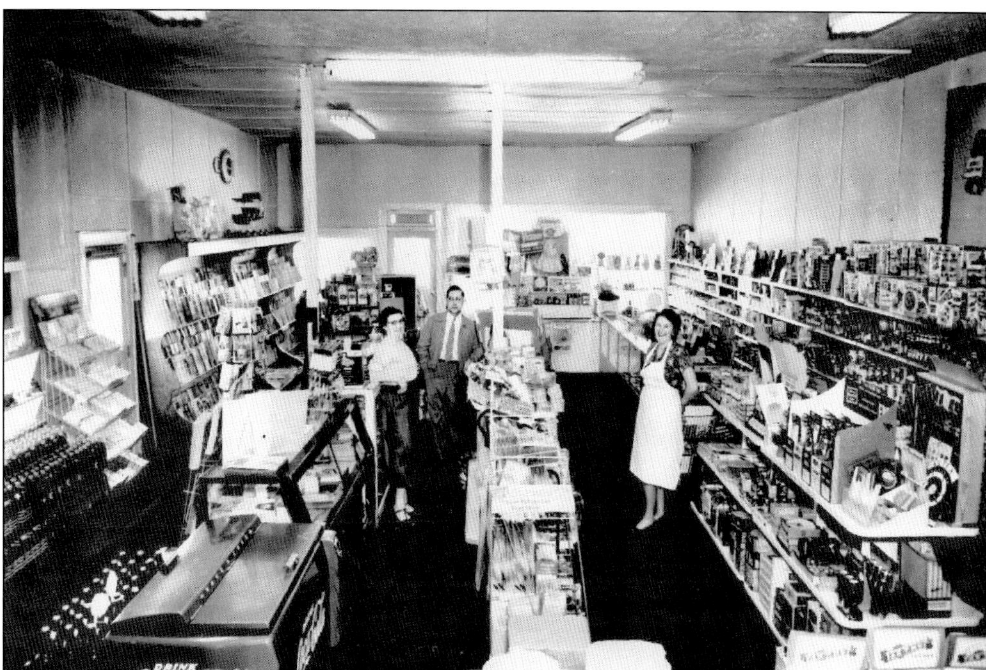

There were quite a few shelves of goods from which customers could choose inside the Handy Shop. Shown are proprietors Mr. and Mrs. Walter Camp on the left. (Courtesy of Dick Duez.)

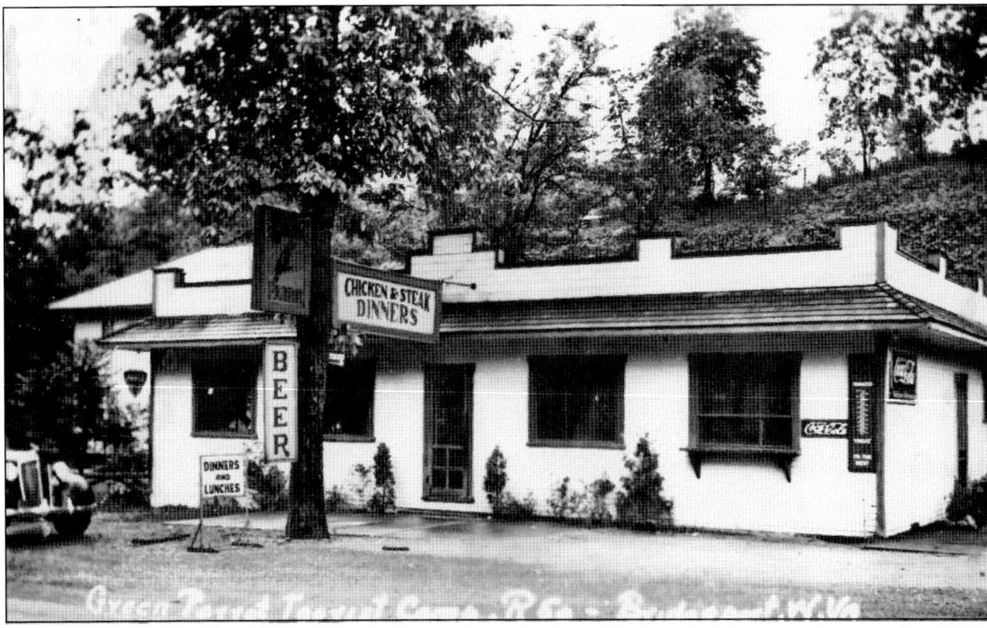

The Green Parrot Tourist Camp, which was built by Pete Hall probably some time in the 1930s, greeted travelers on U.S. 50, then just outside Bridgeport's city limits. (Courtesy of Dick Duez.)

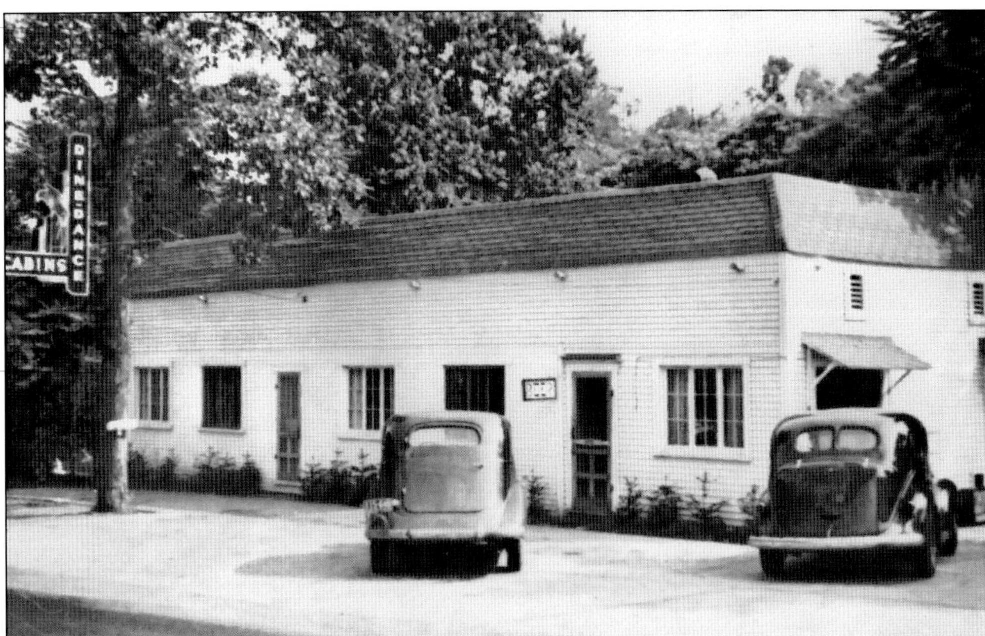

In later years, the Green Parrot was quite the popular place for sandwiches, beer, and a large dance floor, and people from miles around were frequent visitors. It was operated by Bob Fesler, whose DeSoto automobile can be seen in the parking lot at right. (Courtesy of Dick Duez.)

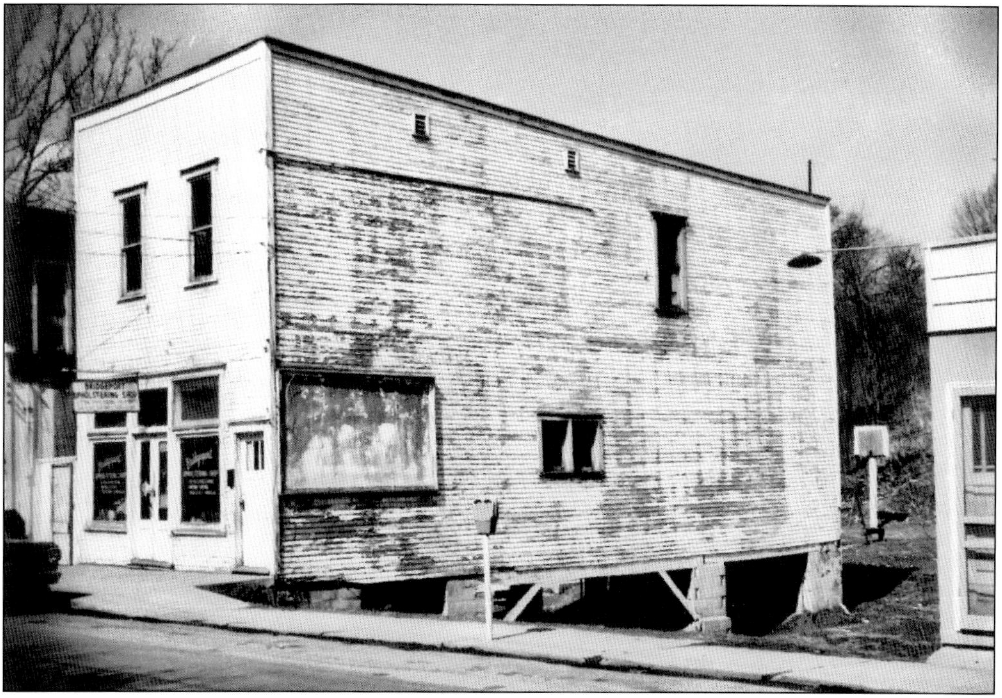

Allman's Upholstery Shop is shown in 1961. Benny's Boot Hill eventually located in the same building. (Courtesy of Dick Duez.)

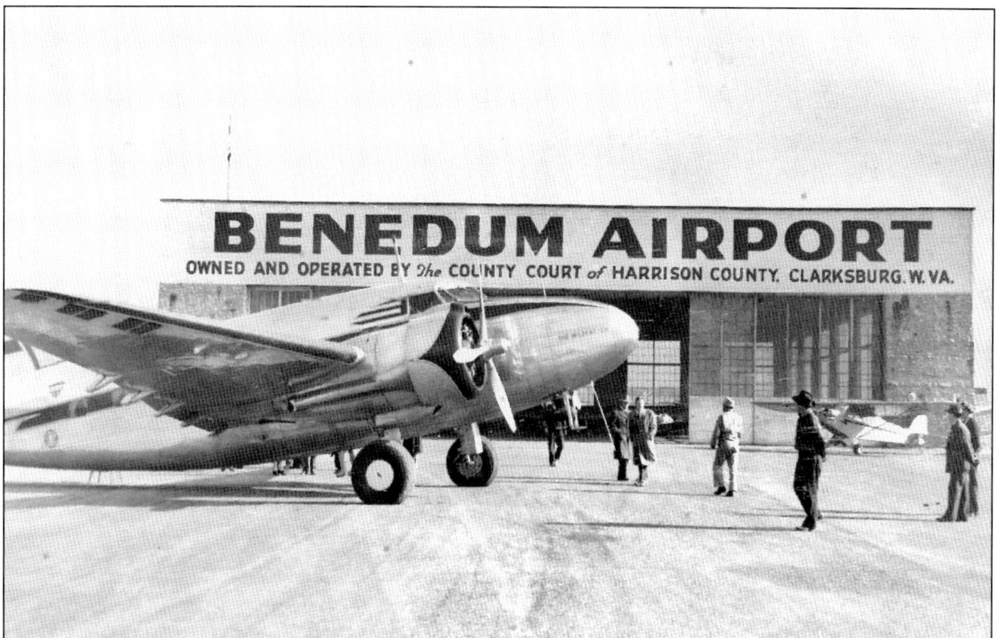

Michael Benedum's plane, the *Wildcatter*, has just landed at Benedum Airport in Bridgeport, c. 1954. (Courtesy of Benedum Civic Center.)

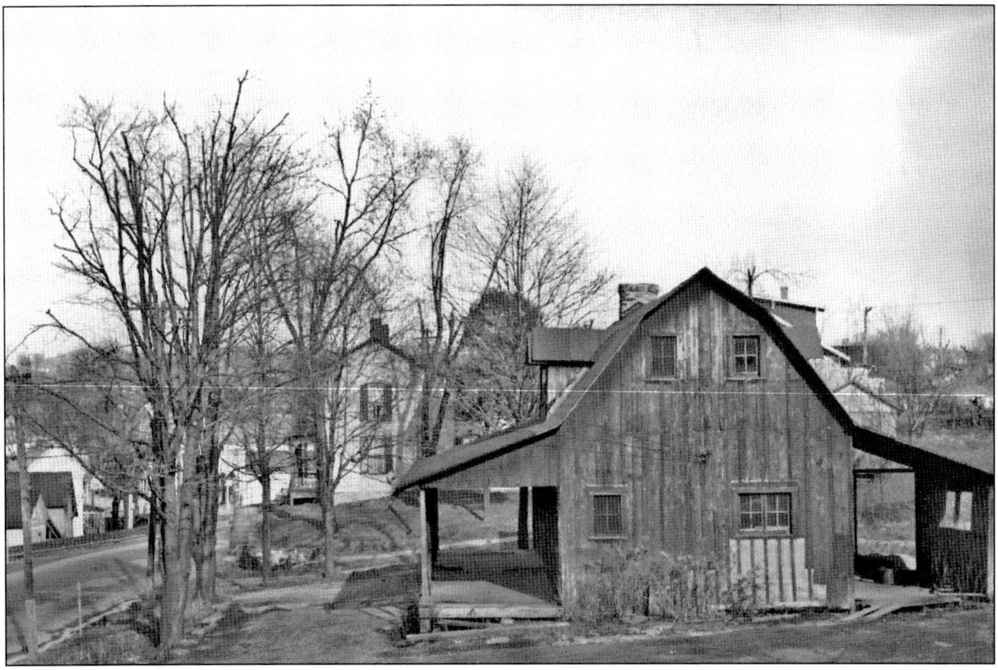

Here's a view of the building that housed the Millstone Restaurant on West Main Street near its intersection with Virginia Avenue in Bridgeport. The photograph, looking eastward, was taken in 1953. Delicious home-cooked food was the specialty of the restaurant. (Courtesy of Dick Duez.)

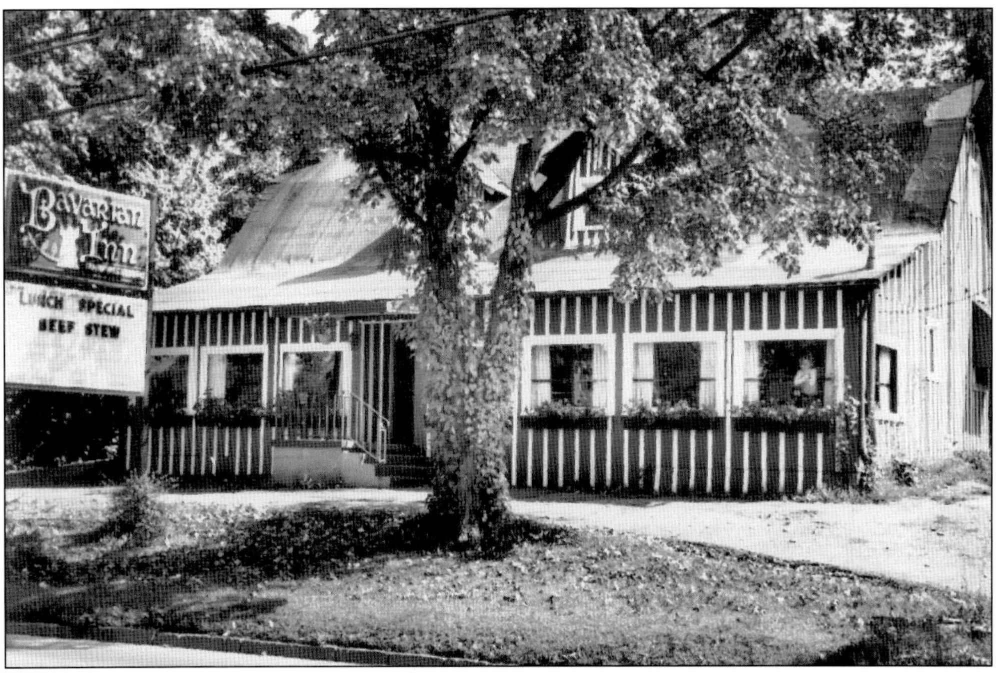

The Bavarian Inn once occupied the barn-shaped building that housed the Millstone Restaurant. Other businesses that have occupied the building include a photography shop, a drugstore, and a bicycle shop. (Courtesy of Dick Duez.)

Seen at Benedum Airport around 1954 are, from left to right, Michael Benedum; his sister, Sophia; and banker and publisher Cecil B. Highland. (Courtesy of Benedum Civic Center.)

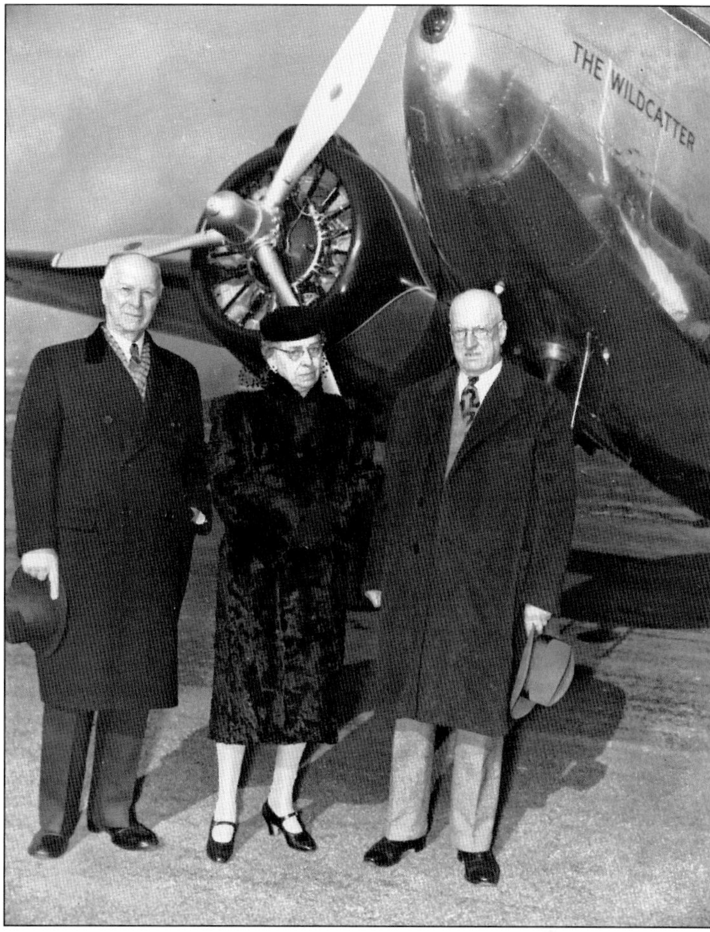

Although Bridgeport has never had a downtown section as such, here are just some of the businesses along West Main Street. (Courtesy of Dick Duez.)

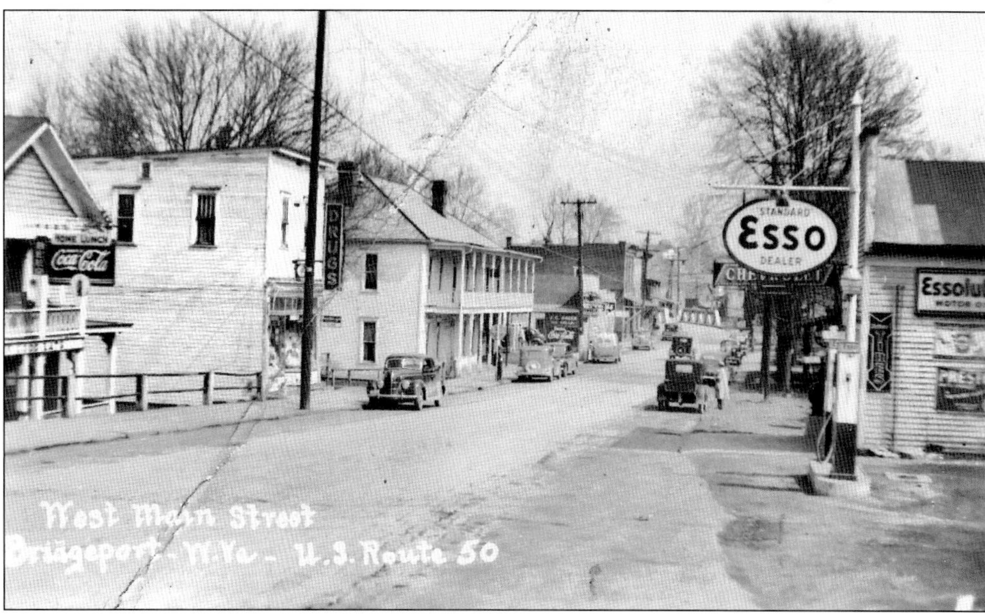

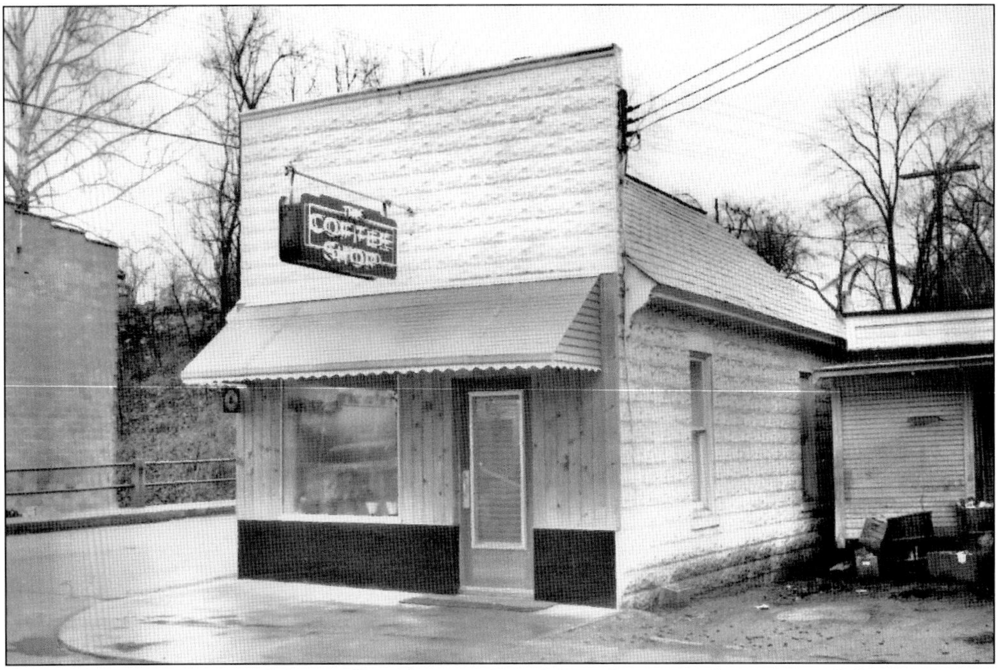

Here's an exterior view of the Coffee Shop on East Main Street at the corner of Center Street. The building was at one time the city jail. (Courtesy of Dick Duez.)

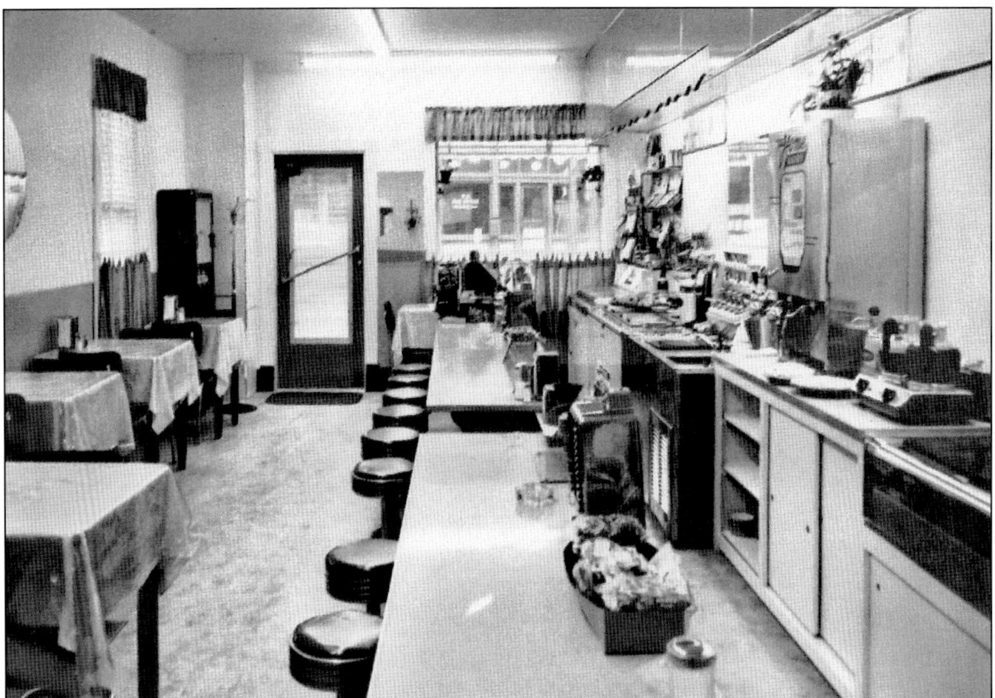

This photograph shows the interior of the Coffee Shop before the lunch crowd arrives. (Courtesy of Dick Duez.)

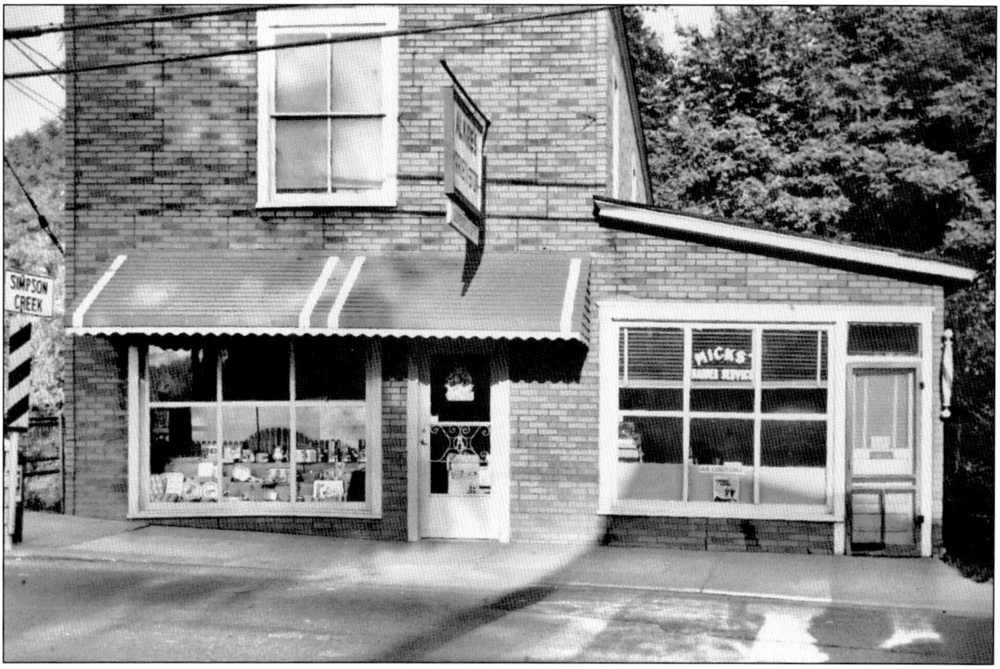

Alkire's Variety Store was on West Main Street at the bridge in mid-town Bridgeport. Alkire's was considered much like a dime store. At the right is Mick's Barber Shop, owned by Bill Mick. (Courtesy of Dick Duez.)

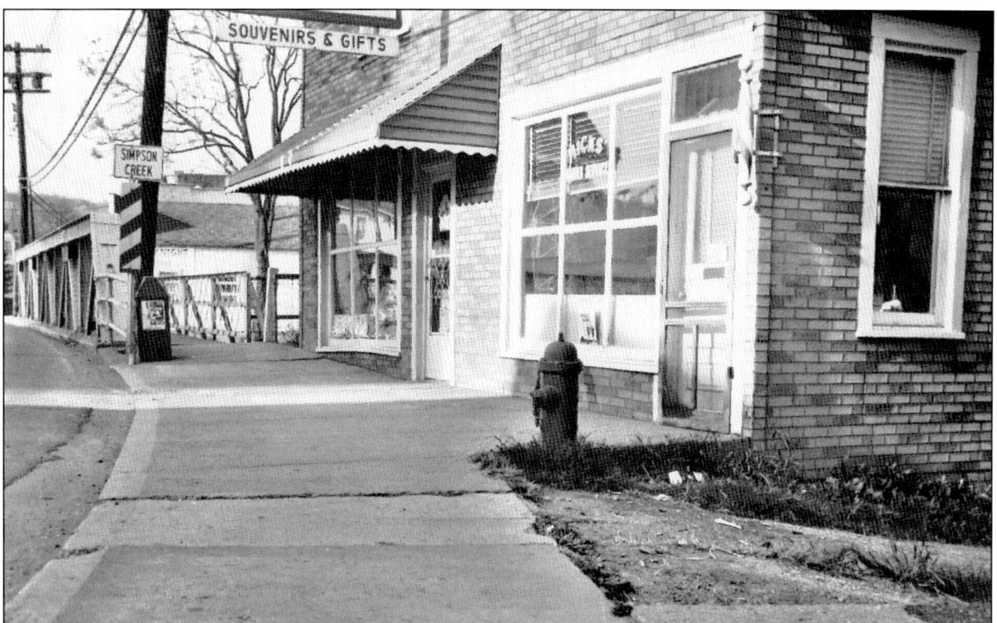

Here is a front view of Alkire's Variety Store and Mick's Barber Shop in Bridgeport. (Courtesy of Dick Duez.)

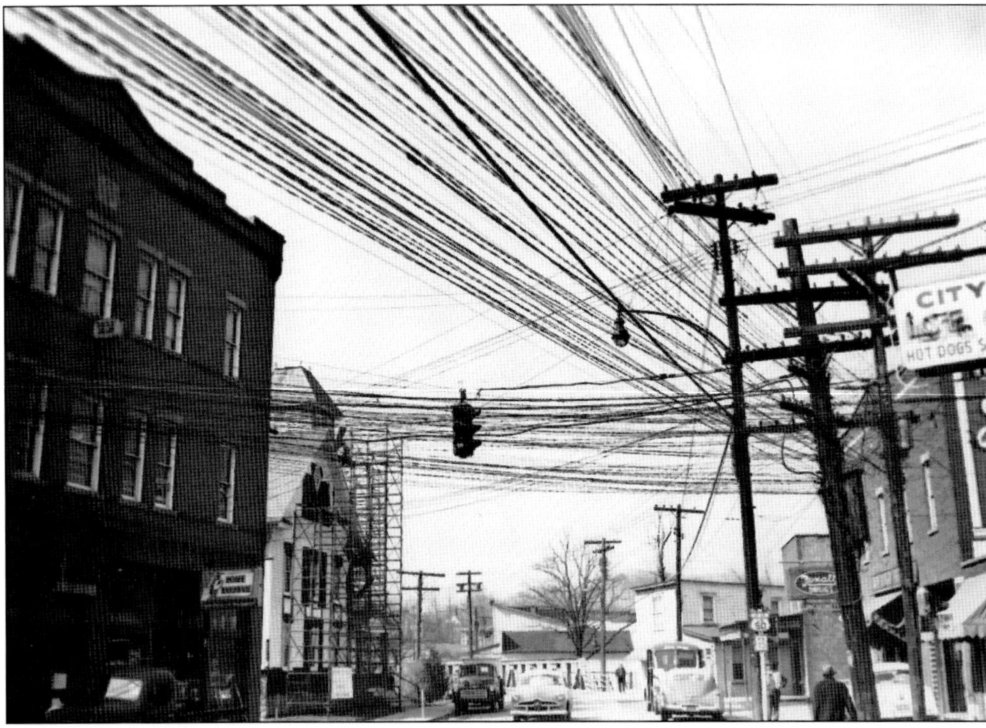

This is mid-town Bridgeport, looking west from the Center Street intersection with East Main. (Courtesy of Dick Duez.)

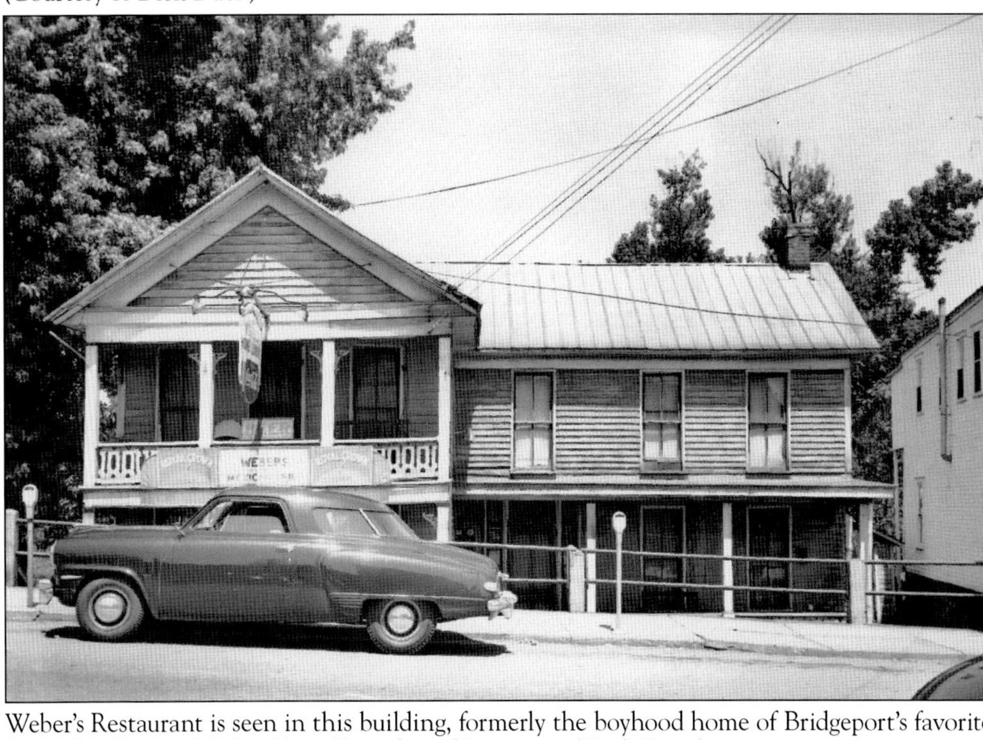

Weber's Restaurant is seen in this building, formerly the boyhood home of Bridgeport's favorite son, oil wildcatter Michael Late Benedum. (Courtesy of Dick Duez.)

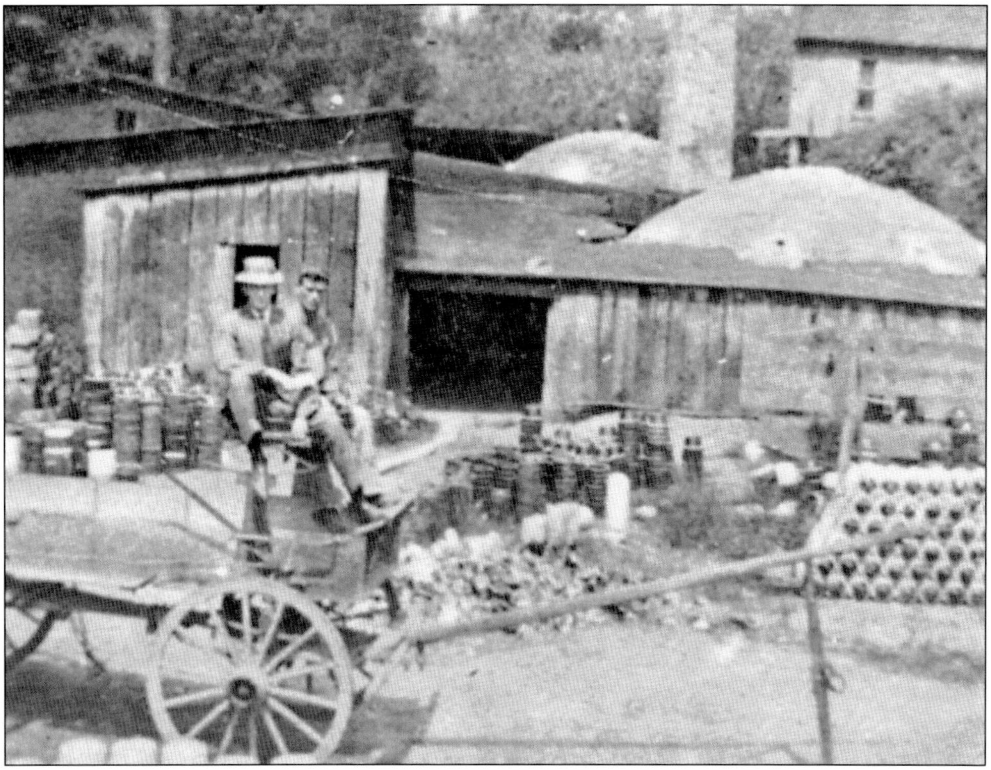

This man steers his horse-drawn wagon in front of the pottery at the end of South Davis Street. The pottery was first operated by Bing Sandusky, but E. O. Russell bought the business in the late 19th century. (Courtesy of Dick Duez.)

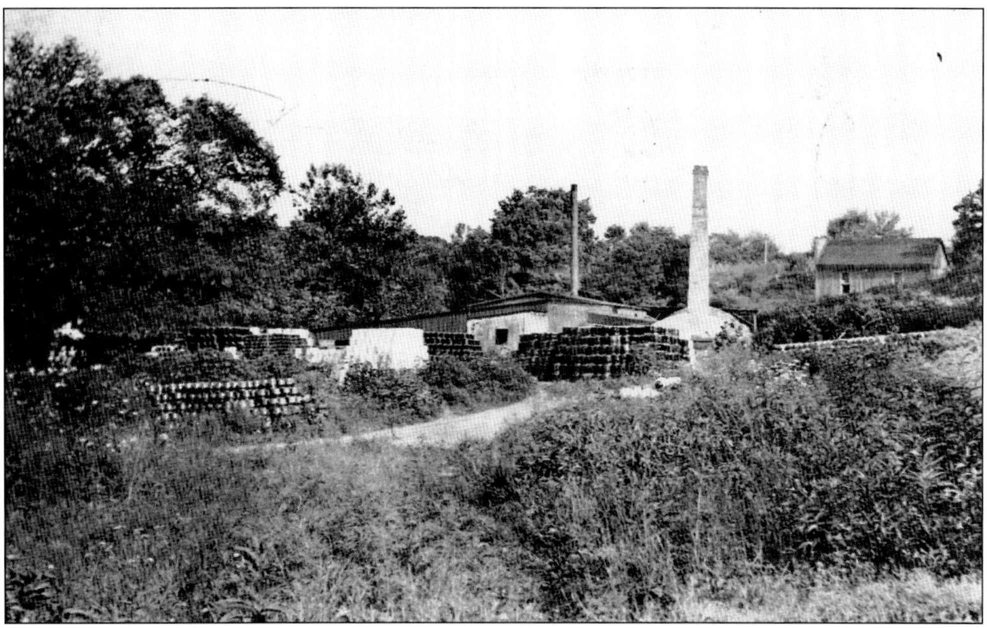

Here is another view of the pottery, which was incorporated as the West Virginia Pottery Company in April 1907 with C. H. Warner as president. (Courtesy of Dick Duez.)

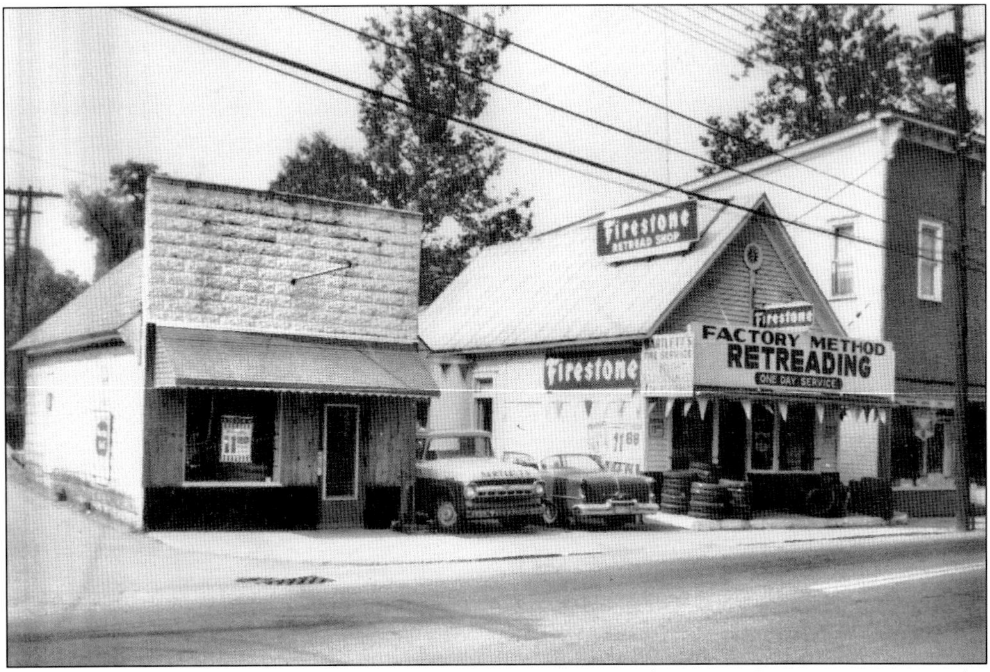

Looking northward on East Main Street at its intersection with Center Street, one can see the old Firestone Tire store, with the small building that once housed the Bridgeport Jail at left. (Courtesy of Dick Duez.)

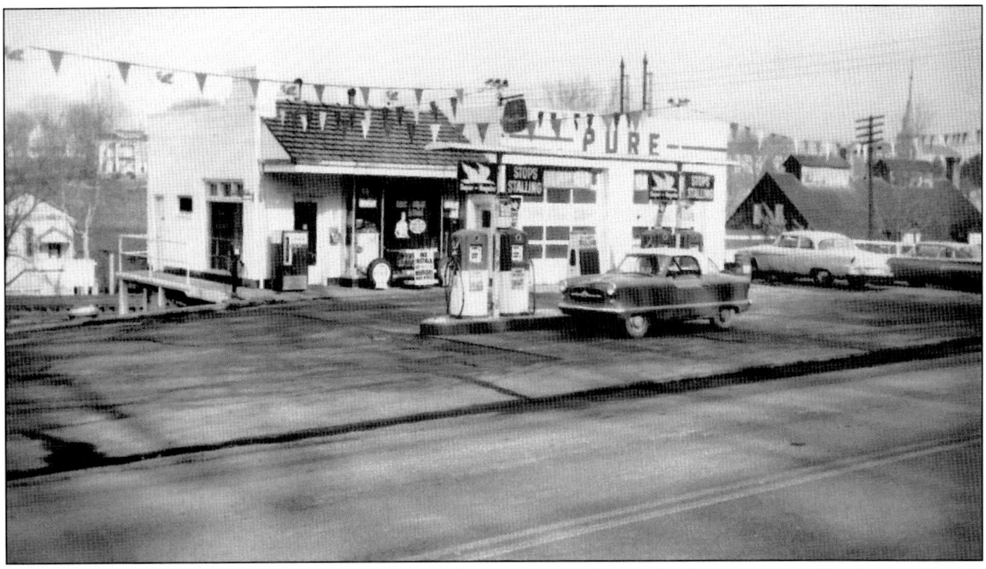

What appears to be a rare Metropolitan Sunbeam automobile, which was owned by Terry Bland, is at the pumps at the Pure Oil service station on East Main Street in Bridgeport. Since the station closed, virtually no other service station at the location has managed to stay in business very long. (Courtesy of Dick Duez.)

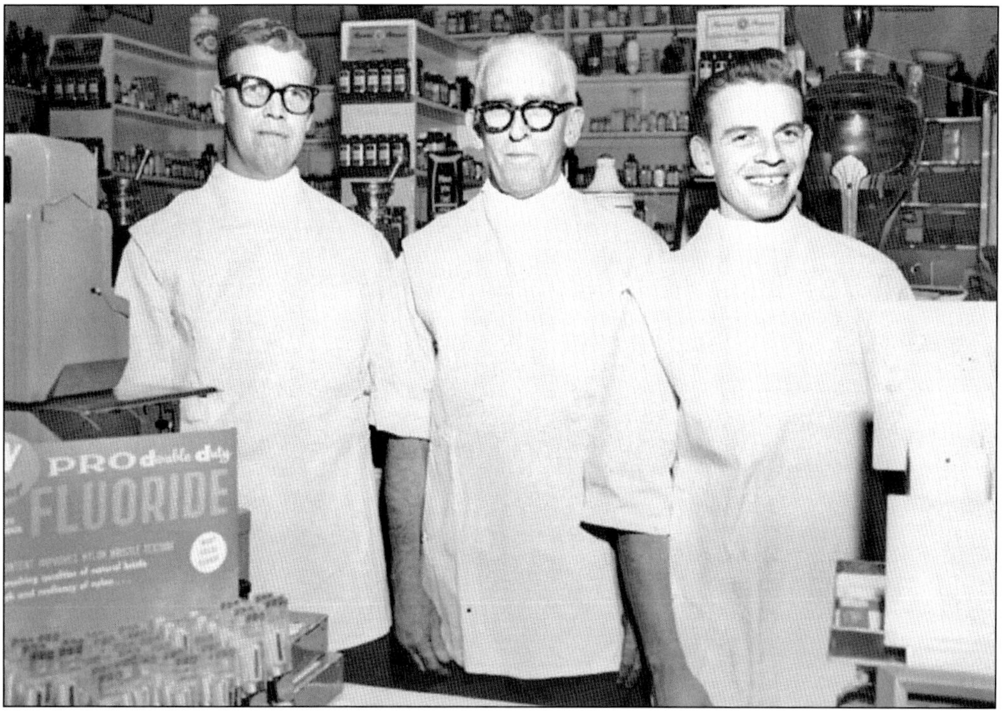

Furbee's Rexall Pharmacy was in good hands and all in the family with this trio of druggists. From left to right are Carl Furbee Jr., Carl Furbee Sr., and Jim Furbee. The photograph was taken in the late 1950s. (Courtesy of Dick Duez.)

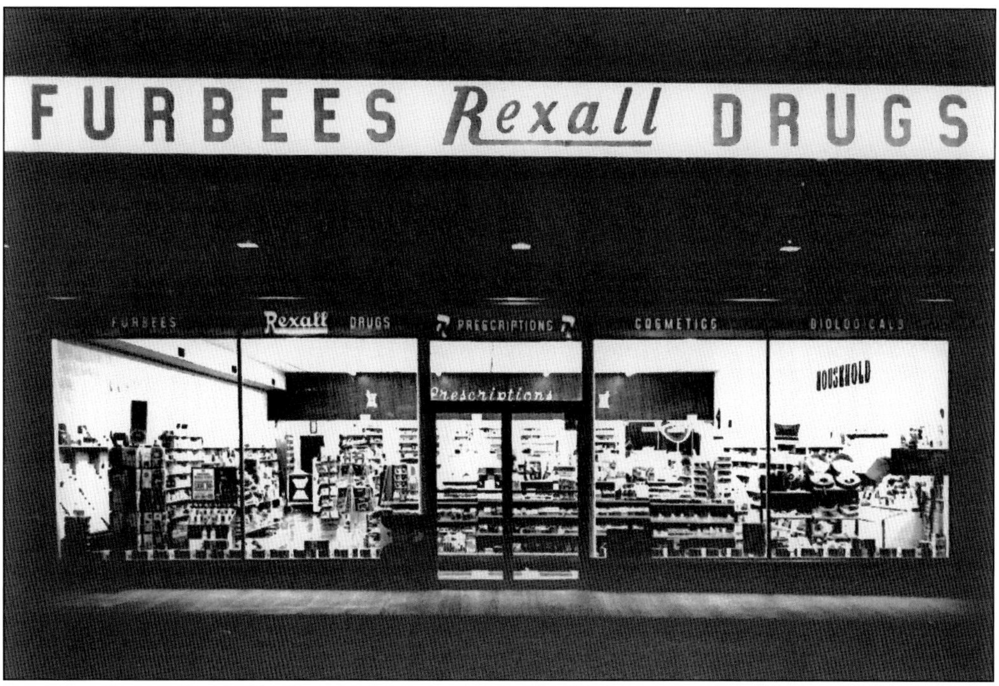

In 1962, when Valley Hills Shopping Center was built along Routes 50 and 58, Furbee's Pharmacy located its shop there. Here it is seen alight in evening hours. (Courtesy of Dick Duez.)

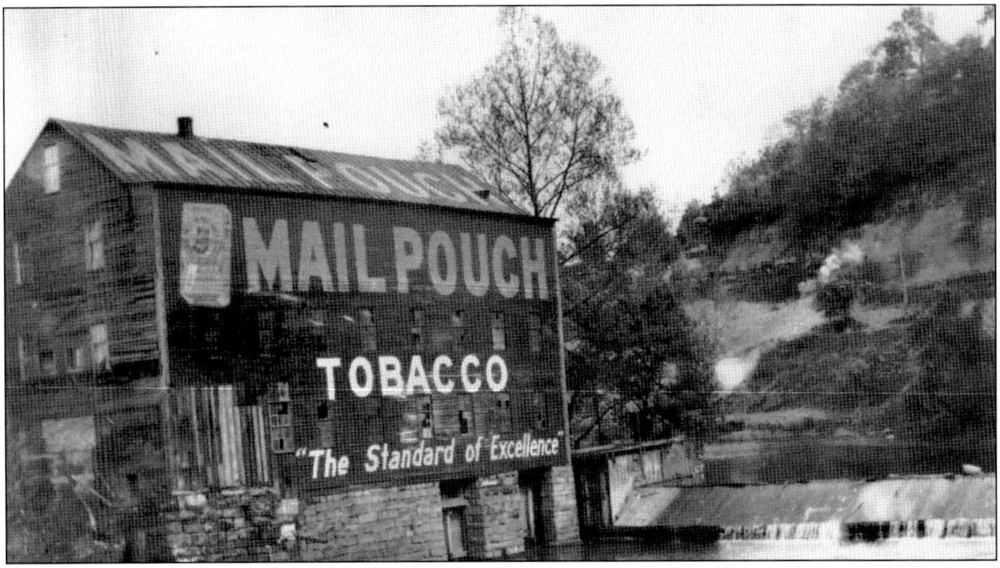

The Old Mill, with its painted Mail Pouch Tobacco sign, was just off Water Street in the bend of Simpson Creek. Its real name was the Davidson and Hurry Mill, and it was known to be in business in 1881. (Courtesy of Dick Duez.)

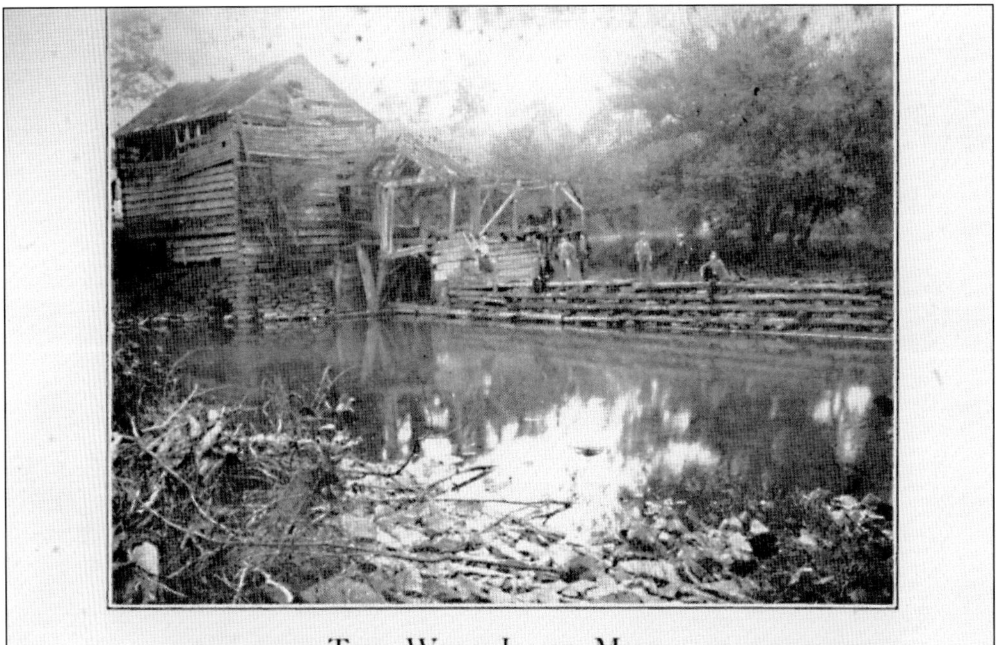

The Webb-Lang Mill was constructed on Simpson Creek near Oral Lake at some time prior to 1784 by Thomas Webb. It was located near what is now the intersection of State Route 76 and the Oral Lake turnoff about two miles east of Bridgeport. (Courtesy of Dick Duez.)

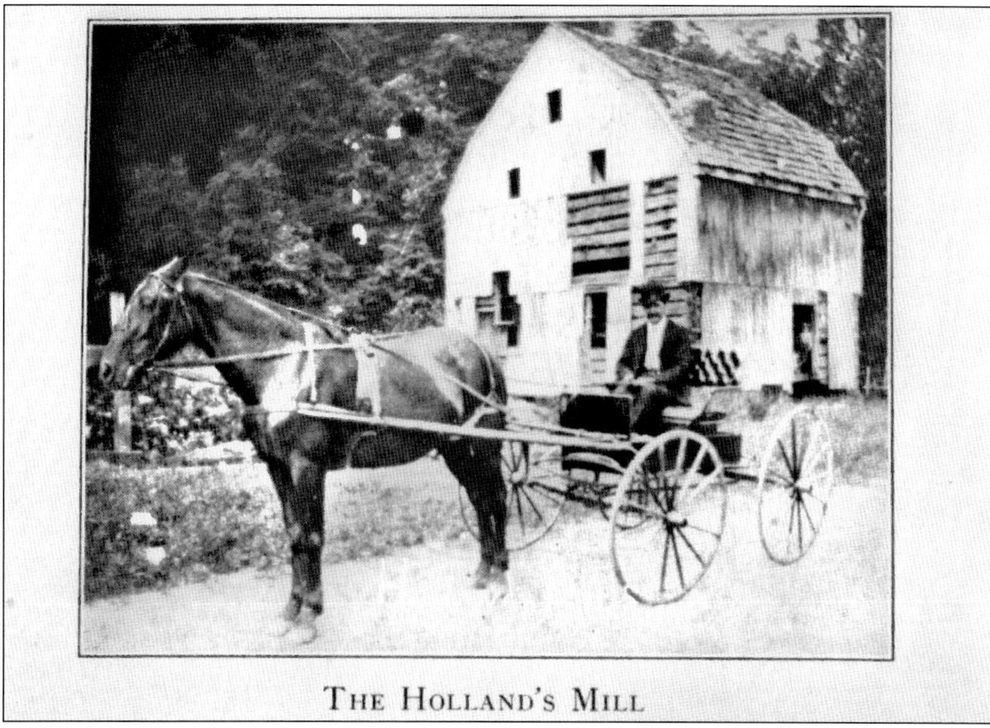

This mill, which was built by Col. Benjamin Wilson to grind grain, saw lumber, and manufacture wool, was sold by Daniel Wilson to Solomon Holland. A steam engine was equipped to the mill by Holland. Holland's Mill was believed to be the first mill in Harrison County to be run by steam. The mill was sold to Lemuel Jarvis and Jefferson J. Smith, and after Smith died in 1893, Holland's Mill was demolished. (Courtesy of Dick Duez.)

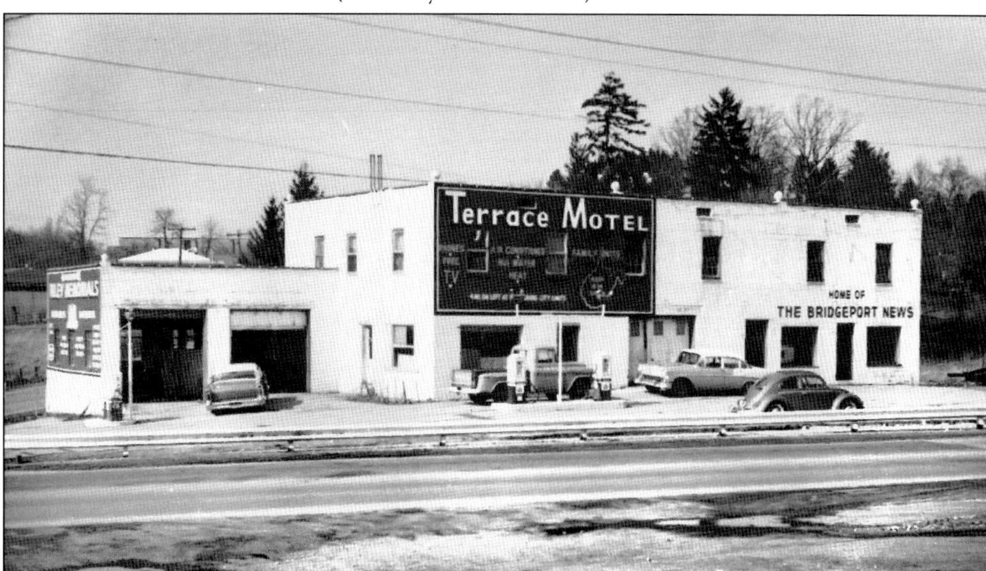

Cecil Golden operated this service station/automobile repair shop at the northeast corner of the U.S. 50–old Route 73 intersection. The old *Bridgeport News*, a weekly newspaper in the late 1950s, can be seen at right. (Courtesy of Dick Duez.)

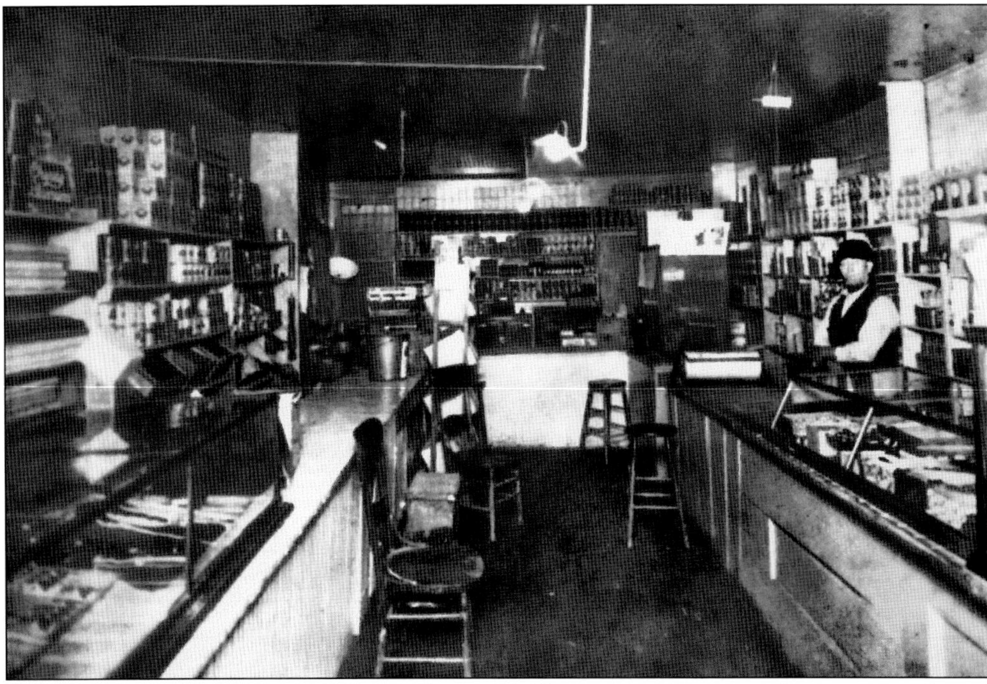

The Newton Wright general store in Bridgeport sold a variety of merchandise in its day. It can't be absolutely determined whether or not the gentleman behind the counter is Newton Wright himself. (Courtesy of Dick Duez.)

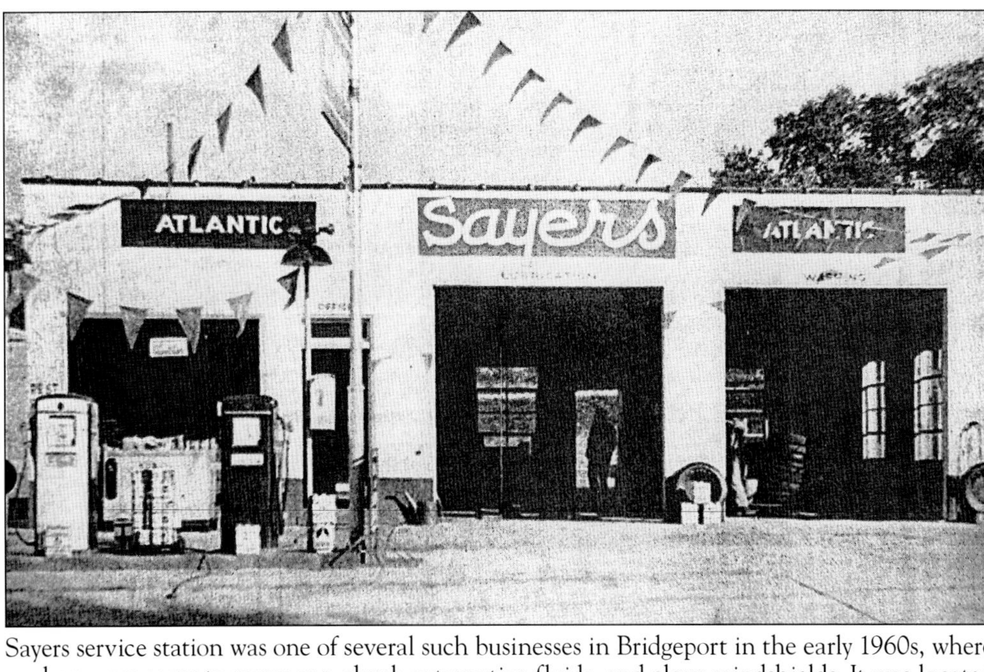

Sayers service station was one of several such businesses in Bridgeport in the early 1960s, where workers were eager to pump gas, check automotive fluids, and clean windshields. It was located in a building across from the present-day Dairy Queen. (Courtesy of Dick Duez.)

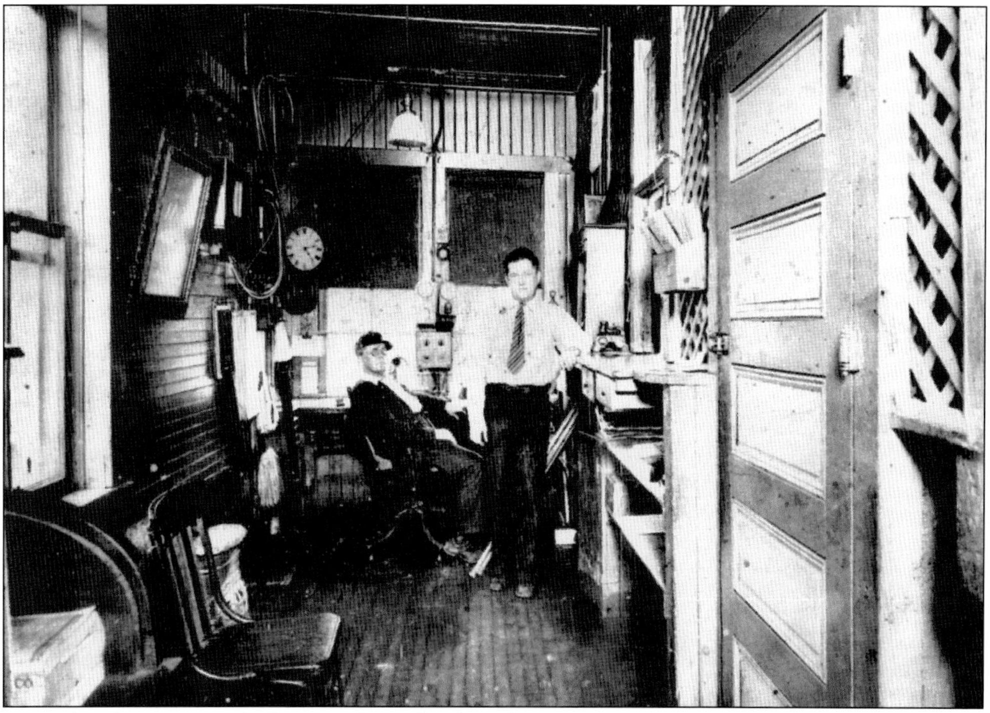

B&O freight agent J. A. Deegan (standing) and W. S. Law, a telephone operator, pose for a photographer on April 30, 1928. (Courtesy of Dick Duez.)

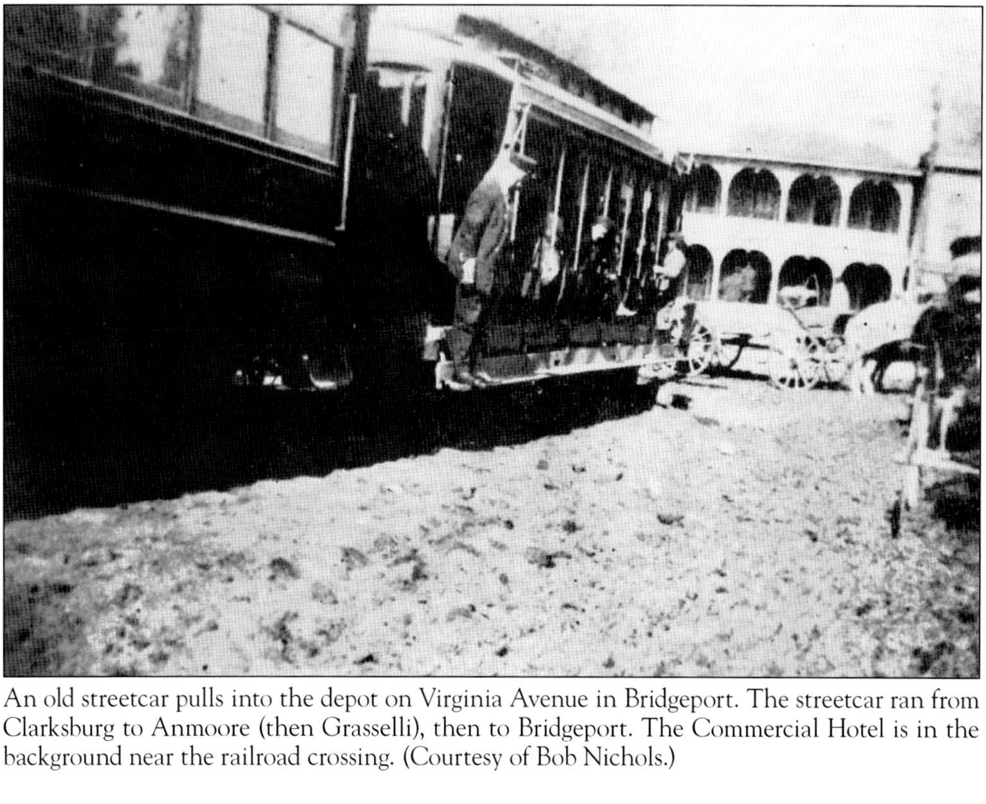

An old streetcar pulls into the depot on Virginia Avenue in Bridgeport. The streetcar ran from Clarksburg to Anmoore (then Grasselli), then to Bridgeport. The Commercial Hotel is in the background near the railroad crossing. (Courtesy of Bob Nichols.)

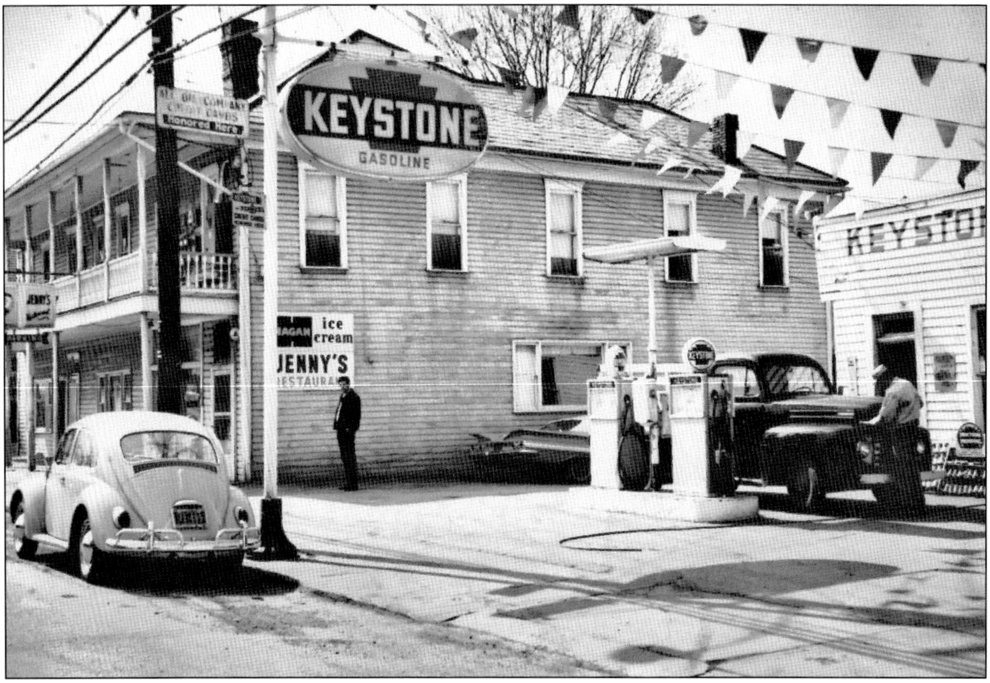

The popular Jenny's Restaurant on West Main Street in Bridgeport is seen here with the Keystone Gasoline filling station owned by Bob Andrews beside it. (Courtesy of Dick Duez.)

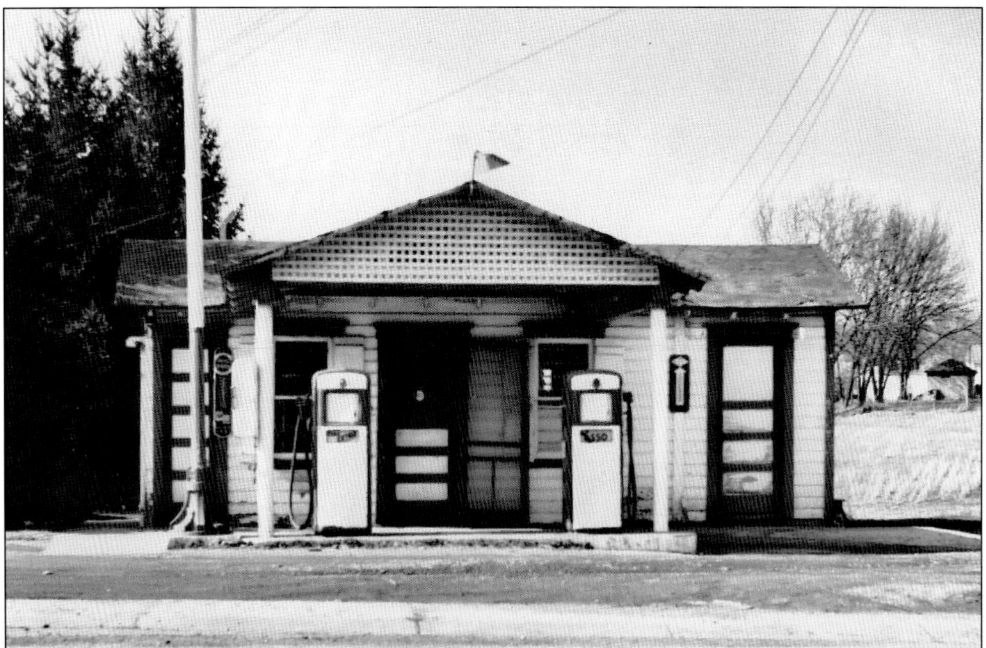

Lowe's Service Station was on the northwest side of the U.S. 50–Route 73 intersection for many years, until it was demolished in 2006. (Courtesy of Dick Duez.)

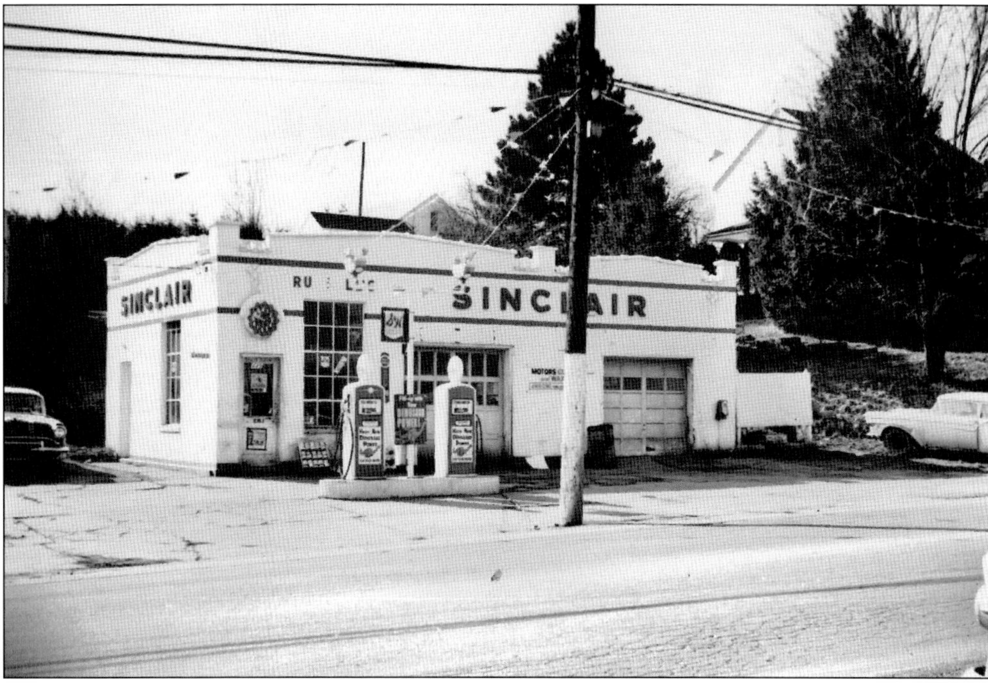

Russell's Sinclair filling station is on East Main Street (U.S. 50) at the bottom of Fifth Street in this 1962 photograph. (Courtesy of Dick Duez.)

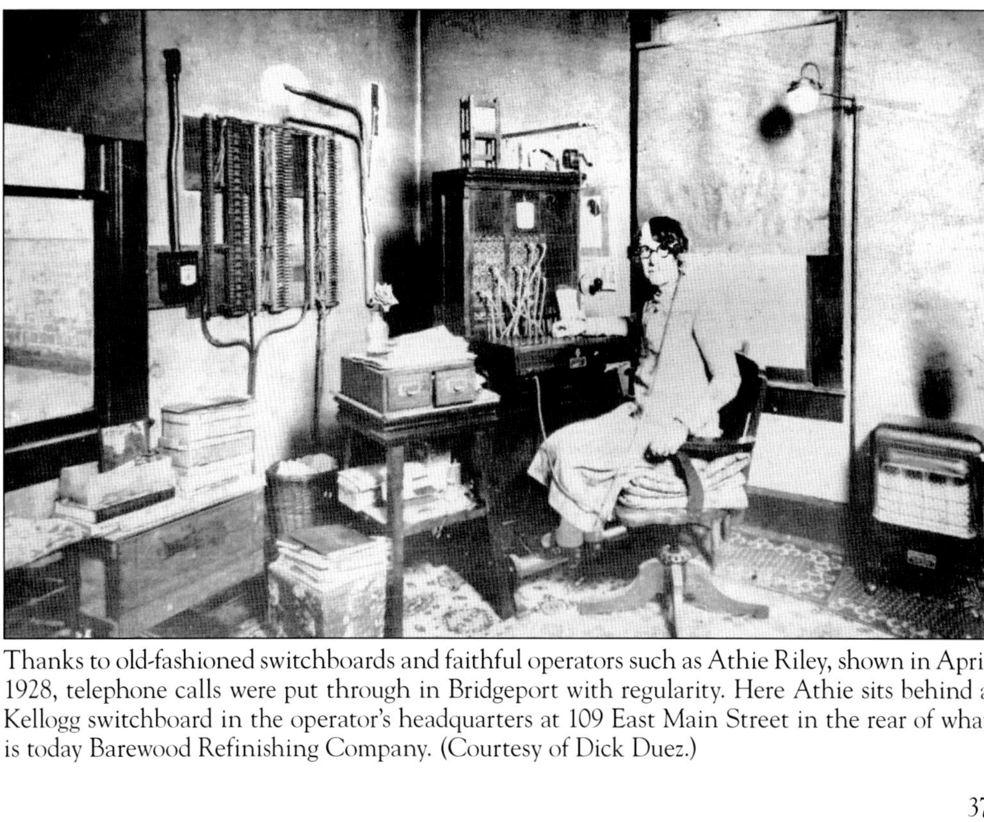

Thanks to old-fashioned switchboards and faithful operators such as Athie Riley, shown in April 1928, telephone calls were put through in Bridgeport with regularity. Here Athie sits behind a Kellogg switchboard in the operator's headquarters at 109 East Main Street in the rear of what is today Barewood Refinishing Company. (Courtesy of Dick Duez.)

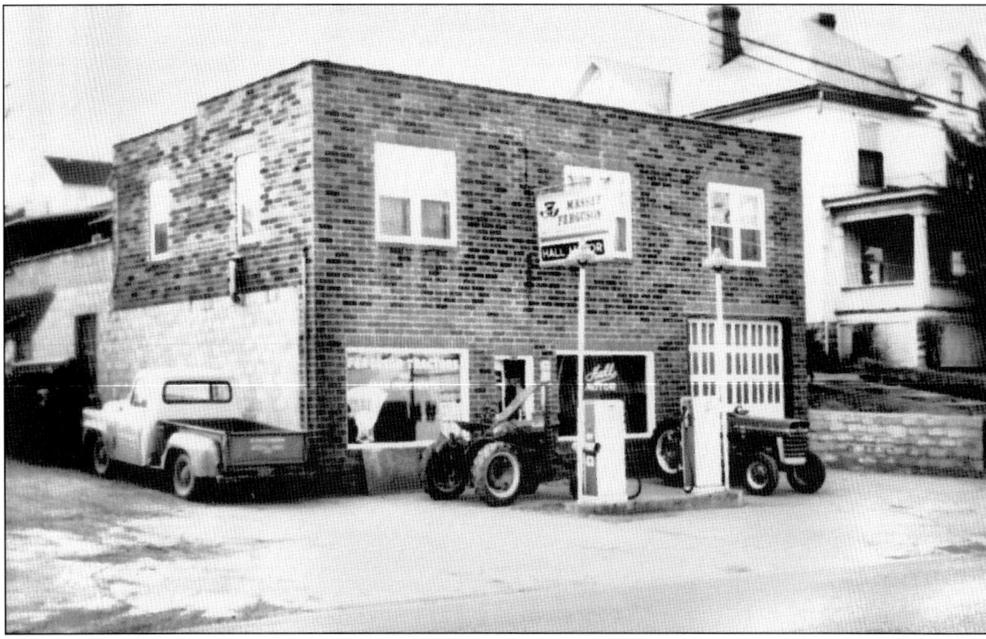

A familiar sight on East Main Street was this brick building, which housed Hall Motor Company, a business that serviced tractors and other farm equipment. (Courtesy of Dick Duez.)

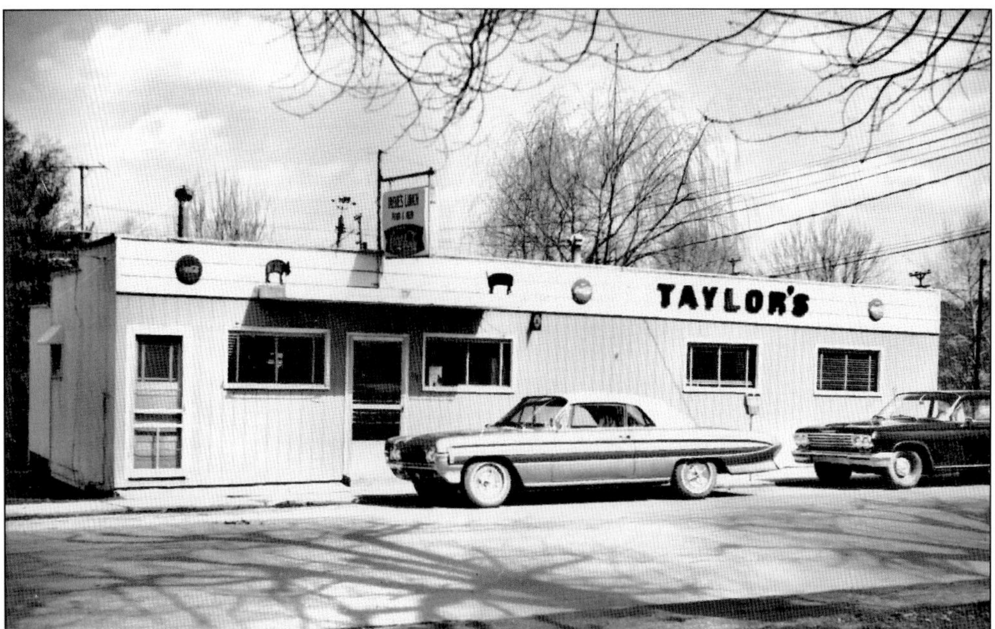

Taylor's Restaurant, also on East Main Street, was a popular eatery in Bridgeport in the 1950s and 1960s. (Courtesy of Dick Duez.)

Two

DOCUMENTS, MONUMENTS, AND MARKERS

There have been so many well-known Bridgeport residents who did their part to form or maintain the city that monuments to only some of them will be seen on the pages to follow. One very prominent Bridgeporter, Michael Late Benedum, who died in July 1959, is buried in the Pittsburgh area, where he finished his successful career.

Included in these pages are letterheads for receipts of older businesses in the city as well as small portions of letters and diaries of people who had gone off to battle in the War Between the States from 1861 to 1865. There's a specimen of a train schedule as well as a water bill from Bridgeport Municipal Water Works. Old-time postcards are also shown. There's even a page of advertisements taken from a former newspaper in the city, the *Bridgeport Independent*. Interestingly enough, there is also a reward poster made by the sheriff of Harrison County for a robber-arsonist. Highway historical markers, popular throughout the entire state of West Virginia, are in evidence in Bridgeport. These include the Benedum Civic Center, John Powers's Fort, and the Simpson Creek Covered Bridge. The text on the signs provides a mini–history lesson on each site. Perhaps one day, there will be even more historical markers in Bridgeport, such as for the William Johnson house, the Gov. Joseph Johnson house, and the Bridgeport Cemetery.

One will also see the epitaphs of such notable Bridgeporters as Gov. Joseph Johnson, Col. Benjamin Wilson, and Joseph Davisson, who are buried in the Bridgeport Cemetery, believed to be the oldest cemetery in Harrison County. In addition, there is a plaque installed on the exterior wall of the old Baptist meetinghouse that was located in the cemetery.

At one time, standing on Main Street was a multi-sided tribute to Bridgeport residents who had lost their lives in battle in many of the wars in which America was involved. More of each of these might have been desired for this chapter, but it was believed that a sampling would be sufficient for the cause.

PAGE TWO INDEPENDENCE

INDEPENDENCE
PUBLISHED WEEKLY

J. P. Bower .... Editor
Bob Cook ...... Asst. Editor

Build Bridgeport Bigger Better

Send all news items to J. Pat Bower, Box G, % of the *Independence*, Bridgeport, W. Va.

News and Shopping Guide

Bridgeport, W. Va.

LITTLE LEAGUE STANDINGS

	Won	Lost
Moose	6	0
Clearlite	4	1
Elks	4	1
Lost Creek	4	1
Shinnston	4	1
Zeising	4	2
Workingman's	3	3
Tucker's	2	4
Cities	1	4
K. of C.	1	4
West Milford	0	5
Lumberport	0	6

Attention Bridgeport!

— EDITORIAL —

We have made a modest beginning on what we hope will be helpful publication for the community. This paper, with your support, can grow into a real service to the town of Bridgeport.

The majority of the merchants of the community have, as they have always in the past, given their wholehearted support to ths newspaper and it is now the responsibility of the citizens themselves to supply their support.

Our merchants have been interested enough in your welfare to support the INDEPENDENCE. We humbly request that you return this favor by patronizing the advertising merchants of the INDEPENDENCE.

Money spent outside of the community is lost capital to this city. Therefore it is the duty of each citizen to patronize the merchants of Bridgeport whenever possible. In this manner the wealth and progress of our fair city may be insured. Why not let the merchants know that you are standing behind them in every way?

We have started from the bottom of the ladder and with your support we will work our way up rung by rung. We shall earnestly strive to improve this paper from week to week, and with your aid and sustenance we feel confident it will be a success.

Buy In Bridgeport

Reliable Prescription Service

FURBEE'S PHARMACY

The Rexall Store

DIAL 2-2980 Bridgeport, W. Va.

FREE

WE WILL TEST THE TREAD OF YOUR TIRES AND SHOW YOU THE CONDITION OF THEM

BUY NEW GUARANTEED PURE TIRES ON EASY TERMS

DON DUKE'S

PURE OIL SERVICE

Be Sure With Pure

The Delicatessen

The Delicatessen owned by Elizabeth Thorp

Delcious home baked pies and cakes just like mother always makes

ICE CREAM, CANDY, CAKES, SMOKES

AND PICNIC SUPPLIES

208 MAIN STREET, BRIDGEPORT

This page shows an array of advertisements from a page of the old *Bridgeport Independent* newspaper in July 1960. Don Duke's service station and Furbee's Pharmacy are among the advertisers. (Courtesy of Fred Layman.)

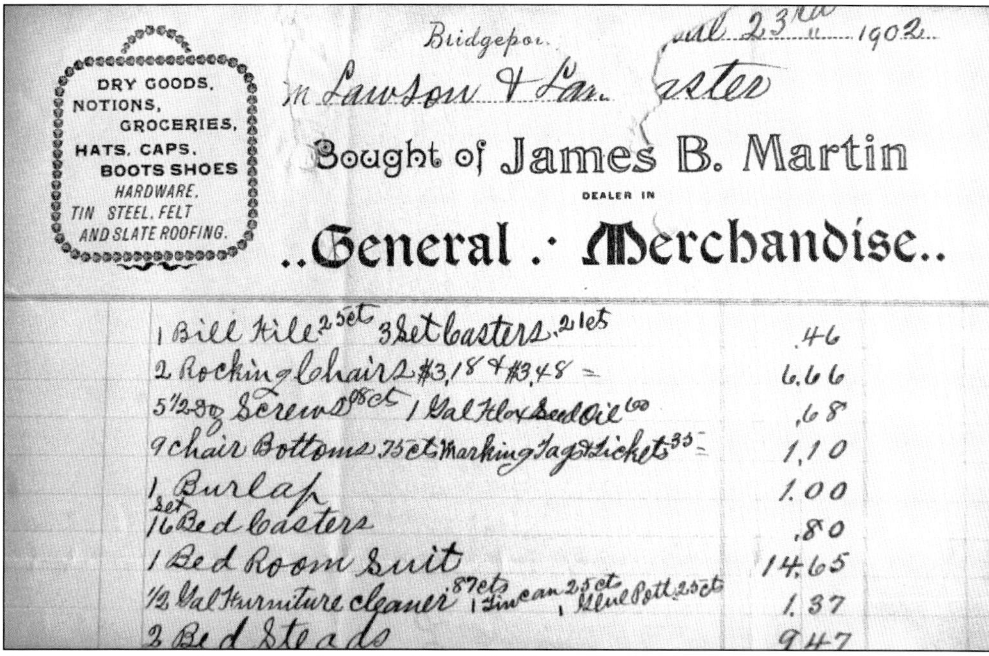

DRY GOODS,
NOTIONS,
GROCERIES,
HATS, CAPS,
BOOTS SHOES
HARDWARE,
TIN STEEL, FELT
AND SLATE ROOFING.

Bridgepor... ...23rd ... 1902

M Lawson & Lancaster

Bought of James B. Martin

DEALER IN

..General .· Merchandise..

1 Bill File 25ct 3 set casters 21ct	.46
2 Rocking Chairs $3.18 & $3.48 =	6.66
5½ doz Screws 08ct 1 Gal Flax Seed Oil 60	.68
9 chair Bottoms 75ct Marking Tag & Tickets 35 =	1.10
1 Burlap	1.00
16 set Bed Casters	.80
1 Bed Room Suit	14.65
½ Gal Furniture cleaner 87cts 1 Tin can 25ct 1 Glue Bott 25ct	1.37
2 Bed Steads	9.47

Above is a copy of a receipt from the James B. Martin business. He was a dry goods general merchant. (Courtesy of Dick Duez.)

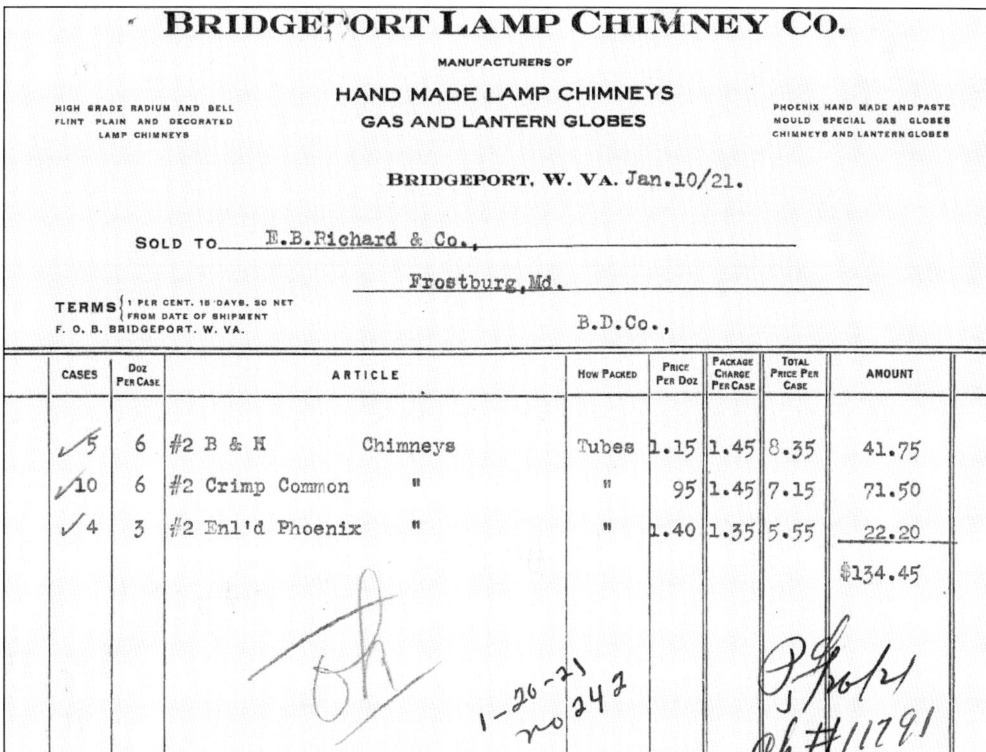

BRIDGEPORT LAMP CHIMNEY CO.

MANUFACTURERS OF

HAND MADE LAMP CHIMNEYS
GAS AND LANTERN GLOBES

HIGH GRADE RADIUM AND BELL FLINT PLAIN AND DECORATED LAMP CHIMNEYS

PHOENIX HAND MADE AND PASTE MOULD SPECIAL GAS GLOBES CHIMNEYS AND LANTERN GLOBES

BRIDGEPORT, W. VA. Jan.10/21.

SOLD TO E.B.Richard & Co.,
Frostburg,Md.

TERMS { 1 PER CENT. 10 DAYS. 30 NET FROM DATE OF SHIPMENT
F. O. B. BRIDGEPORT, W. VA.

B.D.Co.,

CASES	DOZ PER CASE	ARTICLE	HOW PACKED	PRICE PER DOZ	PACKAGE CHARGE PER CASE	TOTAL PRICE PER CASE	AMOUNT
✓5	6	#2 B & H Chimneys	Tubes	1.15	1.45	8.35	41.75
✓10	6	#2 Crimp Common "	"	95	1.45	7.15	71.50
✓4	3	#2 Enl'd Phoenix "	"	1.40	1.35	5.55	22.20
							$134.45

1-26-21
no 247

Ck #11791

This receipt was from the lamp plant, a business in which merchant John Dunkin was a partner. (Courtesy of Dick Duez.)

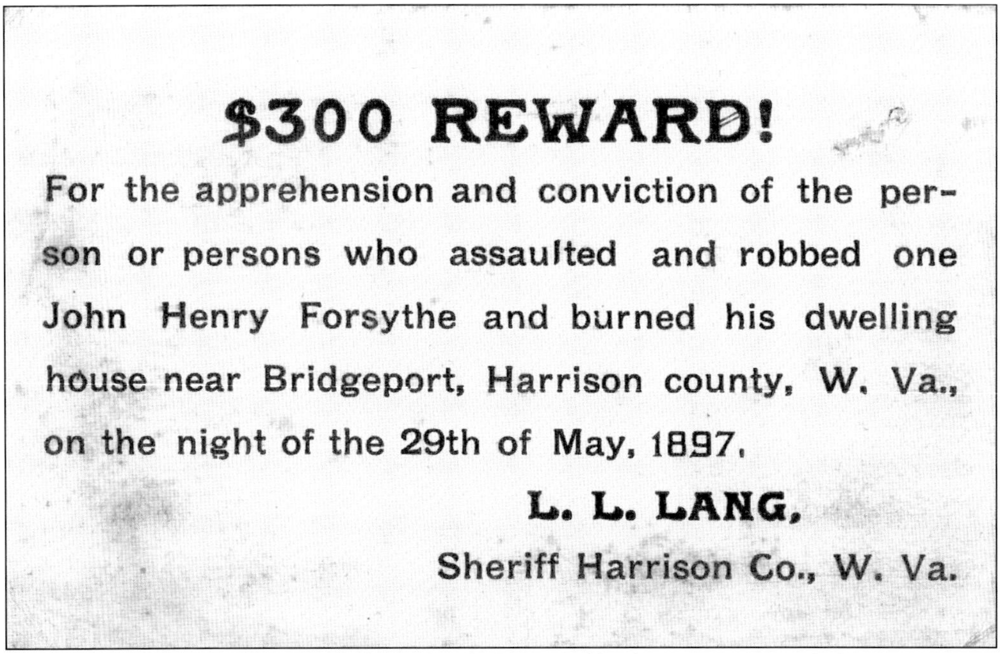
$300 REWARD!

For the apprehension and conviction of the person or persons who assaulted and robbed one John Henry Forsythe and burned his dwelling house near Bridgeport, Harrison county, W. Va., on the night of the 29th of May, 1897.

L. L. LANG,
Sheriff Harrison Co., W. Va.

Here's a message that made for a different kind of postcard back in 1897—one of a bit more serious nature, to be sure. (Courtesy of Dick Duez.)

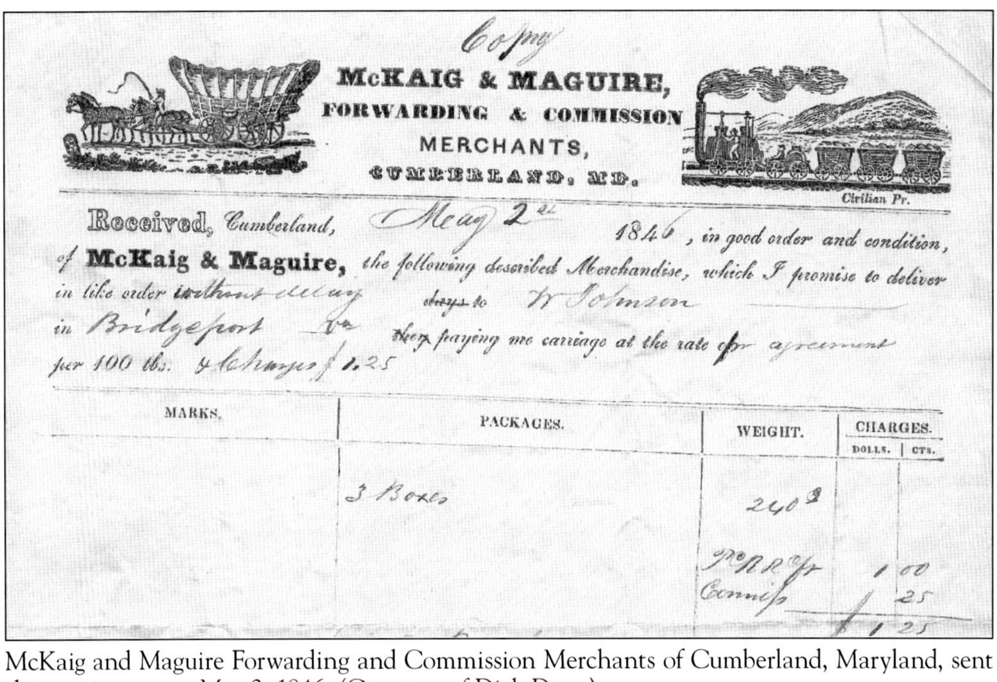
Copy

McKAIG & MAGUIRE,
FORWARDING & COMMISSION
MERCHANTS,
CUMBERLAND, MD.

Clrilian Pr.

Received, *Cumberland,* May 2d 1846, *in good order and condition,* of **McKaig & Maguire,** *the following described Merchandise, which I promise to deliver in like order* without delay *days to* W Johnson in Bridgeport Va *they paying me carriage at the rate* of agreement *per 100 lbs.* & charges $ 1.25

MARKS.	PACKAGES.	WEIGHT.	CHARGES. DOLLS.	CTS.
	3 Boxes	240		
		P. RR Co fr	1	00
		Comm		25
			1	25

McKaig and Maguire Forwarding and Commission Merchants of Cumberland, Maryland, sent this receipt out on May 2, 1846. (Courtesy of Dick Duez.)

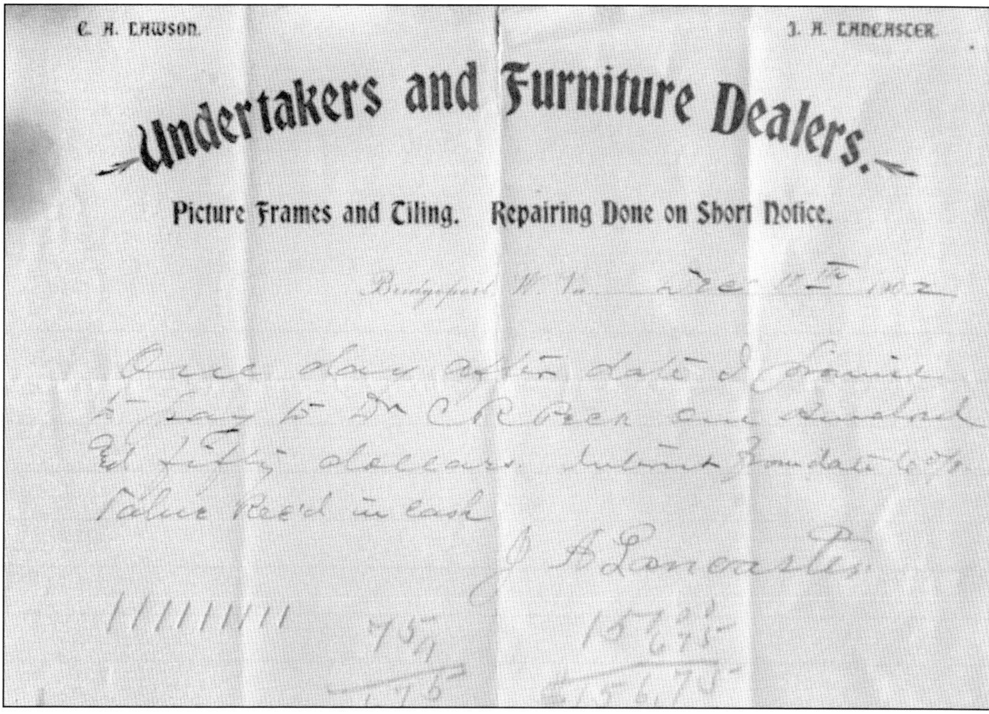
C. A. LAWSON. J. A. LANCASTER.

Undertakers and Furniture Dealers.

Picture Frames and Tiling. Repairing Done on Short Notice.

This is a receipt from an undertaker, the former name of a funeral director or mortician. (Courtesy of Dick Duez.)

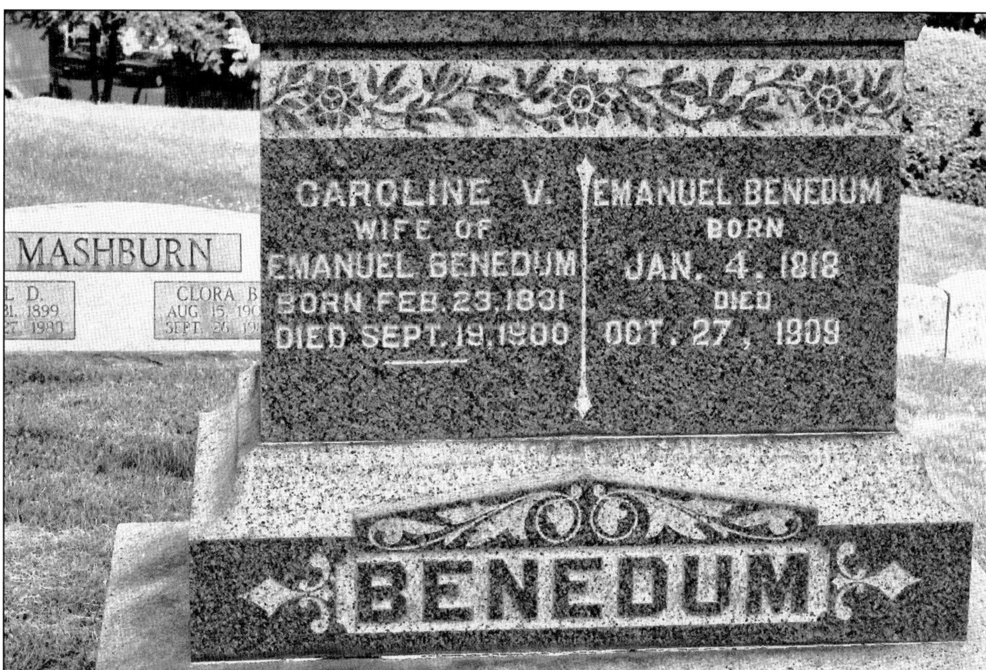

The words on this monument in the Bridgeport Cemetery briefly memorialize Caroline and Emanuel Benedum, the parents of Michael L. Benedum. (Courtesy of Benedum Civic Center.)

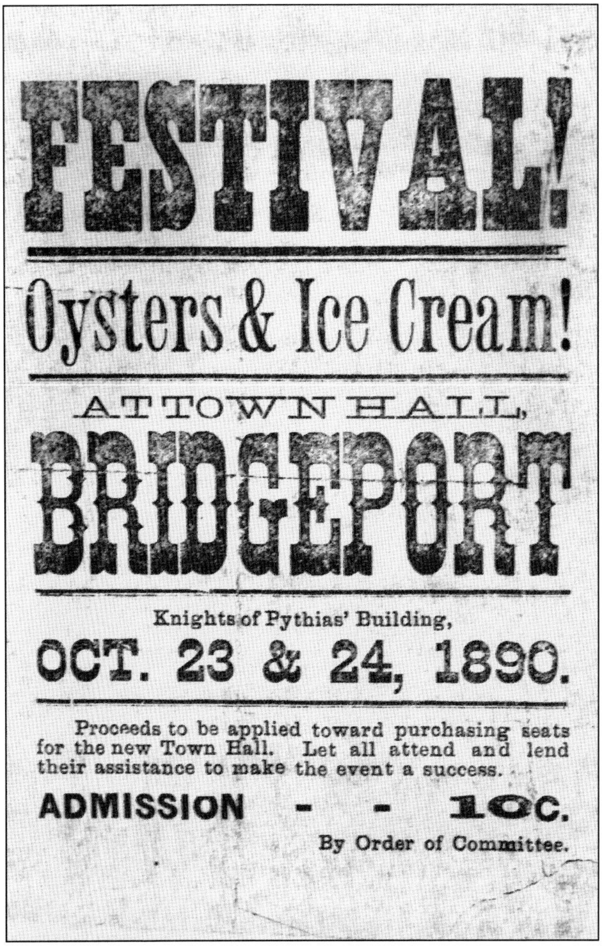

Oysters and ice cream! That sounds like a rather unlikely combination by today's standards, perhaps, but in the 1890s, it was quite an attraction, and it was made available during a festival at the Bridgeport Town Hall in the Knights of Pythias Building for the admission price of a dime. The event was held October 23 and 24, 1890. (From author's collection.)

This postcard was addressed to J. C. Johnson of Bridgeport, dated 1874. Note that the spelling of the last name as "Johnston" was in error. (Courtesy of Dick Duez.)

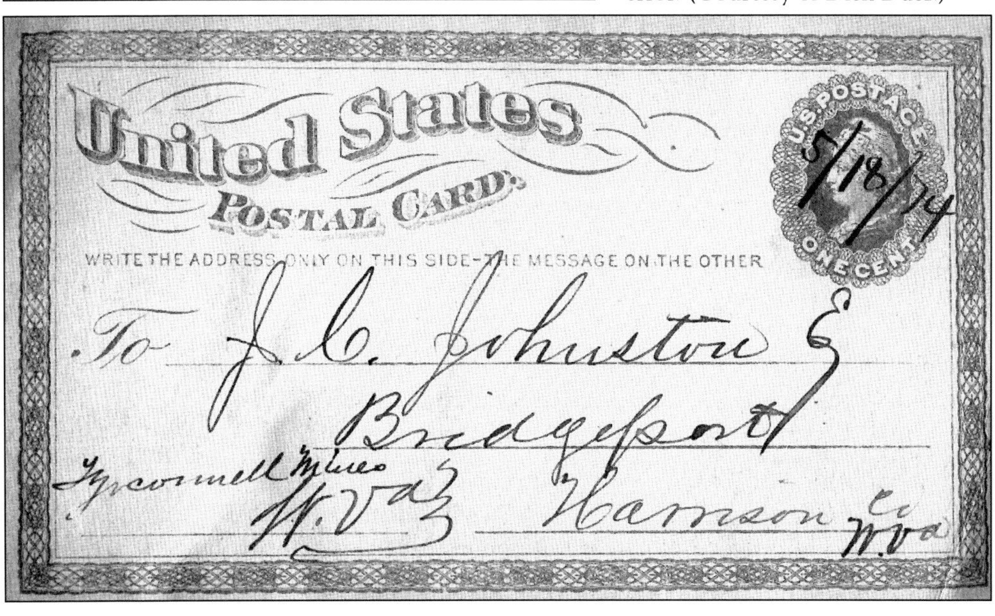

This is a railroad contract with Thomas Johnson as agent. It was dated April 17, 1861, near the start of the War Between the States. (Courtesy of Roger Hardy.)

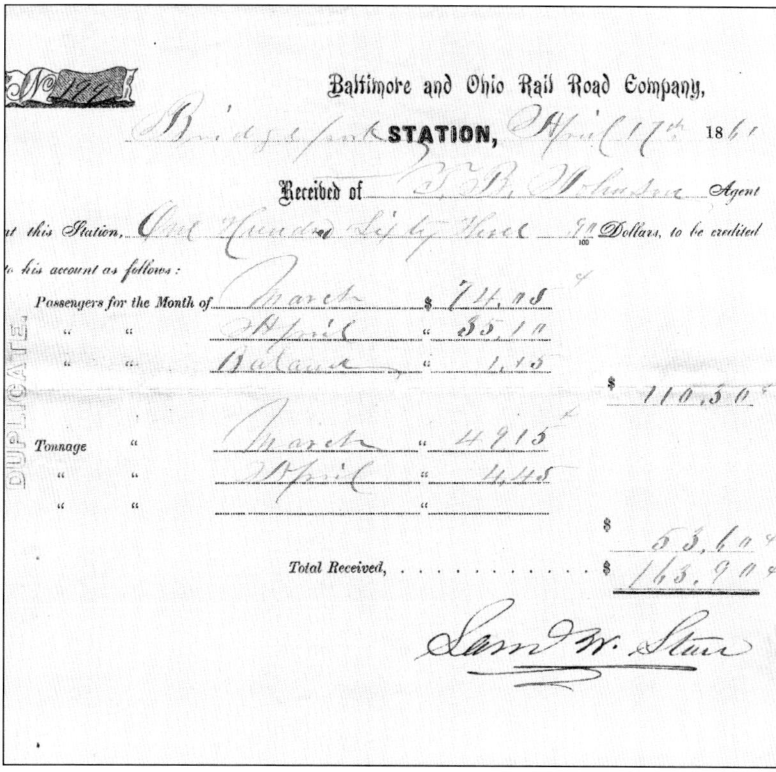

No. 1771

Baltimore and Ohio Rail Road Company,

Bridgeport STATION, April 17th 1861

Received of T. B. Johnson Agent

at this Station, One Hundred Sixty Three 90/100 Dollars, to be credited to his account as follows:

Passengers for the Month of	March	$ 74.05		
" "	April	" 35.10		
" "	Balance	" 1.15		
			$	110.30
Tonnage "	March	" 49.15		
" "	April	" 4.45		
" "		"		
			$	53.60
Total Received,			$	163.90

DUPLICATE.

Saml W. Starr

The Davidson and Hurry partnership, which was associated with a mill at the end of Water Street, sent this receipt to one of its customers back in the 19th century. (Courtesy of Dick Duez.)

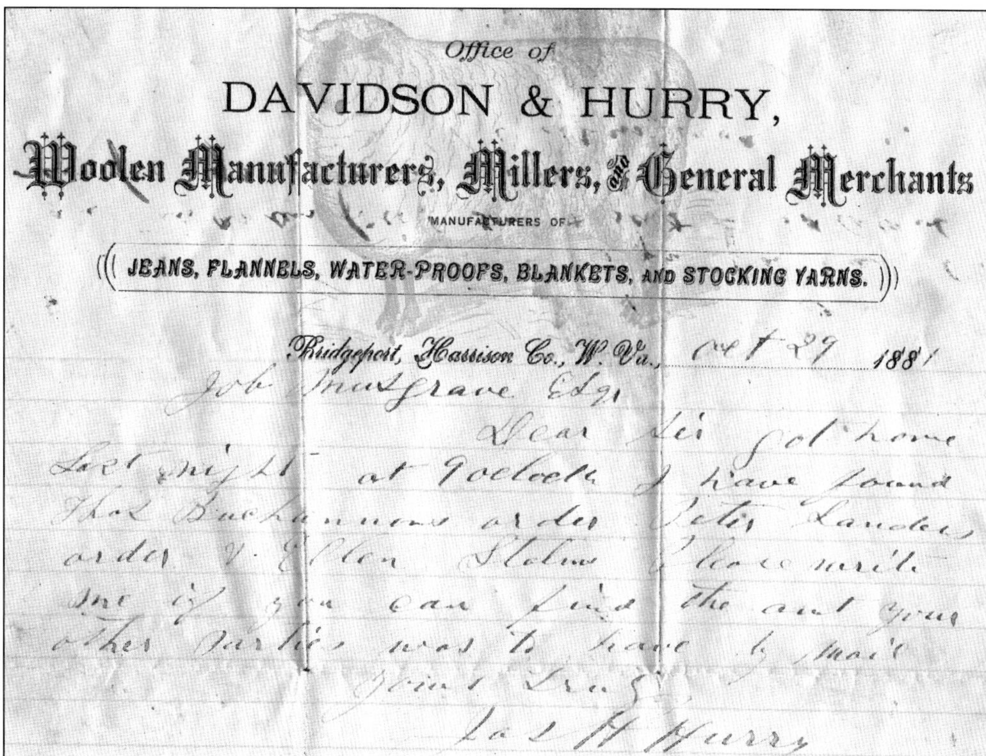

Office of

DAVIDSON & HURRY,

Woolen Manufacturers, Millers, and General Merchants

MANUFACTURERS OF

JEANS, FLANNELS, WATER-PROOFS, BLANKETS, AND STOCKING YARNS.

Bridgeport, Harrison Co., W. Va., Oct 29 1881

Job Musgrave Esq

Dear Sir got home last night at 9 oclock I have found that Buchannons order Peter Sandes order & Ellen Stalus Please write me if you can find the amt your other parties was to have by mail

Yours Truly

Jas H Hurry

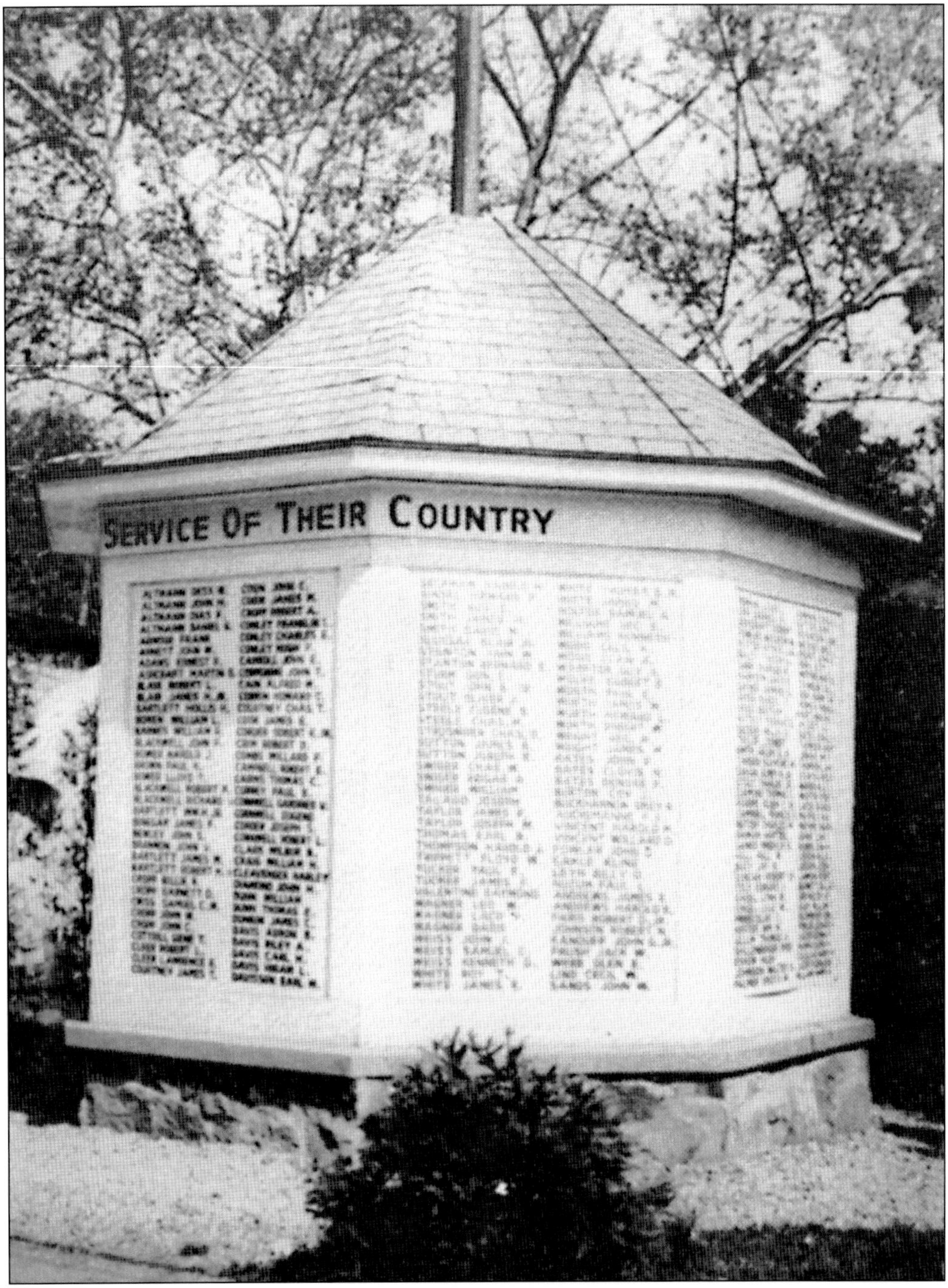

For years, this hexagonal monument to soldiers from Bridgeport who gave their lives in battle for their country stood along East Main Street near the old school walkway. (Courtesy of Dick Duez.)

Joseph Johnson was governor of Virginia from 1852 to 1855, prior to when West Virginia became a state. He was a resident of Bridgeport who lived just east of lower Johnson Avenue. Pictured is his tombstone. (Courtesy of Dick Duez.)

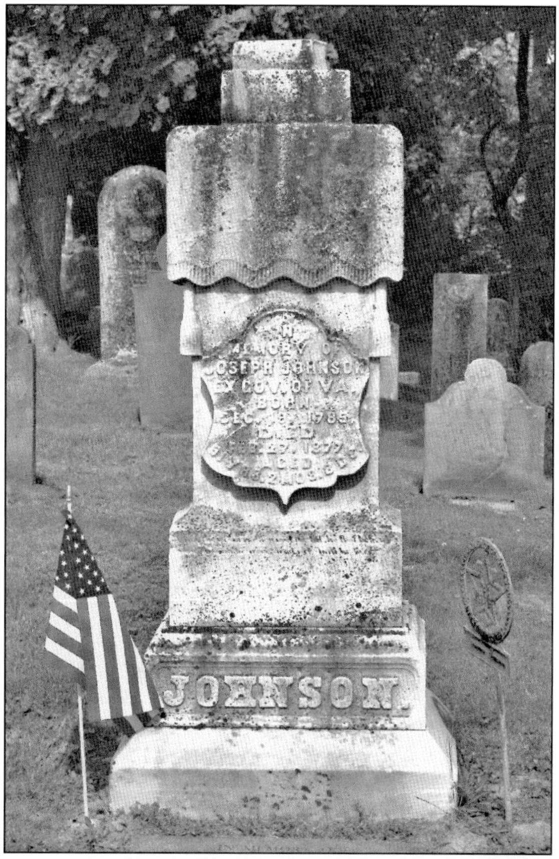

Governor Johnson is remembered in an epitaph on the tombstone. (Courtesy of Dick Duez.)

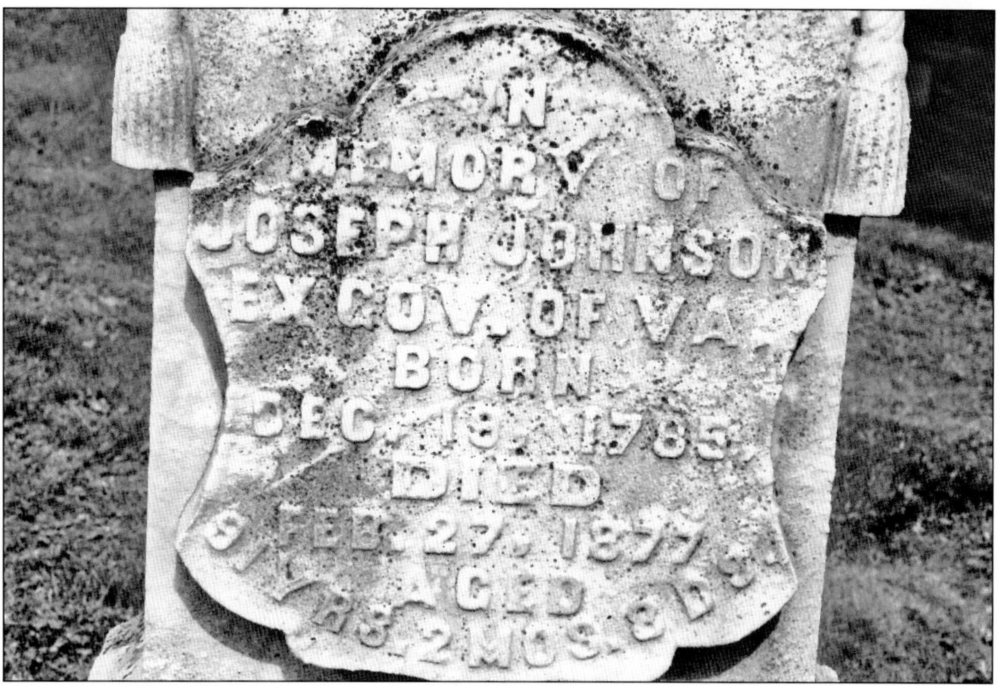

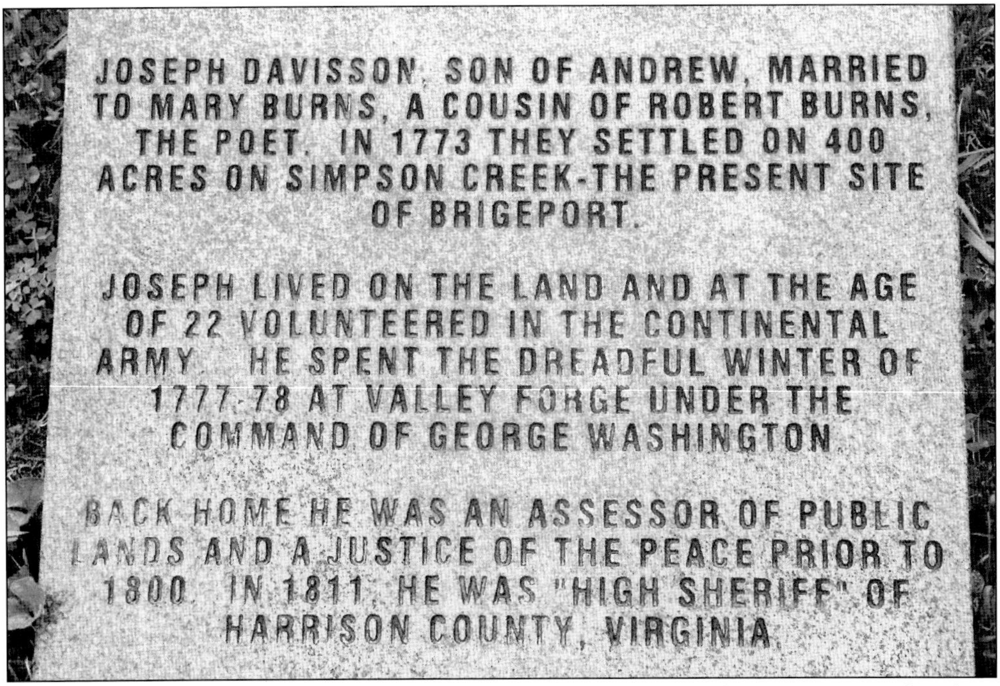

In a relatively few words, this inscription on the flat gravestone of Joseph Davisson, son of Andrew Davisson, in Bridgeport Cemetery, notes his adventures in the Revolutionary War and his life back in Bridgeport. (Courtesy of Dick Duez.)

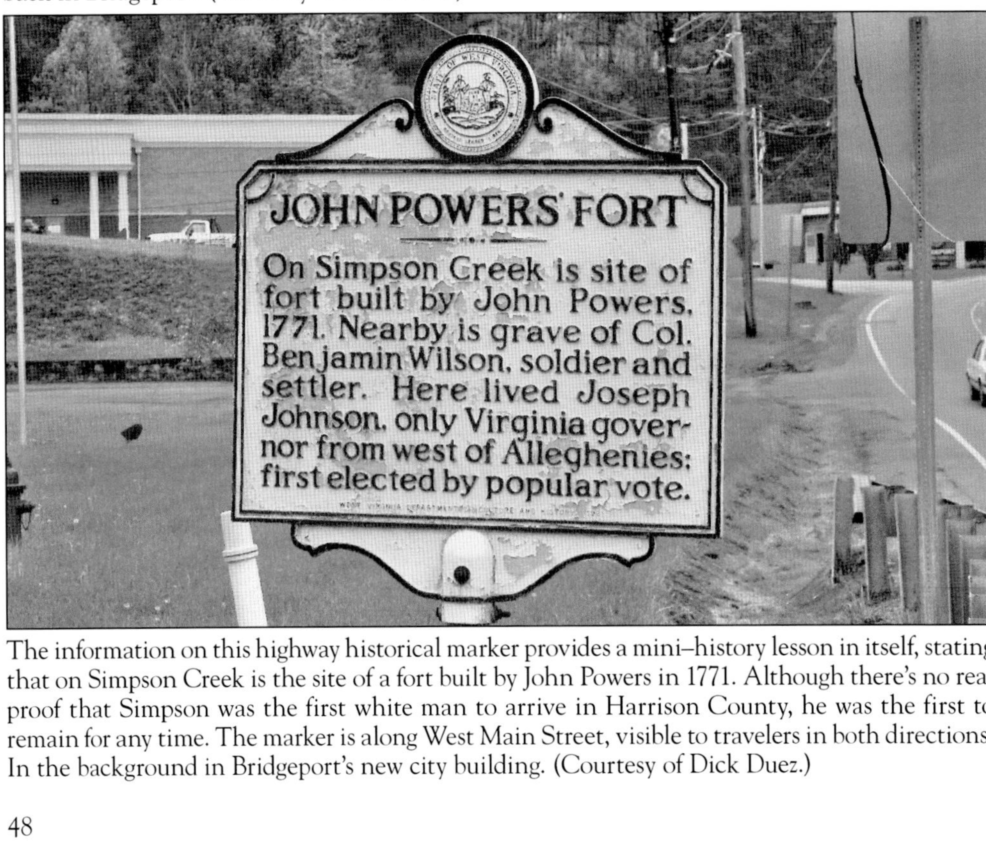

The information on this highway historical marker provides a mini–history lesson in itself, stating that on Simpson Creek is the site of a fort built by John Powers in 1771. Although there's no real proof that Simpson was the first white man to arrive in Harrison County, he was the first to remain for any time. The marker is along West Main Street, visible to travelers in both directions. In the background in Bridgeport's new city building. (Courtesy of Dick Duez.)

J. C. Johnson wrote these diary pages when he was 23 years of age. They reflect two days in his life during the War Between the States. (Courtesy of Dick Duez.)

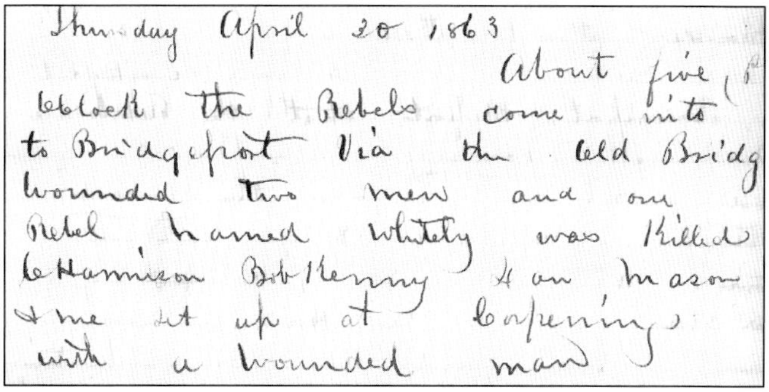
Thursday April 20 1863
About five O'clock the Rebels come into Bridgeport via the old Bridge wounded two men and one Rebel named Whitely was killed. Harrison Bob Kenny Hon Mason & me set up at Copenings with a wounded man

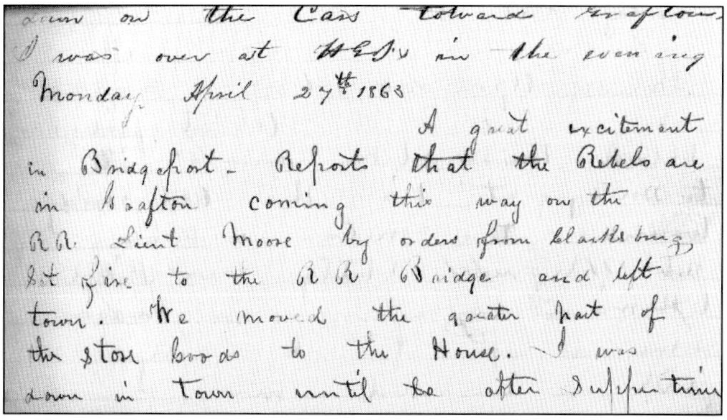
down on the Cars toward Grafton. I was over at H.E.S's in the evening
Monday April 27th 1863
A great excitement in Bridgeport. Report that the Rebels are in Grafton coming this way on the R.R. Lieut Moore by orders from Clarksburg set fire to the R R Bridge and left town. We moved the greater part of the store goods to the House. I was down in town until be after supper time

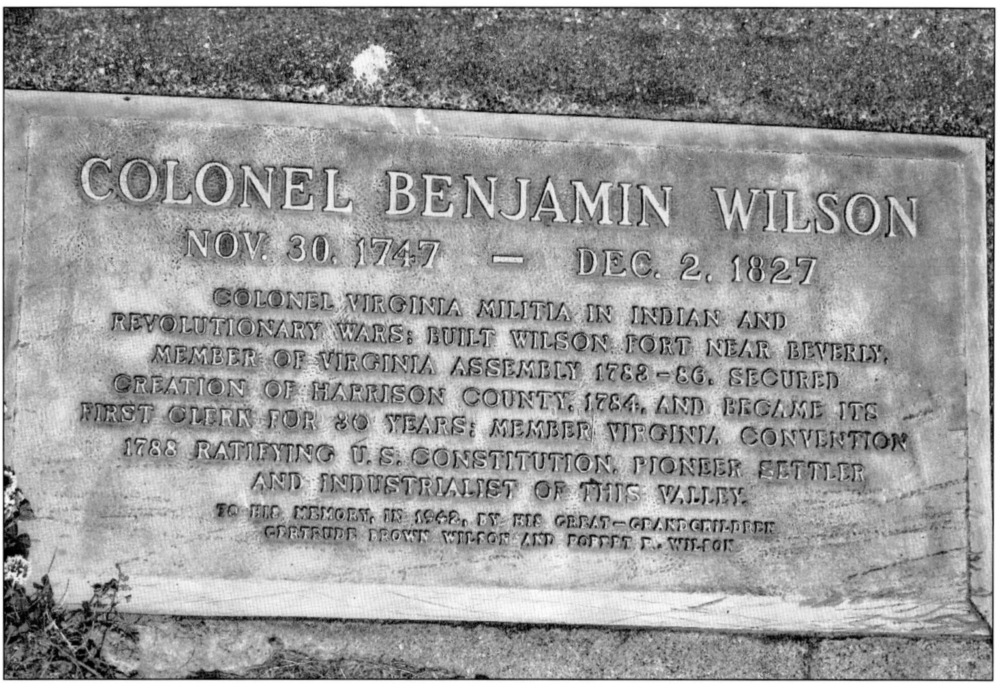

This is the epitaph on the gravestone of Col. Benjamin Wilson, who lived to the age of 80. Among the numerous things for which the colonel was well known was his leadership of settlers in pursuing the Native American captors of their wives and children and the destroyers of their homes. His son, Benjamin Wilson II, was a clerk of the Harrison County Circuit Court. (Courtesy of Dick Duez.)

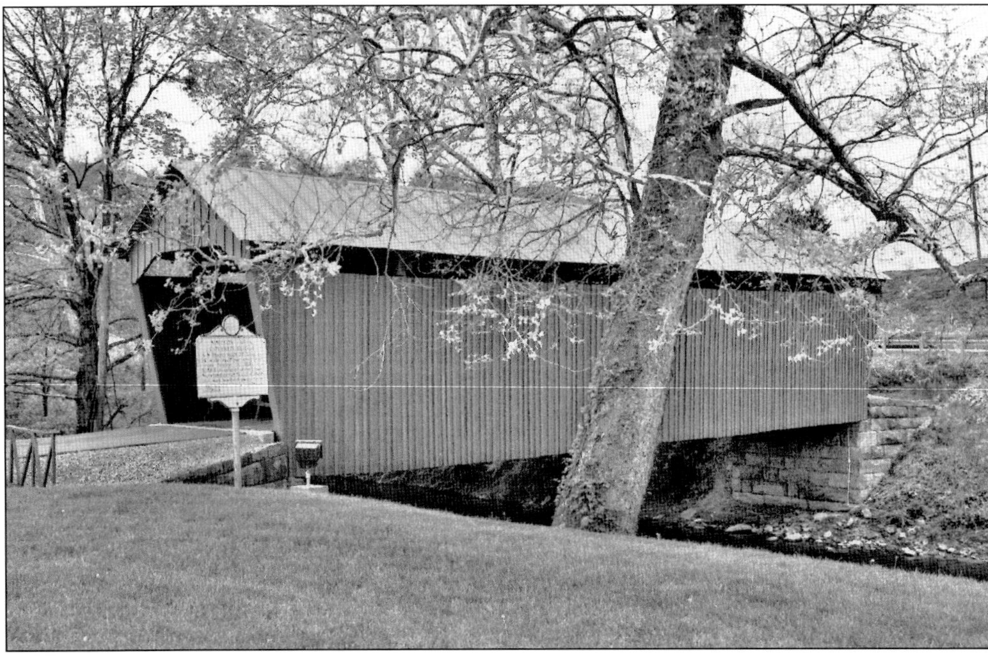

The Simpson Creek Covered Bridge, located just off Harrison County Route 24 (the Meadowbrook Road), closed to vehicular traffic several years ago. It is probably the best known of the covered bridges that have ever been located in the county and was a direct link between the Meadowbrook Road and Murphy's Run Road, a county route. The highway marker providing information about the span can be seen from a distance. (Courtesy of Dick Duez.)

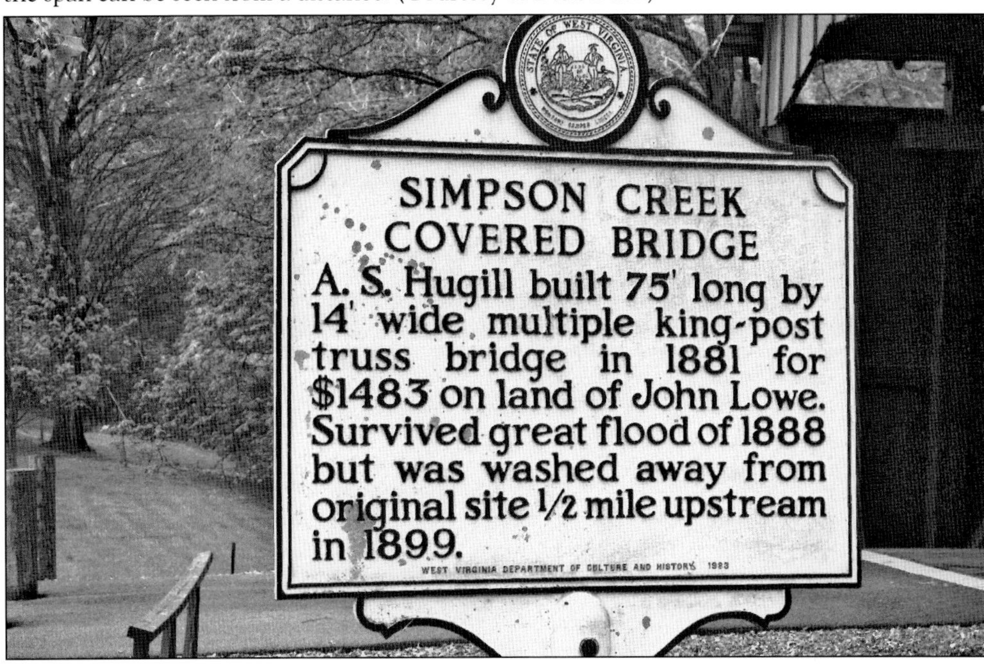

This is a closer look at the highway marker for the Simpson Creek Covered Bridge, which was built by A. S. Hugill back in 1881 at the cost of $1,483. The marker lists the dimensions of the wooden bridge, which was on the John Lowe property. (Courtesy of Dick Duez.)

This is the start of a letter dealing with the proposed building of old State Route 73, from Morgantown to Bridgeport. The letter was sent from Richmond, Virginia, on March 16, 1849, to William Johnson from his son-in-law, John Burdett, who was in the state senate. In essence, the letter states that a bill was passed to build a new road from Morgantown to Bridgeport and that the state would cover three-fifths of the $10,000 cost of construction but urged all interested citizens to raise the other two-fifths in order to get the road built. (Courtesy of Dick Duez.)

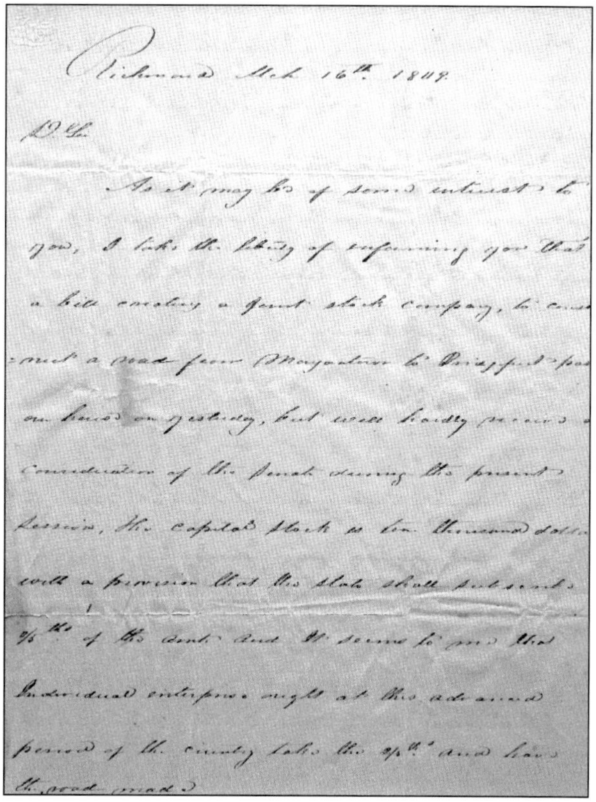

Richmond Mch 16th. 1849.

D. Sir

As it may be of some interest to you, I take the liberty of informing you that a bill creating a joint stock company, to construct a road from Morgantown to Bridgeport passed our house yesterday, but will hardly receive consideration of the Senate during the present session, the capital stock is ten thousand dollars with a provision that the State shall subscribe 3/5ths of the stock and it seems to me that individual enterprise might at this advanced period of the county take the 2/5ths and have the road made.

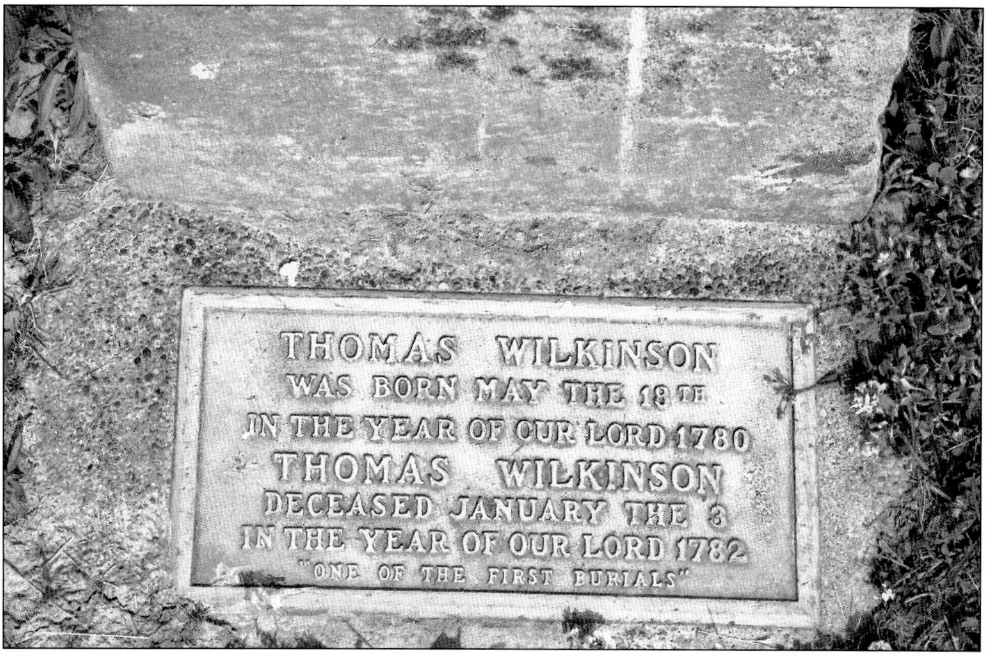

The Thomas Wilkinson stone is a replacement plaque in the lower Baptist section of the Bridgeport Cemetery. Thomas Wilkinson was but two years of age at the time of his death. The inscription does not indicate the cause of the child's death. (Courtesy of Dick Duez.)

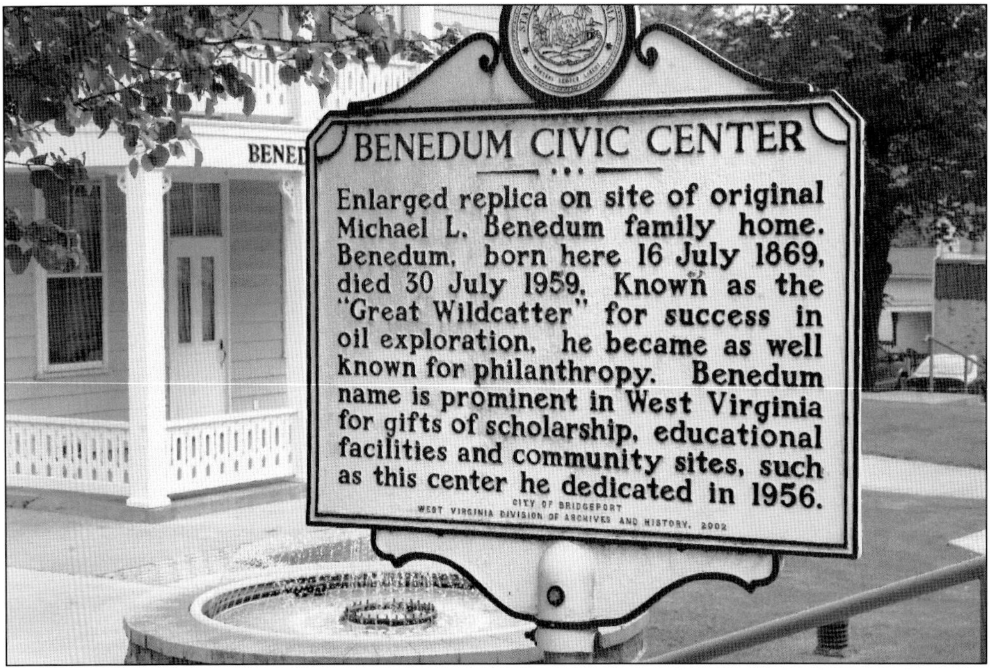

Prominently standing in front of the Benedum Civic Center in Bridgeport is this historical marker that memorializes the life of Michael Late Benedum, the great wildcatter who lived to the age of 90. As the words state, the Benedum name is prominent throughout the entire state for gifts of scholarship and other worthwhile endeavors. (Courtesy of Dick Duez.)

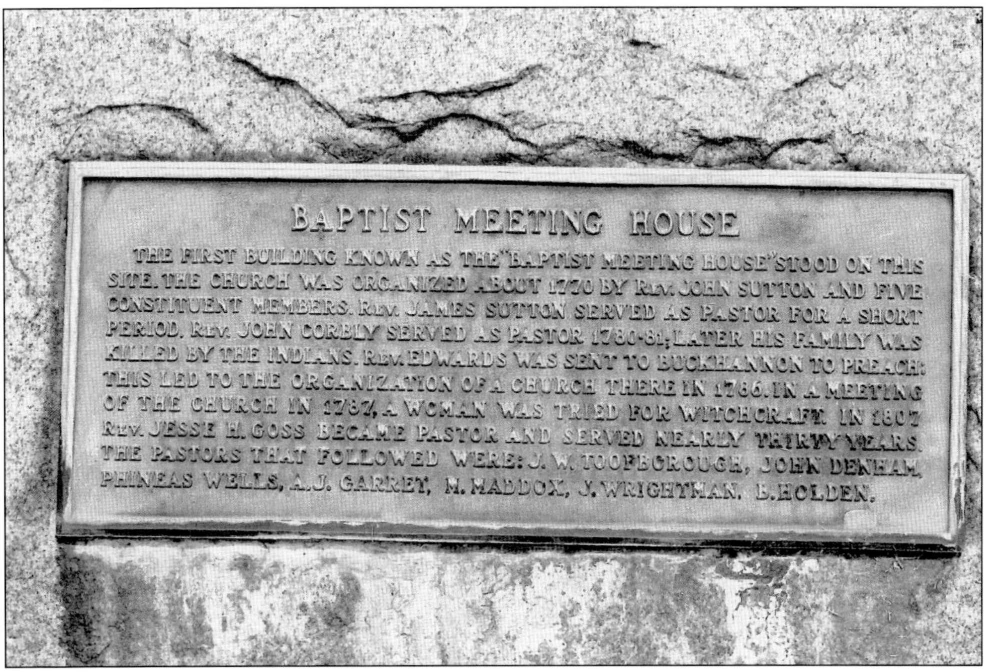

These words were inscribed on a plaque on what was known as the Baptist Meeting House or Simpson's Creek Meeting House, which stood near a burial ground on a portion of what is now the Bridgeport Cemetery. (Courtesy of Dick Duez.)

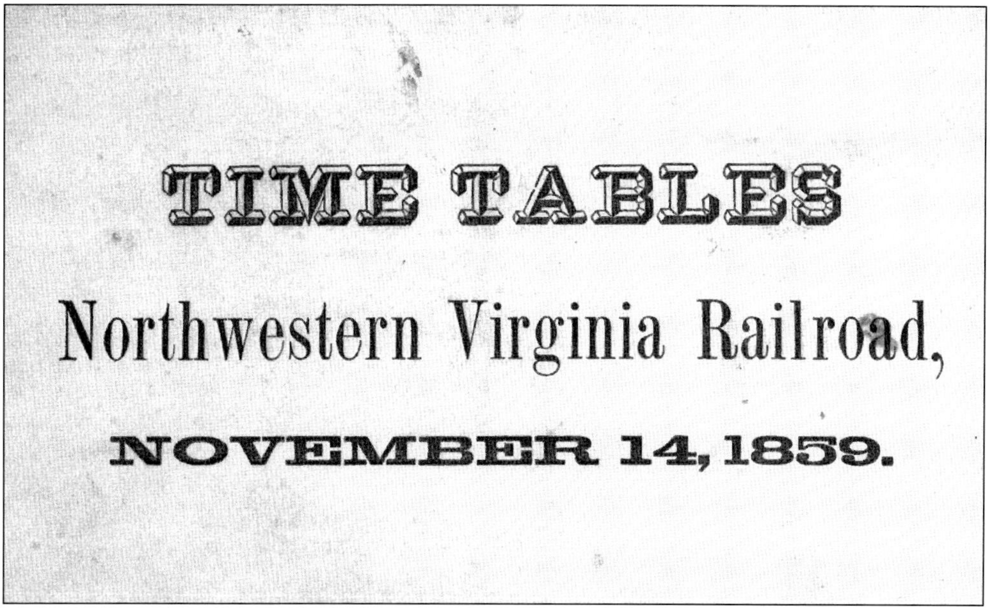

TIME TABLES

Northwestern Virginia Railroad,

NOVEMBER 14, 1859.

This sign tops the schedule of trains between Grafton and Parkersburg, of course including Bridgeport. It was on the Northwestern Virginia Railroad. (Courtesy of Dick Duez.)

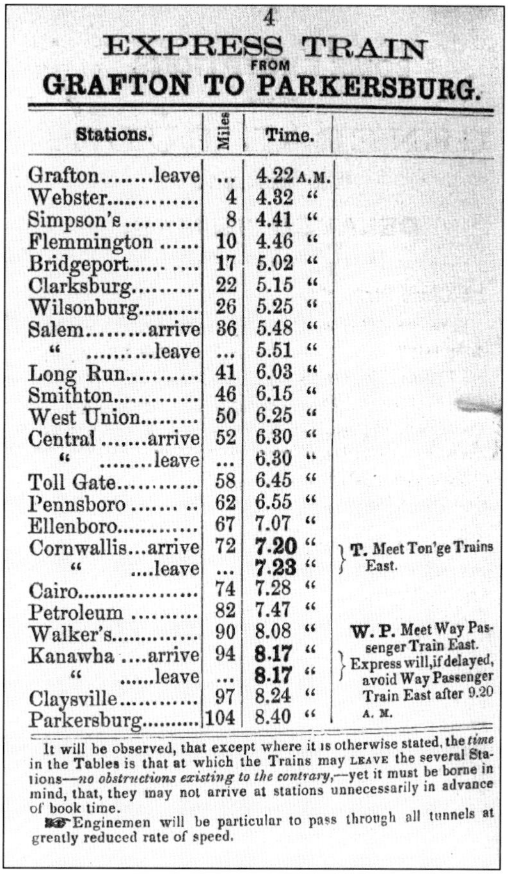

4

EXPRESS TRAIN FROM GRAFTON TO PARKERSBURG.

Stations.	Miles	Time.	
Grafton........leave	...	4.22 A.M.	
Webster.............	4	4.32 "	
Simpson's...........	8	4.41 "	
Flemmington	10	4.46 "	
Bridgeport......	17	5.02 "	
Clarksburg..........	22	5.15 "	
Wilsonburg..........	26	5.25 "	
Salem.........arrive	36	5.48 "	
" ....leave	...	5.51 "	
Long Run...........	41	6.03 "	
Smithton............	46	6.15 "	
West Union.........	50	6.25 "	
Central ....arrive	52	6.30 "	
" ....leave	...	6.30 "	
Toll Gate...........	58	6.45 "	
Pennsboro	62	6.55 "	
Ellenboro............	67	7.07 "	
Cornwallis...arrive	72	**7.20** "	T. Meet Ton'ge Trains East.
" ....leave	...	**7.23** "	
Cairo.................	74	7.28 "	
Petroleum	82	7.47 "	
Walker's.............	90	8.08 "	W. P. Meet Way Passenger Train East.
Kanawha ....arrive	94	**8.17** "	Express will, if delayed, avoid Way Passenger Train East after 9.20 A. M.
" ......leave	...	**8.17** "	
Claysville............	97	8.24 "	
Parkersburg..........	104	8.40 "	

It will be observed, that except where it is otherwise stated, the *time* in the Tables is that at which the Trains may LEAVE the several Stations—*no obstructions existing to the contrary*,—yet it must be borne in mind, that, they may not arrive at stations unnecessarily in advance of book time.

☞Enginemen will be particular to pass through all tunnels at greatly reduced rate of speed.

The time tables for each community on the Northwestern Virginia line showed the number of miles from Grafton and the amount of elapsed time. Bridgeport was 17 miles away from Grafton on the line and was 40 minutes into the trip. (Courtesy of Dick Duez.)

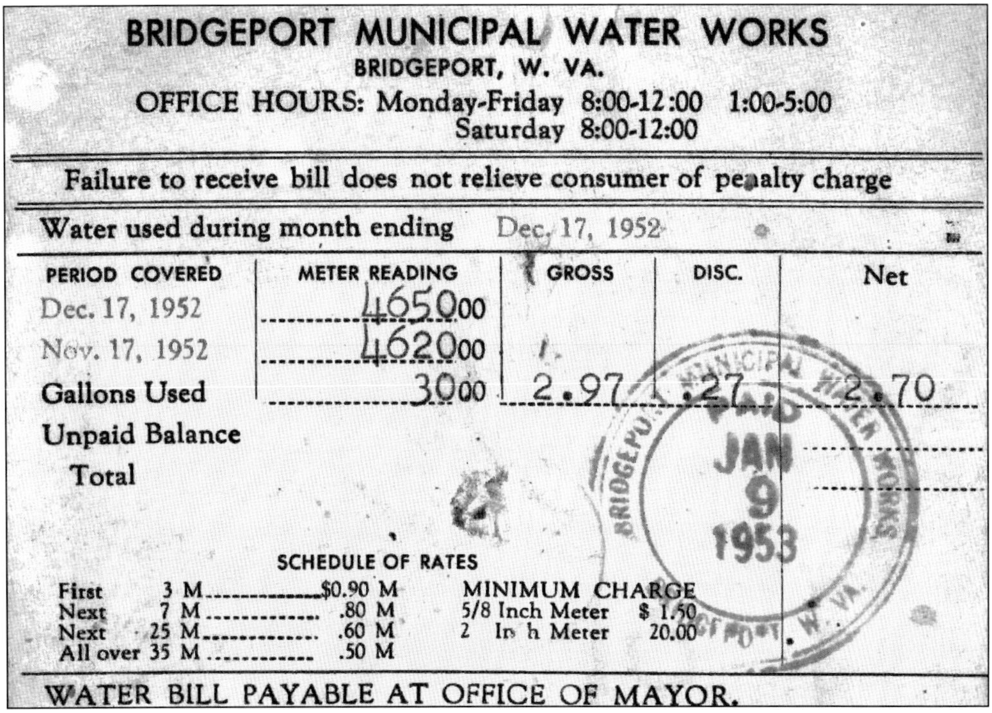

BRIDGEPORT MUNICIPAL WATER WORKS
BRIDGEPORT, W. VA.
OFFICE HOURS: Monday-Friday 8:00-12:00 1:00-5:00
Saturday 8:00-12:00

Failure to receive bill does not relieve consumer of penalty charge

Water used during month ending Dec. 17, 1952

PERIOD COVERED	METER READING	GROSS	DISC.	Net
Dec. 17, 1952	4650 00			
Nov. 17, 1952	4620 00			
Gallons Used	30 00	2.97	.27	2.70
Unpaid Balance				
Total				

SCHEDULE OF RATES

First	3 M	$0.90 M
Next	7 M	.80 M
Next	25 M	.60 M
All over	35 M	.50 M

MINIMUM CHARGE
5/8 Inch Meter $ 1.50
2 Inch Meter 20.00

BRIDGEPORT MUNICIPAL WATER WORKS PAID JAN 9 1953 BRIDGEPORT, W. VA.

WATER BILL PAYABLE AT OFFICE OF MAYOR.

Somebody received a water bill on a postcard from the Bridgeport Municipal Water Works. The water bills were payable at the office of the mayor of Bridgeport, and customers were to bring their cards with them when paying. Note that the water offices were open Saturday mornings as well as on weekdays. (Courtesy of Dick Duez.)

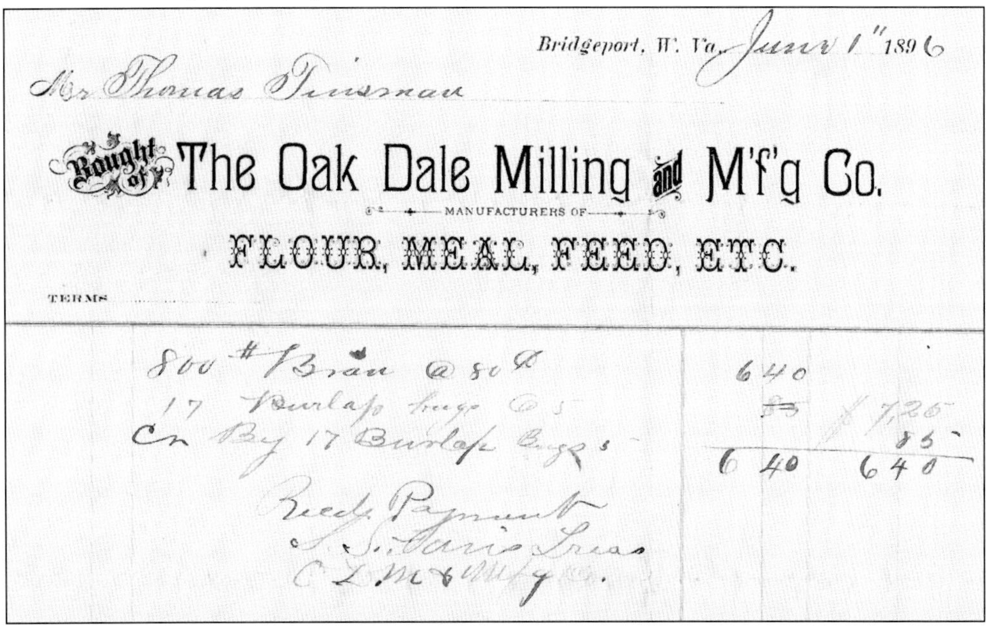

Bridgeport, W. Va., June 1st 1896

Mr Thomas [illegible]

Bought of The Oak Dale Milling and M'f'g Co.
MANUFACTURERS OF
FLOUR, MEAL, FEED, ETC.

TERMS

800 # Bran @ 80¢	6 40	
17 Burlap bags @ 5	85	7.25
Cr By 17 Burlap bags		85
	6 40	6 40

Rec'd Payment
[illegible] Treas
O. D. M & Mfg Co.

A customer of the Oak Dale Milling and Manufacturing Company in Bridgeport received this bill. The company sold flour, meal, feed, and similar items. The Davidson Hurry Mill was acquired by that company in 1895, at which time a planing mill was added. (Courtesy of Dick Duez.)

Three

The People, Then and Now

More than anything else, the history of Bridgeport is a progression of its people and an account of their various activities. The descendants of a number of the town's original settlers continue to live in and around Bridgeport. In fact, some of the original land claims still belong to the claimant's descendants. Some of the very first people in Bridgeport were the Woodland Indians, who had different ideas about owning the land than white men. Some historians have stated that the Native Americans made trouble for white men, but it wasn't the natives who recorded the history.

The first white man in Bridgeport of whom we are aware was a fur trapper named John Simpson, who named Simpson Creek after himself back around 1764. About 1770, settlers came to live in Bridgeport, many of whom built forts. The builders of one fort built a pontoon bridge near where the Main Street bridge is located today, and so the settlement received the name Bridge Fort, but this was changed years later.

James Anderson, another early settler, owned 400 acres of land from where Worthington Drive is located to where Simpson Creek runs toward I-79. In 1787, he built a mill on Simpson Creek near the former stockyards. Joseph Davisson owned 400 acres in the area where the old high school was located.

In 1815, Joseph Johnson presented legislation to the Virginia General Assembly to create a town to be called Bridgeport, and the act was passed in early 1816. The town's first mayor was John Wright. It wasn't until 1887 that Bridgeport was incorporated.

In addition to those already mentioned, there were other settlers, including Joseph Wilkinson, who owned 400 acres in southeast Bridgeport. The John Thomas family settled near Boothsville on Thomas Run in the 1770s. Emanuel Benedum had numerous businesses, was a town postmaster, and was a mayor and justice of the peace. He was the father of famous Bridgeport oil wildcatter Michael Late Benedum.

Many others had a hand in Bridgeport's progress over the years—too many to mention them all. The images that follow deal mainly with those from the 18th, 19th, and early 20th centuries.

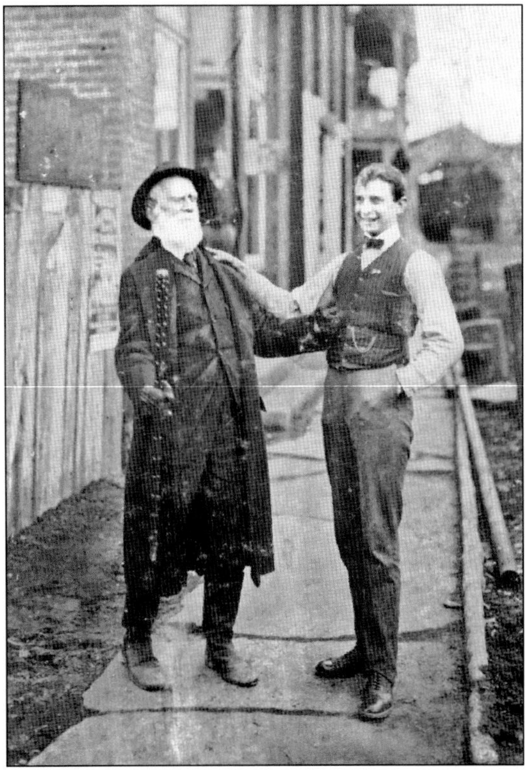

Emanuel Benedum (left), father of Michael Late Benedum, appears above with Allen Fitzhugh, a well-known merchant and one-time postmaster of Bridgeport, in this late-19th-century photograph taken near the present-day Benedum Civic Center. He lived in the old house, the site of the civic center. Note the covered bridge in background. (Courtesy of Dick Duez.)

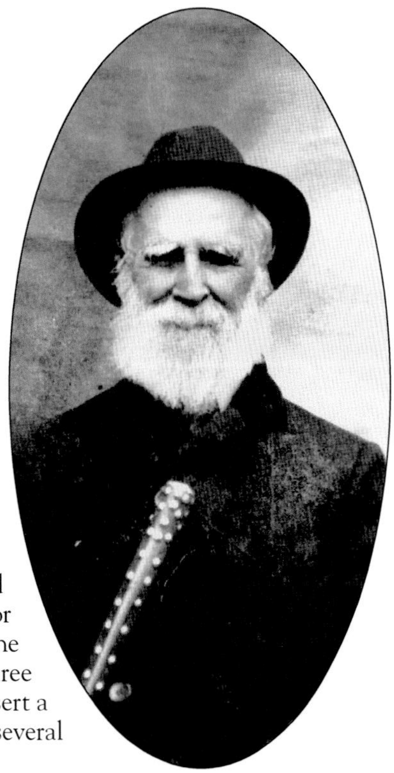

Here's a closer photograph of Emanuel Benedum, who lived in the house later restored by his son, Michael Benedum, for the Bridgeport Civic Center. He sold his general store at the beginning of the 1880s to concentrate working on his three farms. In each of the elder Benedum's canes, he would insert a tack for every argument he won. It was known that he had several canes. (Courtesy of Benedum Civic Center.)

William Michael Late, M.D., was a prominent physician in Bridgeport in the mid- to late 19th century. He helped found and was first president of the Bridgeport Bank. He was first worshipful master of the Masonic lodge in Bridgeport, which bears his name. He and Dr. William Dunkin were also delegates to the convention in Wheeling in 1863 that voted to make West Virginia a separate state. (Courtesy of Dick Duez.)

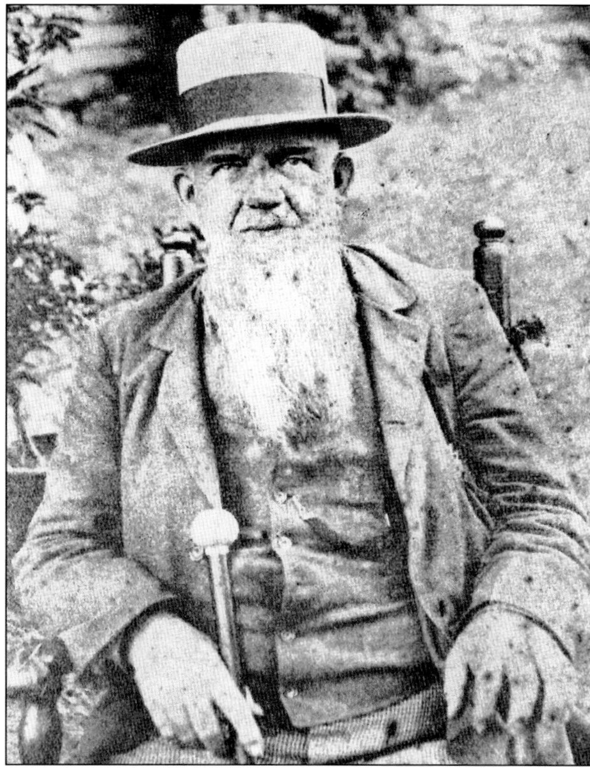

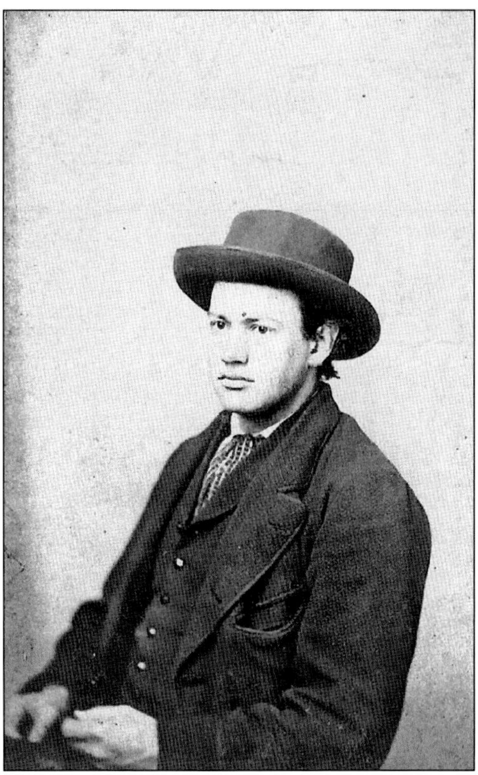

John C. "J. C." Johnson, the son of William Johnson and nephew of Gov. Joseph Johnson, was born in 1840. He would later build the house on the hill opposite the William Johnson home on Virginia Avenue, which continues to stand today and is the residence of Nancy Rush. The father and son owned extensive tracts of land in the Bridgeport area. J. C. was a recent graduate of Bethany College when this photograph was taken in 1862. He was reportedly accused of conspiracy with the Confederacy and was jailed once in 1861 and again in 1862. (Courtesy of Wayne Farley.)

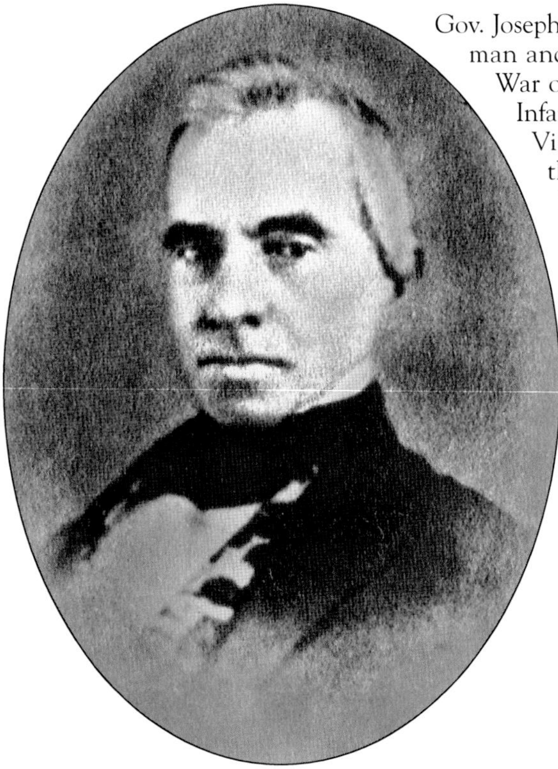

Gov. Joseph Johnson was described as a self-educated man and a well-educated one. He served in the War of 1812 as a captain of the Virginia Light Infantry and File Company of Harrison County, Virginia. Six years later, he was elected to the lower house of the Virginia legislature, became Virginia's representative to the U.S. Congress for several terms and took office as Virginia's governor from 1852 through 1855. (Courtesy of Dick Duez.)

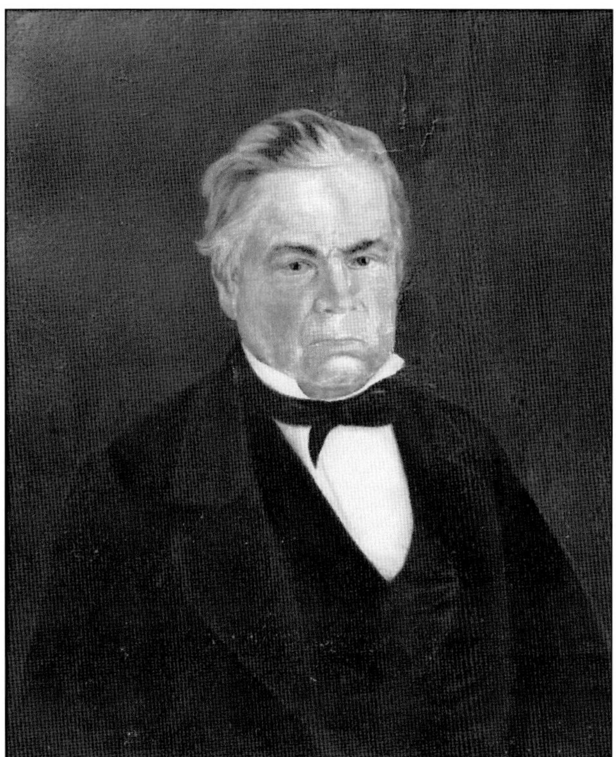

William Johnson was a merchant, the first station agent for the B&O, and Bridgeport's first postmaster. He built the two-story brick home that stands to this day at the corner of West Main Street and Virginia Avenue. He had come to Bridgeport in the very early 1800s from New York with his brother, Joseph. (Courtesy of Bridgeport Public Library.)

Virtually no information is available about Solomon Johnson, right, a brother of Joseph and William, who is believed to have moved to Baltimore and died there in 1864. (Courtesy of Dick Duez.)

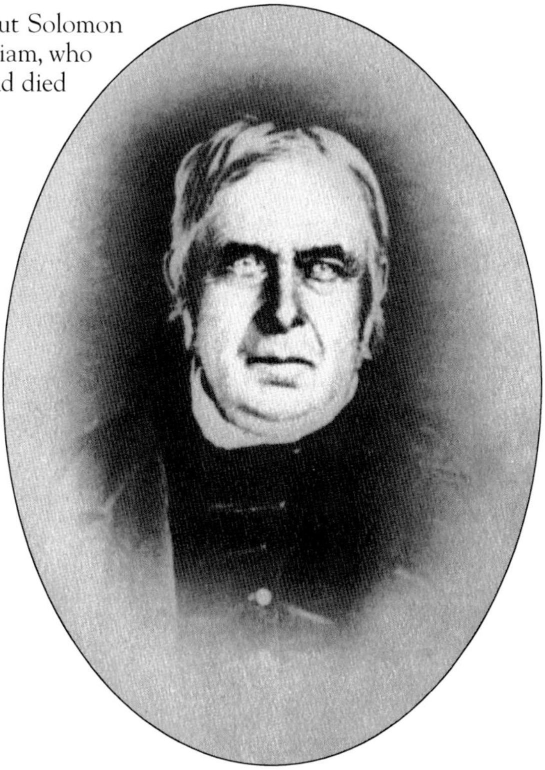

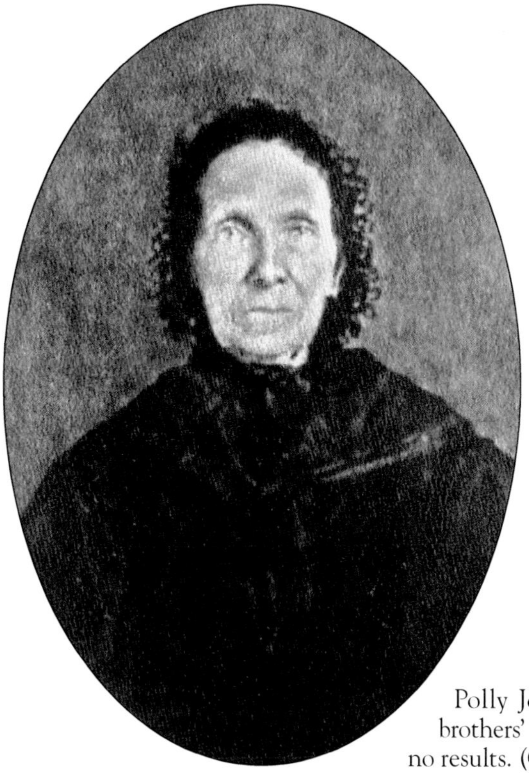

Polly Johnson Wright, above, was the Johnson brothers' sister, but further research on her life produced no results. (Courtesy of Dick Duez.)

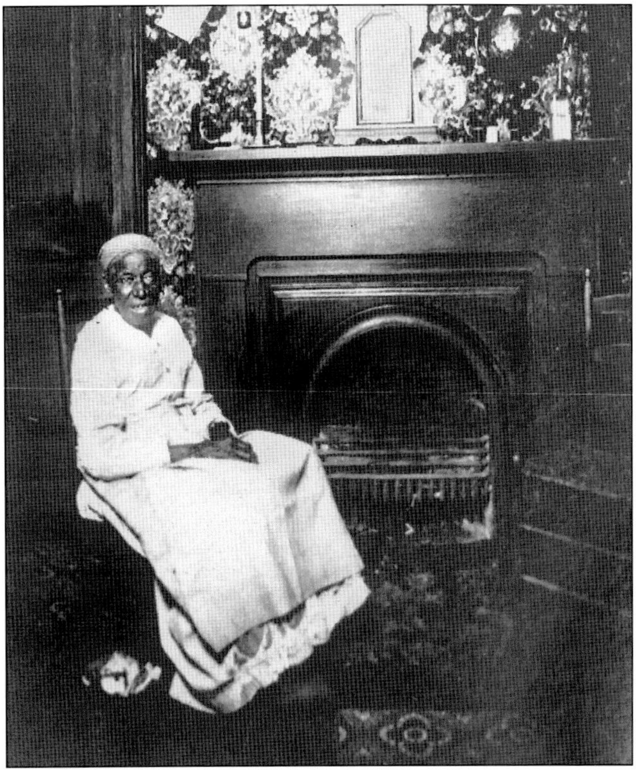

This image of "Aunt Sook," a slave woman, was taken from a rare postcard. Her real name was Sophia Westfall. She and her daughter, Jane, were acquired not long before the War Between the States by George Higinbotham, a rich Simpson Creek farmer. The Higinbotham farm is now the Bridgeport Country Club. She was said to be a good friend of the Lowe family in Shinnston, whom she would frequently visit on horseback. (Courtesy of Rose Davis.)

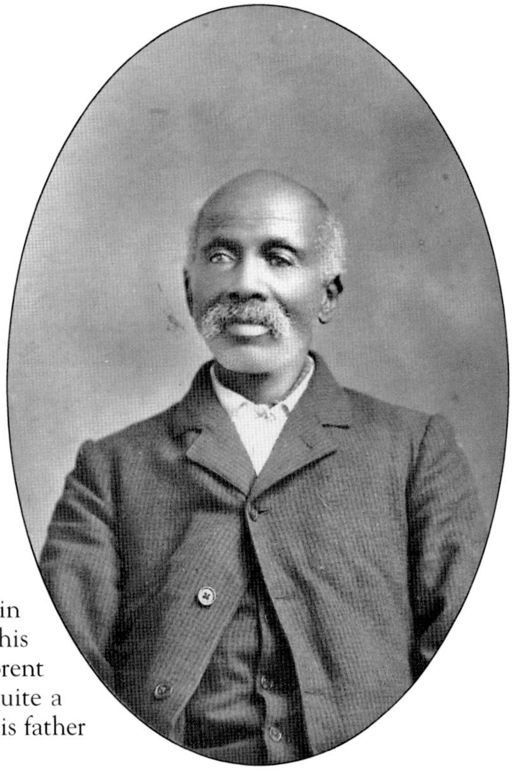

Jefferson Spencer Brent (1832–1922) was slave in the Bridgeport area for William Johnson and his family. After the War Between the States, Brent stayed on with the Johnsons and became quite a prominent figure in the city of Bridgeport. His father was Spencer Brent. (Courtesy of Dick Duez.)

This is Rebecca Wheeler Johnson, the second wife of William Johnson. Olive Waldo was Johnson's first wife. (Courtesy of Roger Hardy.)

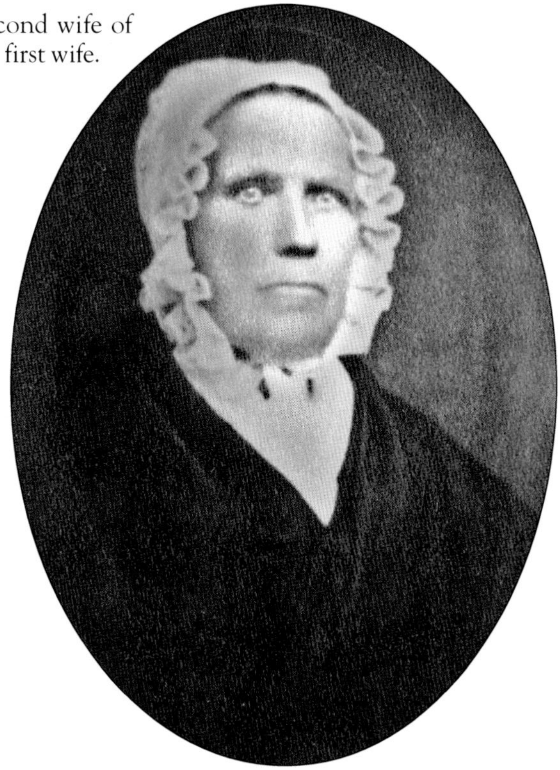

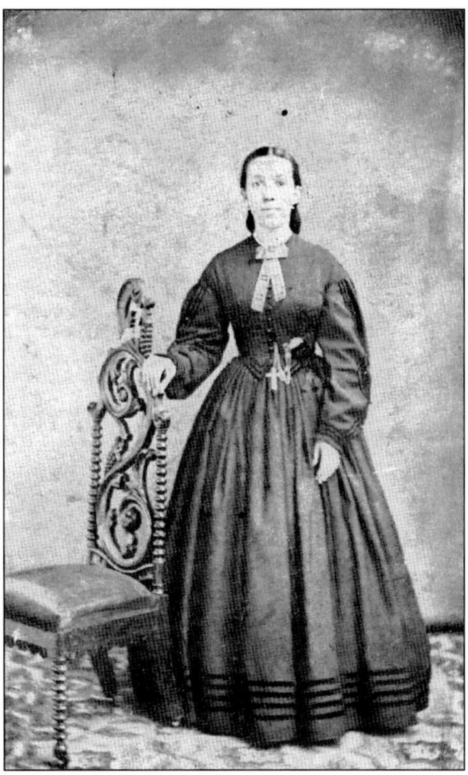

A full portrait of Patty Winters Johnson, taken in 1865, appears above. Information on her relationship to the Johnson brothers or their families is lacking. (Courtesy of Roger Hardy.)

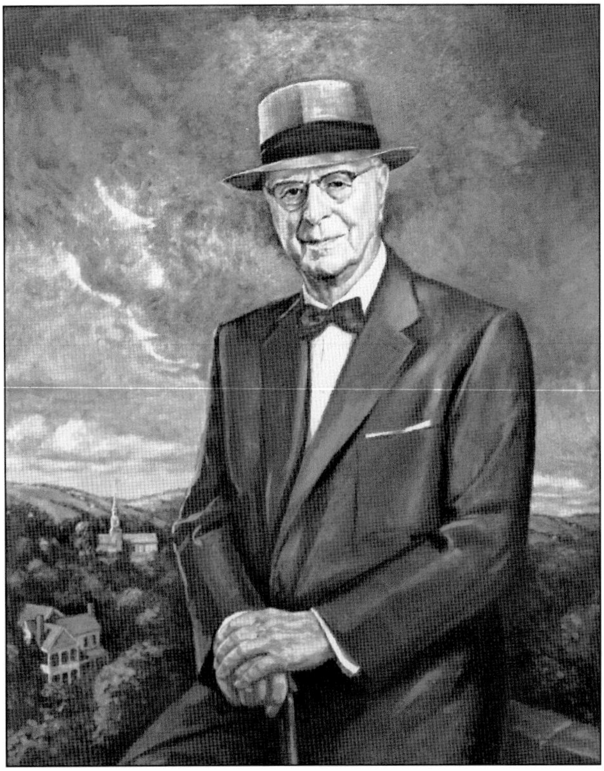

Michael Late Benedum, a native of Bridgeport, appears in this portrait. He was named for Dr. William Michael Late, who delivered him. Although he endured considerable economic hardship in his younger life, working with his father and taking numerous other jobs, he joined with Joe C. Trees in 1900 to form the Benedum Trees Oil Company in West Virginia. They struck oil in Illinois five years later, and his life decidedly turned around. The admired oil wildcatter became quite a philanthropist, giving millions of dollars for charitable purposes and worthy causes. A festival is held every July in his name. He died in 1959 at the age of 90. (Courtesy of Benedum Civic Center.)

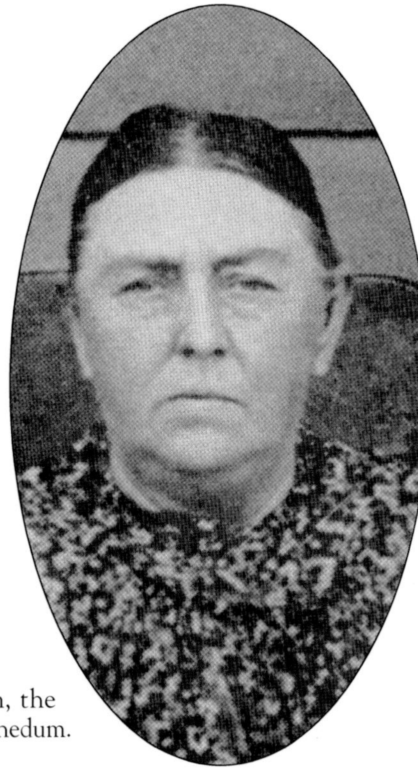

This portrait shows Caroline Southworth Benedum, the mother of Michael L. Benedum and wife of Emanuel Benedum. (Courtesy of Dick Duez.)

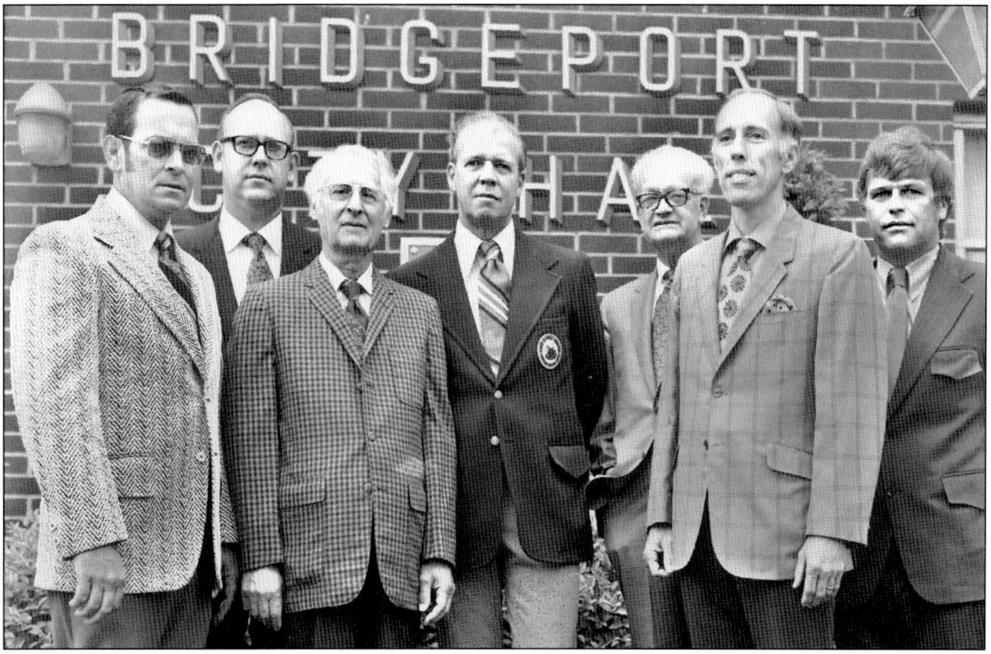

These gentlemen were members of the Bridgeport City Council in 1961. From left to right are Don Duke, Robert Allen, Louis Oliverio, Mayor Carl E. Furbee Jr., Philip N. Sheets, Richard Whiteman, and Jack Hodge. In addition to Furbee, Whiteman and Hodge also served as Bridgeport mayors. (Courtesy of Dick Duez.)

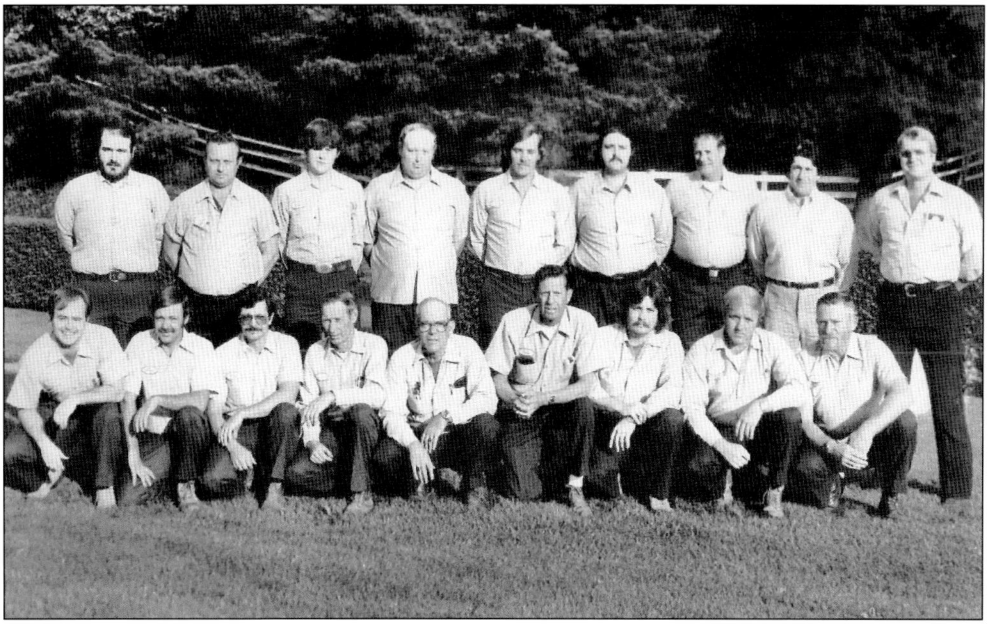

Bridgeport Public Works Department employees, photographed in May 1983, include, from left to right (first row) Greg Talkington, Ron Tate, Ron Hornor, Carson Cottrill Sr., Sam Fortney, John Diamond, Dellot Shields, unidentified, and Uri Grimes; (second row) Mario Oliverio, Willard Hurst, Roy Echard, Carson Cottrill Jr., unidentified, Gary Pullman, Wayne Haggerty, Mike Holmes, and Stephen Tucker. (Courtesy of Dale Shields.)

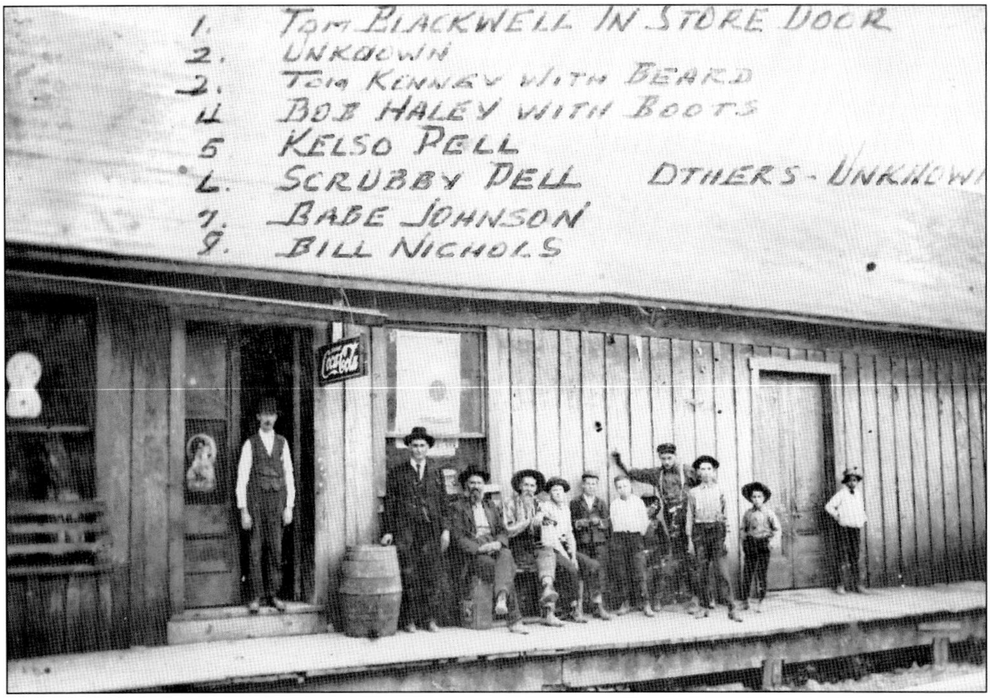

These men and boys seemed to love passing the time on the porch of the B&O depot along Virginia Avenue in the late 19th century. Standing in the doorway is Tom Blackwell. Others are, from left to right, unidentified, Tom Kinney, Bob Haley, Kelso Pell, Dorsey "Scrubby" Pell, Babe Johnson, and Bill Nichols. Others in the photograph were not identified. The photograph was taken by John Blackwell. (Courtesy of Dick Duez.)

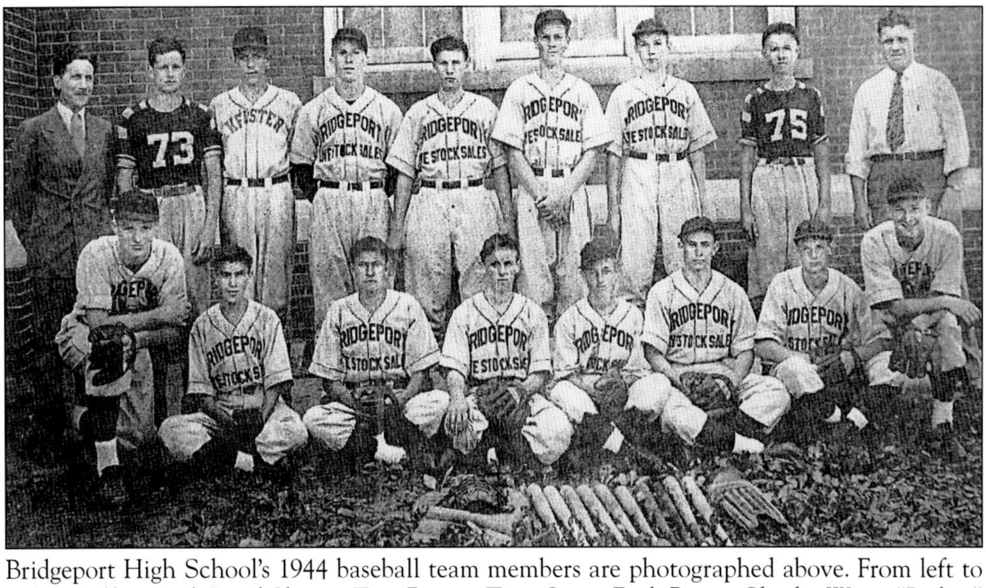

Bridgeport High School's 1944 baseball team members are photographed above. From left to right are (first row) Bond Slusser, Tom Bartos, Ting Cross, Dick Boros, Charlie Wine, "Porkey" Shrader, Charles Clevenger, and Dick Morgan; (second row) principal Norman Tolley, Dorsey McEldowney, Loren Diamond, John Murphy, Bill Douglas, Gene Richardson, Charles Hartzell, Bob Sayers, and coach Pat Hull. (Courtesy of Dick Duez.)

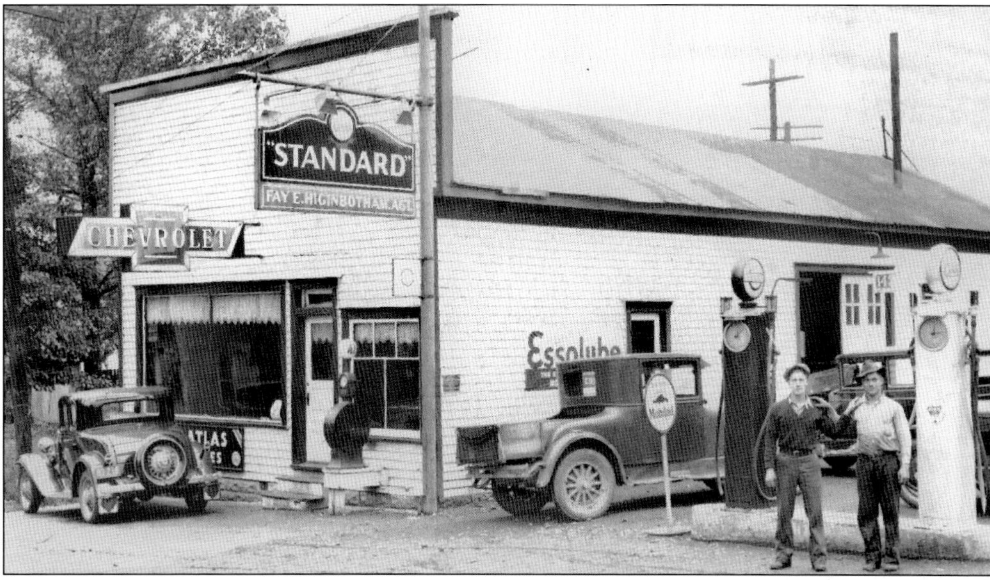

This Chevrolet dealership and Esso filling station were located on the south side of West Main Street in Bridgeport in 1932. Seen standing by the pumps are Forrest Underwood and Glenn Hanna, owners. Hanna's new Chevrolet sports coupe, which had a price tag of less than $600, is parked in front of the business. In addition to being well known in the automobile business, he was also prominent in the real estate business. (From a private collection.)

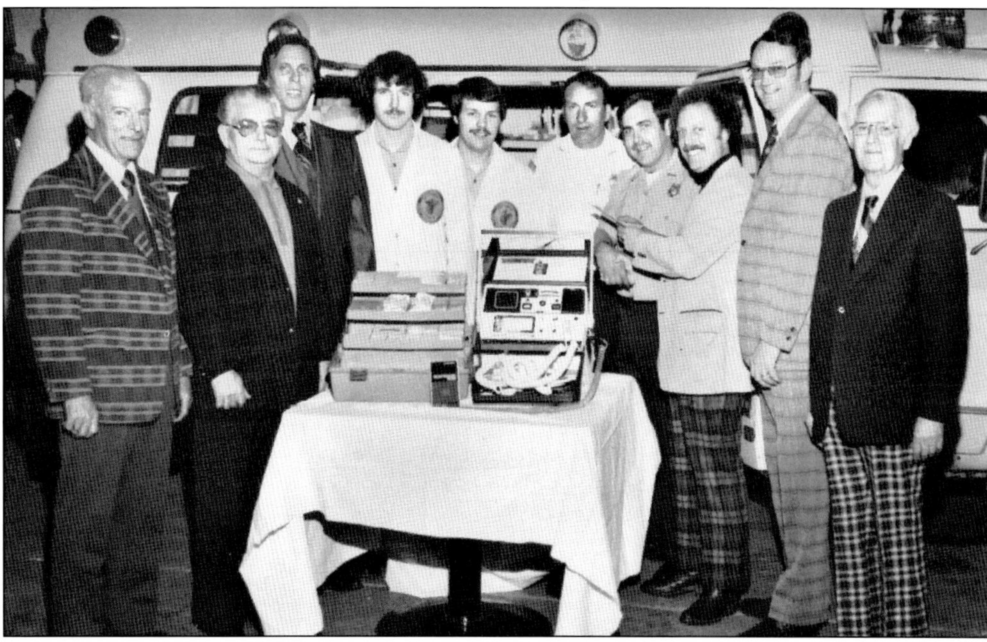

In April 1978, the Bridgeport Lions Club presented a Life Pac, an electronic device used to help save the lives of cardiac patients, to the Bridgeport Volunteer Fire Department. Standing in front of the fire department's ambulances are, from left to right, an unidentified gentleman; Jim Ash and Wally Neely of the Lions Club; fire and rescue personnel Matt Wageman, Rusty Conley, fire chief Bud Calfee, Larry Parks, and Denny Hathaway; Lion Louis Oliverio; and an unidentified Lion member. (Courtesy of Dick Duez.)

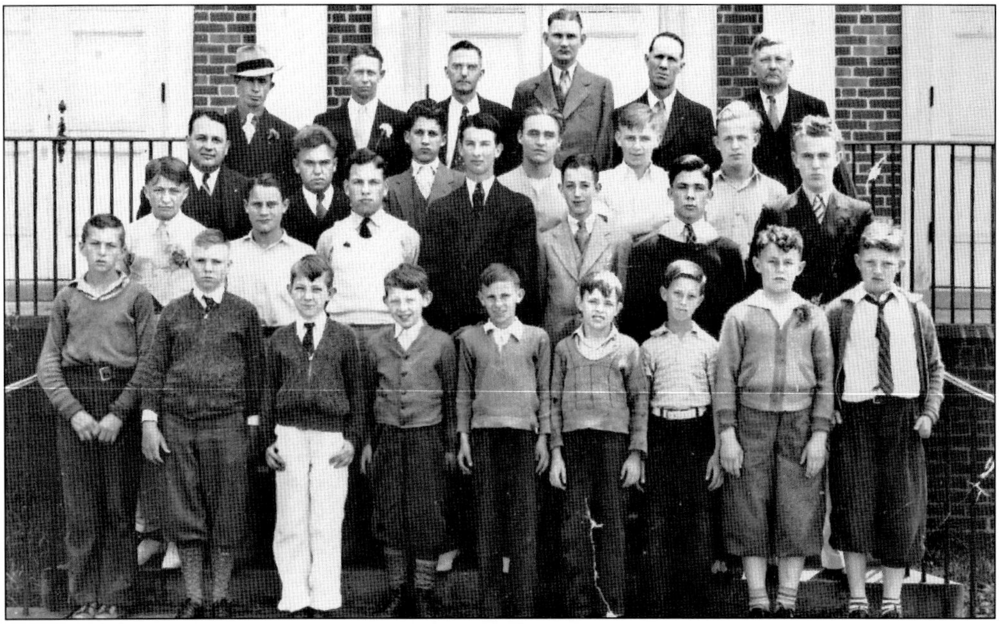

Members of Boy Scout Troop 69 stand on the steps of the Simpson Creek Baptist Church some time in the 1940s. From left to right are (first row) Bill Bowen, Carl Linn, Bill Lodge, John Lodge, Bobby Woofter, "Jumbo" Reed, Jim Taylor, Calvin Herrington, and Jim Dunkin; (second row includes) John Fowler, Jim "Bucky" White, Reitz Sayres, and John Ayers; (third row) scoutmaster Brooke Riley, Edward Griffin, Willis Warder, Louis Hooper, Tom Kinney, and Delmer Fesler; (fourth row) "Rep" Sinsel, Leonard Fowler, W. B. "Bill" Snyder, Earl Kester, Delbert McDaniel, and I. D. Mason. (Courtesy of Benedum Civic Center.)

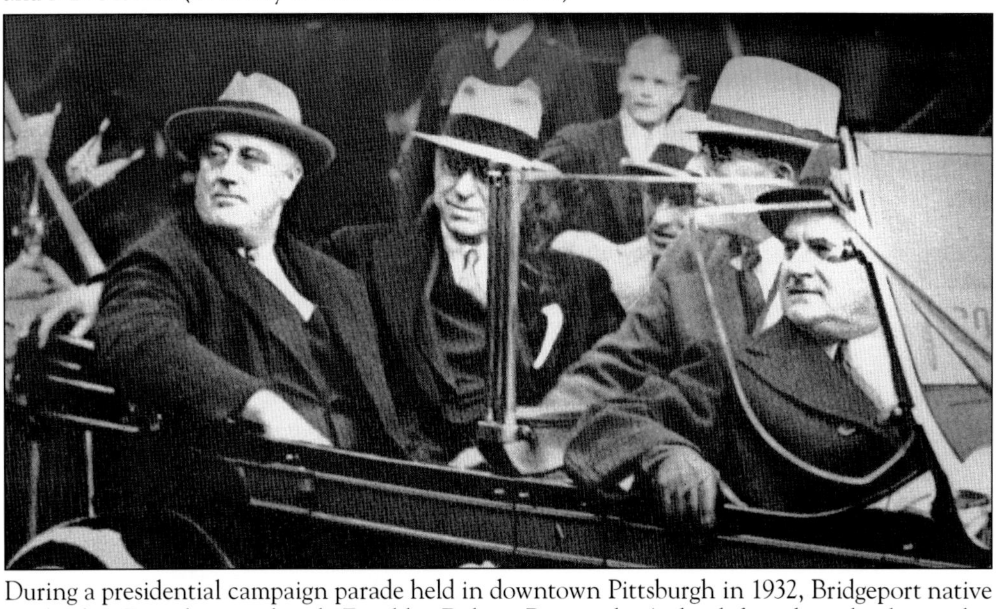

During a presidential campaign parade held in downtown Pittsburgh in 1932, Bridgeport native Michael L. Benedum sits beside Franklin Delano Roosevelt. At his left and partly obscured is James Roosevelt. Shown on the jump seat of the limousine is David L. Lawrence, Pennsylvania Democratic national committeeman and later Pittsburgh mayor. Behind him is Joseph F. Guffey, later a U.S. senator. (Courtesy of Dick Duez.)

Fr. Charles R. Carroll, right, was assigned the All Saints Catholic Church Parish in 1933, and he remained there until the early 1980s. In 1939, he was holding day masses at his Davisson Avenue residence. During his priesthood at the church, Catholics in Bridgeport acquired the Methodist Church building, called Rachel Chapel, on East Main Street and dedicated it as All Saints Church on May 16, 1954. (Courtesy of Dick Duez.)

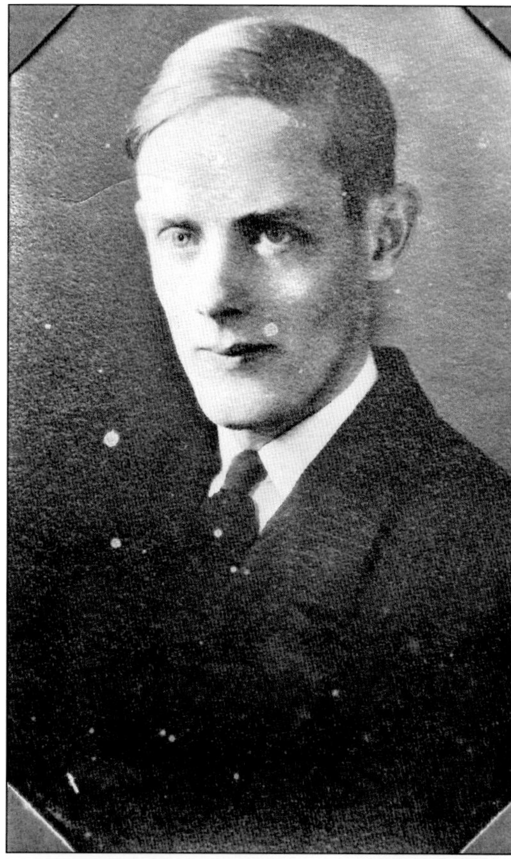

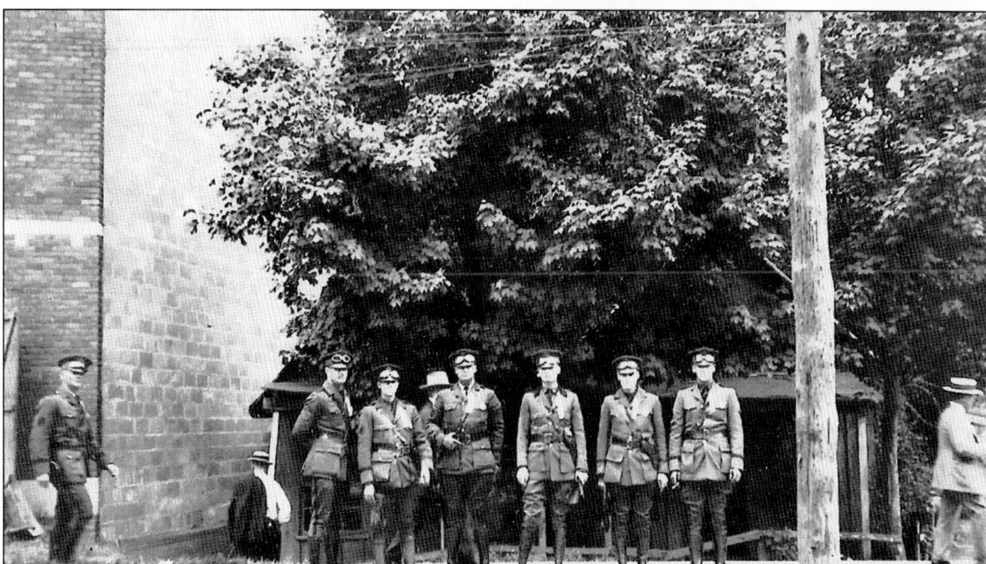

These motorcycle cops played a role in a ceremony marking the opening of U.S. 50 from Grafton to Bridgeport in 1925 at the bottom of Center Street and in front of what is now the Bonamico Building. (Courtesy of Paul Whiteman family.)

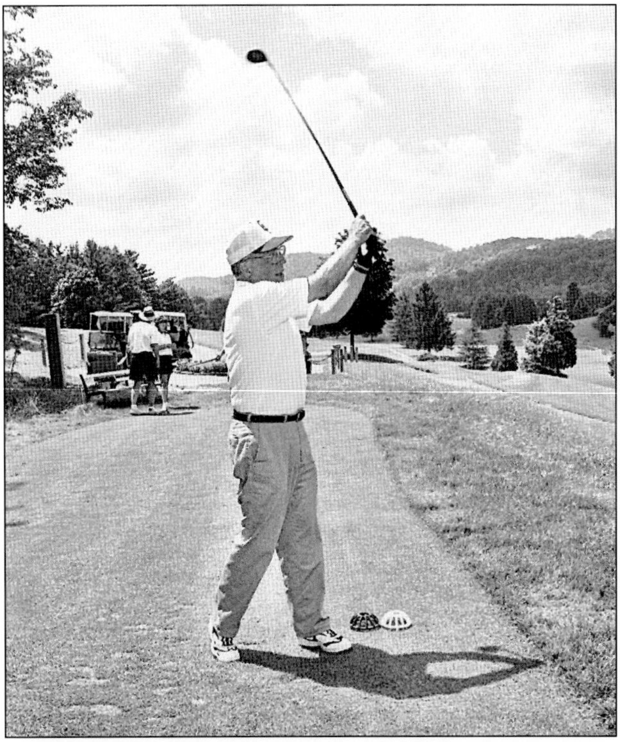

H. Wayne "Smiley" Jamison, beloved longtime head coach of many of the Indians football squads of Bridgeport High School, tees off on the golf course after retiring following many successful seasons. (Courtesy of Bob Nichols.)

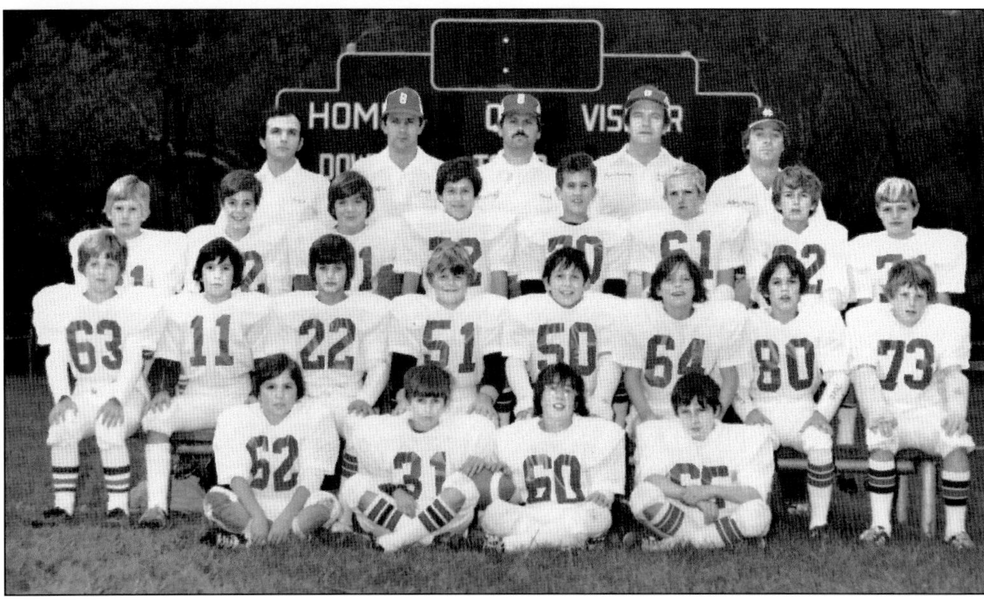

In 1979, the Warriors were one of the first two Pee Wee football teams in Bridgeport. The Redskins were the other team. From left to right are (first row) Brian Green, Reid Bracken, Phil Amos, and Joe Ozalas; (second row) Chris Huey, Greg Oliverio, Claude Ryan, Greg Crak, Chris DeVault, Jim Steinhilber, Matt Duez, and Mike Riggs; (third row) Scott Steffich, Wade Bramer, Josh Peasak, Adrian McCullough, Brian Ayoob, Mark Taylor, Robert Steptoe, and unidentified; (fourth row) coach Charles Hess, John Steffich, Dick Duez, local president Ron Fortney, and Anthony Blount. (Courtesy of Dick Duez.)

Four

HISTORIC HOMES

Bridgeport has seen a number of new housing developments within its boundaries and in its environs, and they are fine, modern structures. This chapter, however, deals more with some of the old homesteads that have stood for many years.

At the top of the list of historic homes is the two-story, redbrick home of William Johnson, built in 1840. It faces West Main Street on the southwest corner of South Virginia Avenue. Atop the hill on the southeast corner of Main Street and Virginia Avenue was the John "J. C." Johnson home, later the Patton residence and now the home of Nancy Rush, who renovated the house in 2005. Nearby is the J. Newton Wilkinson home, across from the former high school and junior high school. It is the only house in Bridgeport that still has working gaslights, and it has 10 fireplaces.

The former home of Gov. Joseph Johnson was located on Oakdale Street in Bridgeport and was said to have been physically moved across the street at one time. The residence of Emanuel and Caroline Southworth Benedum, on West Main Street, was the birthplace of Michael Benedum in 1869. The house stood where the Benedum Civic Center today stands. There also was a large house on East Philadelphia Avenue built by Gordon Late in 1908 and later owned by Sophia Benedum, Michael's sister.

The Otho Place stood on what is now State Route 58 between Bridgeport and Anmoore. It was later renovated into the Green Acres supper club and is presently Via Veneto, a restaurant where many organizations hold special banquets and functions. A short distance farther toward Anmoore was the Supler Farm. It later became Pieter Poth's Holland Dairy Farm.

On Brushy Fork Road still stands Faris Manor, owned by Robert and Marjorie Faris. Sam Faris originally purchased it in 1916 from the Oak Dale Milling and Manufacturing Company, which had acquired it in 1895 from Davisson and Hurry.

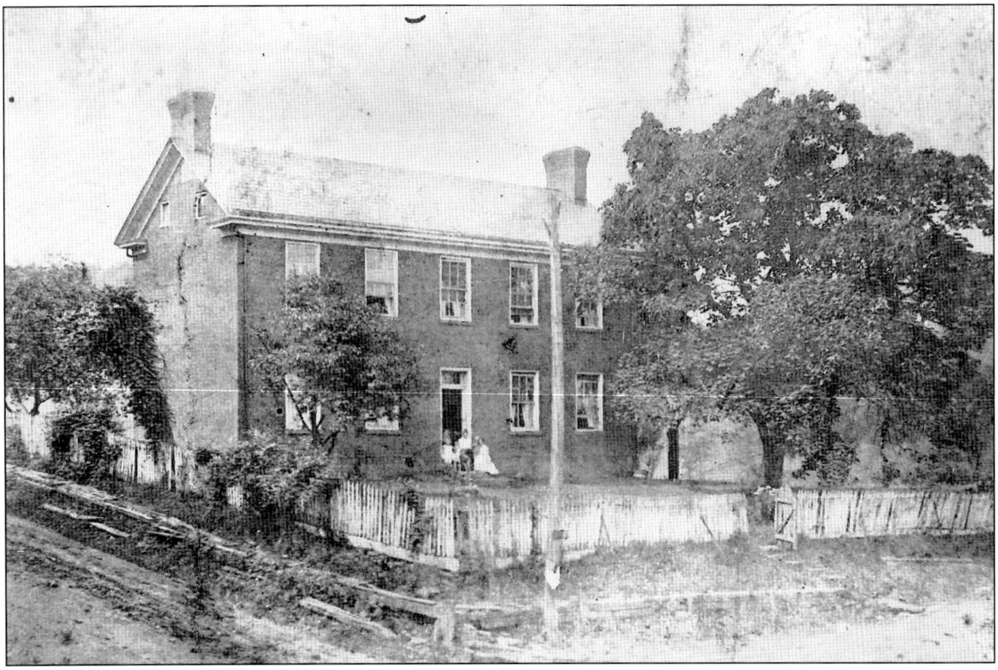

This fine two-story brick home on the southwest corner of West Main Street and Virginia Avenue continues to stand today. It was built by William Johnson in 1840, the year his son, John C. "J. C." Johnson, was born. (Courtesy of Dick Duez.)

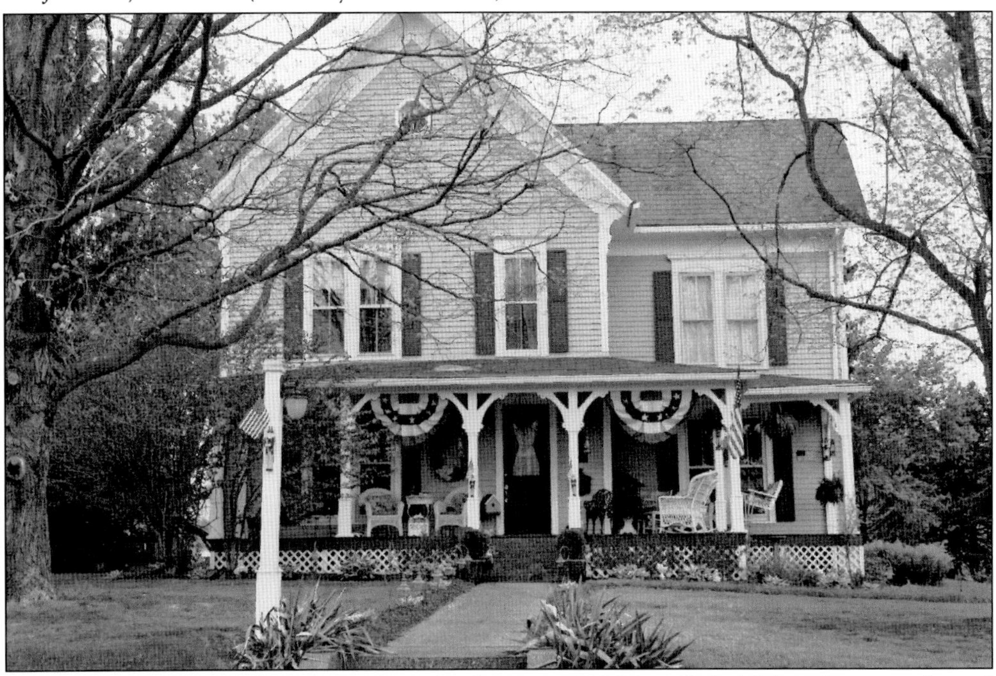

Here's a modern-day look at the A. J. Lodge house at 306 West Philadelphia Avenue, adorned with red, white, and blue bunting below the eaves of the front porch. It stands at the top of Virginia Avenue. Occupied today by the Jennings Monroe family, it may have been built in 1876. (Courtesy of Dick Duez.)

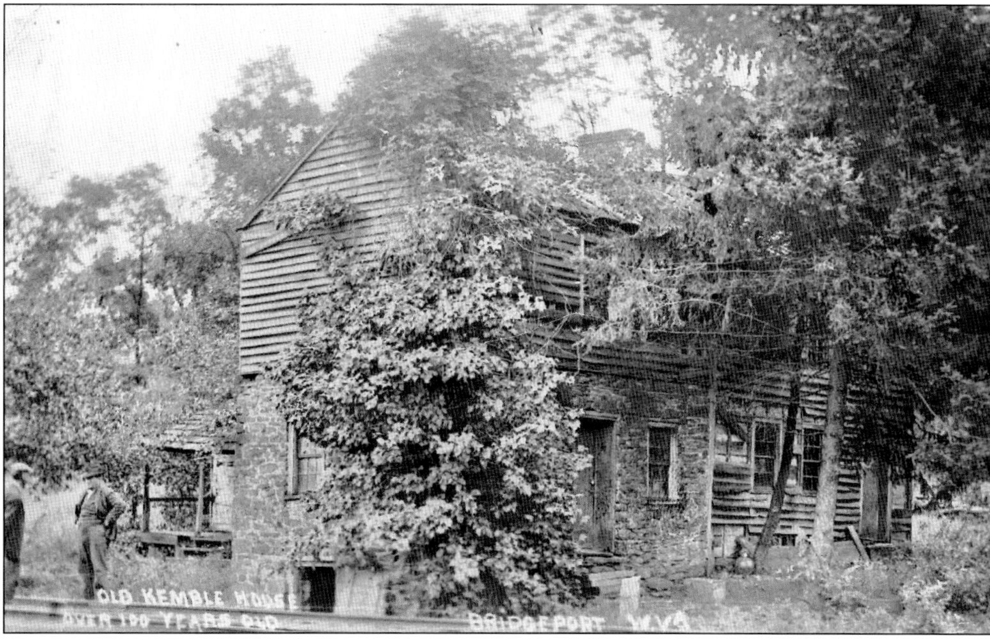

The Kembles most likely built this stone section to the left side of the Davisson house when they came to Bridgeport in 1833. (Courtesy of Dick Duez.)

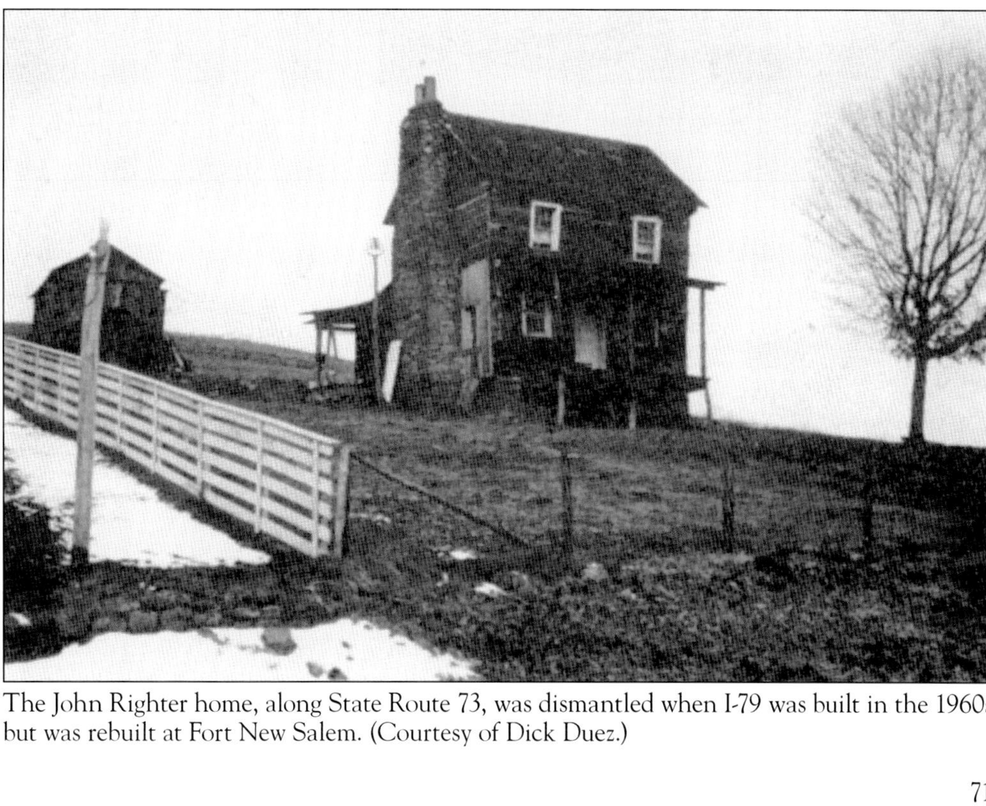
The John Righter home, along State Route 73, was dismantled when I-79 was built in the 1960s but was rebuilt at Fort New Salem. (Courtesy of Dick Duez.)

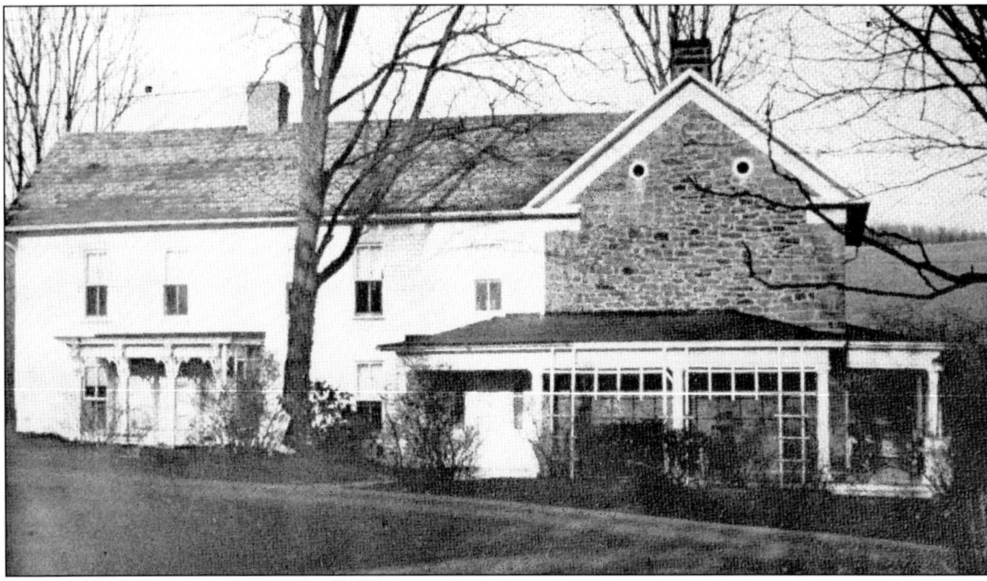

Shown here is Faris Manor, located along the Brushy Fork Road, as it appeared c. 1960. Once a mill, it had been purchased in 1916 by Samuel Sheets Faris. (Courtesy of Dick Duez.)

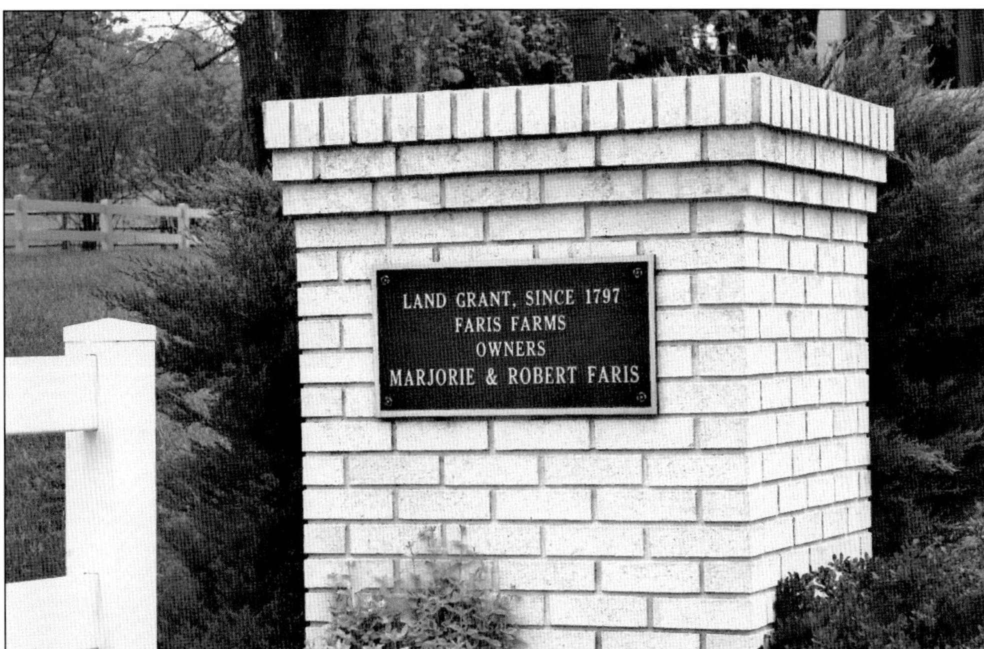

This plaque is on one of the brick pillars at Faris Manor on Brushy Fork Road. When S. S. Faris died in 1922, James Faris's original 400-acre claim had been increased to nearly 2,000 acres. It is the property today of Robert and Marjorie Faris. (Courtesy of Dick Duez.)

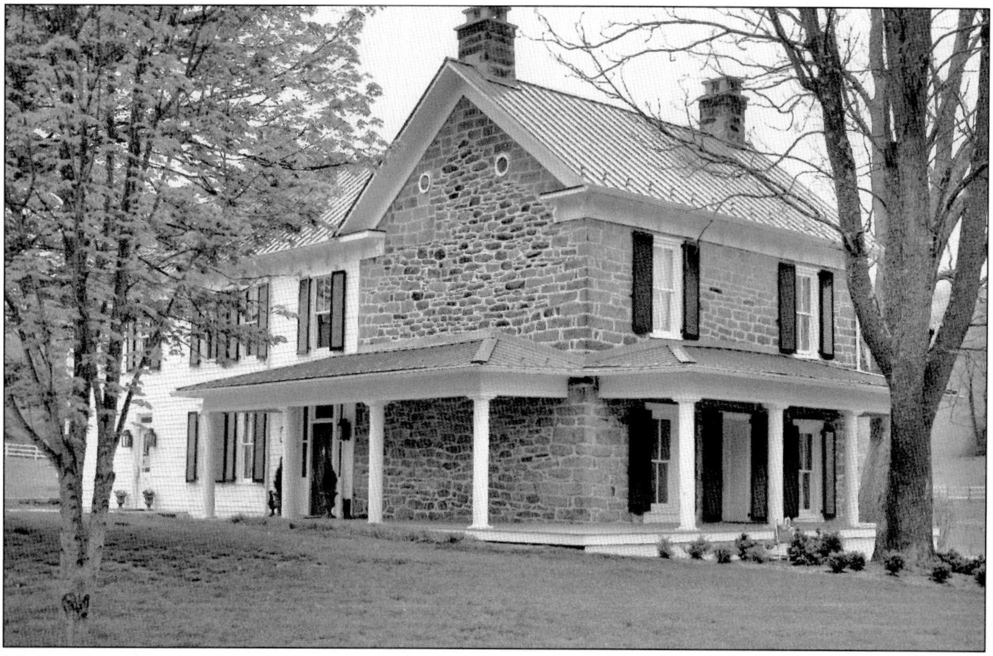

This is a modern view of the old Faris Manor. It was recently renovated, and workers were able to retain its original facade. The house is now occupied by Woody Thrasher, a well-known engineer. (Courtesy of Dick Duez.)

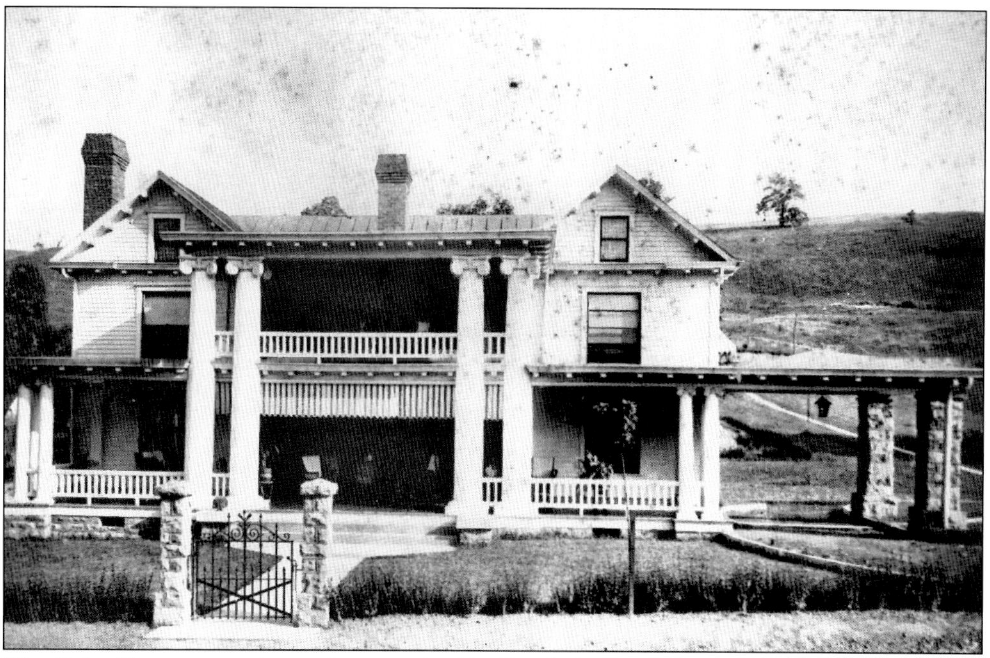

The Otho Place is seen here, photographed by Frank Stout. It stood along what is now State Route 58. In later years, it was owned by Louis Roda and became a restaurant and night club popularly known as Green Acres. In recent years, however, it has become a popular place for dinner meetings and is known as Via Veneto. (Courtesy of Dick Duez.)

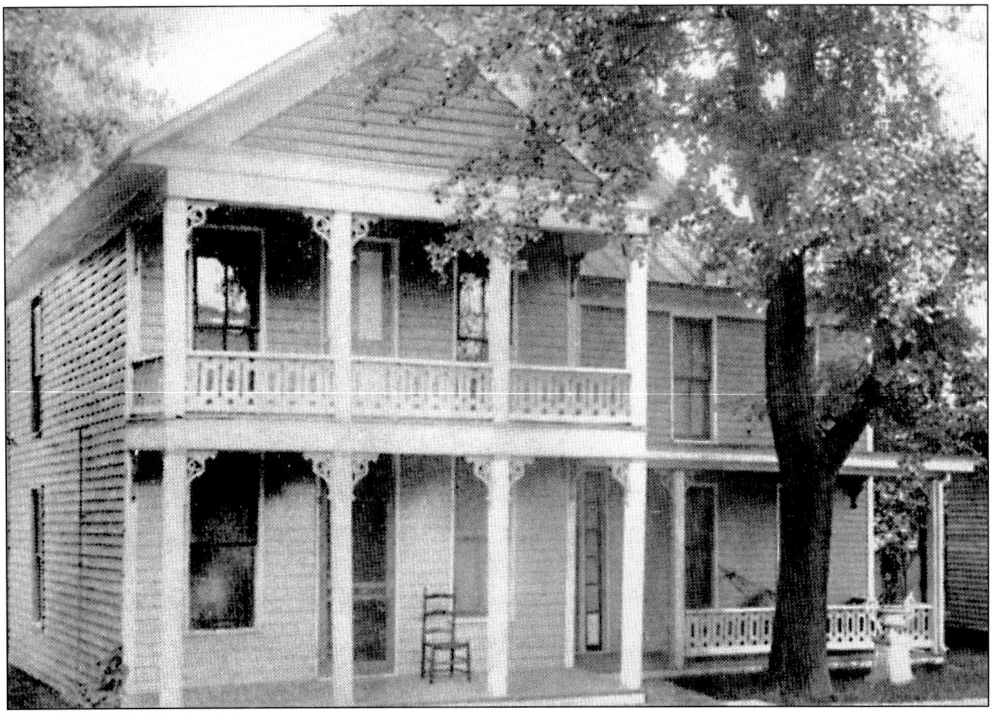

This older view shows a ladder-back chair on the porch of the Emanuel Benedum home on West Main Street. A cast-iron, Victorian-style planter is at the right side of the house. The house may have just been restored by his son, Michael Benedum, soon after his father's death in October 1909. (Courtesy of Dick Duez.)

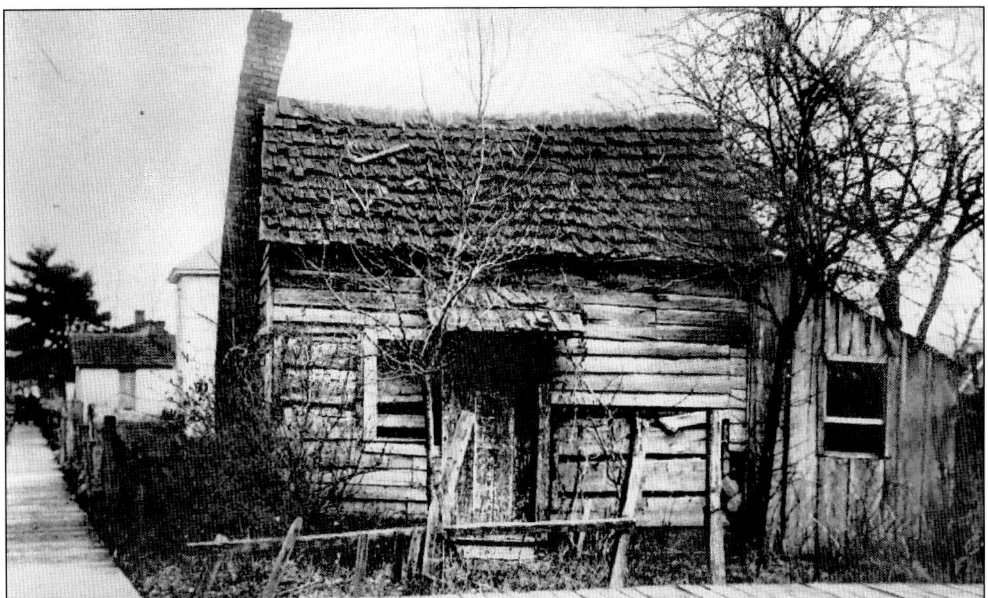

This wooden house was located at the corner of Virginia Avenue and Worthington Drive. The old stockyard building, which was destroyed by fire in January 1965, was later situated on that site. The building above dates back to the 19th century. (Courtesy of Dick Duez.)

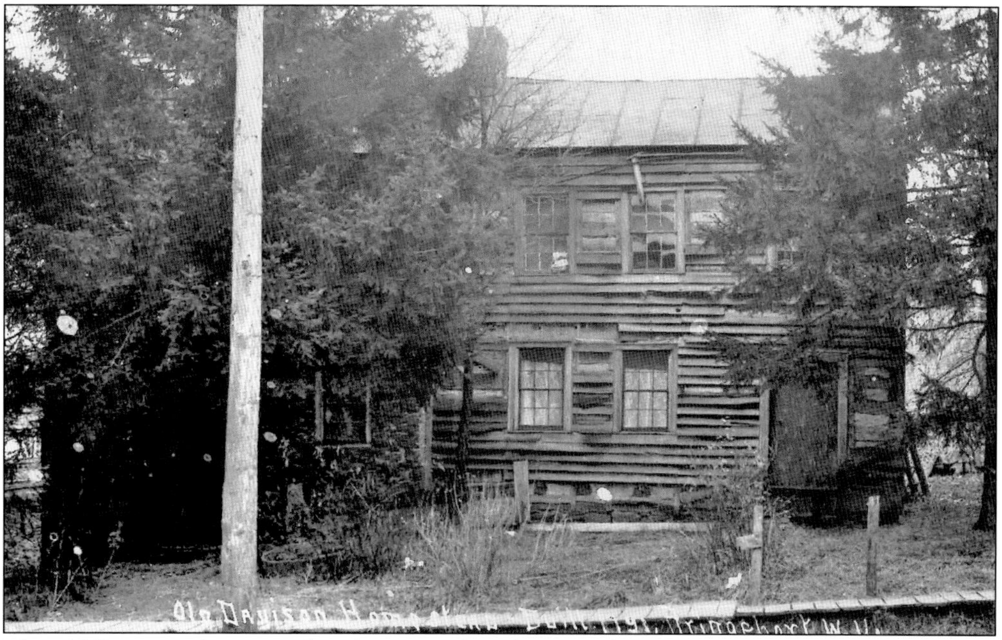

The old Davisson homestead is shown in this photograph. It was built in 1791 in Bridgeport, where the defunct Getty filling station is on West Main Street at Virginia Avenue. (Courtesy of Dick Duez.)

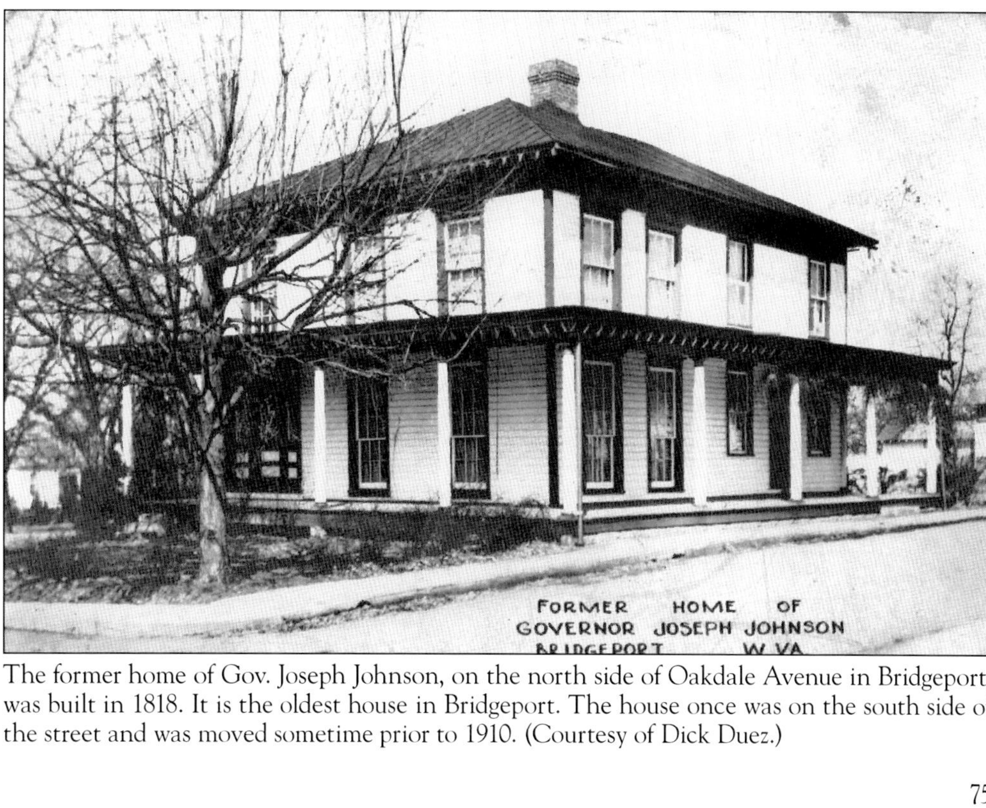

The former home of Gov. Joseph Johnson, on the north side of Oakdale Avenue in Bridgeport, was built in 1818. It is the oldest house in Bridgeport. The house once was on the south side of the street and was moved sometime prior to 1910. (Courtesy of Dick Duez.)

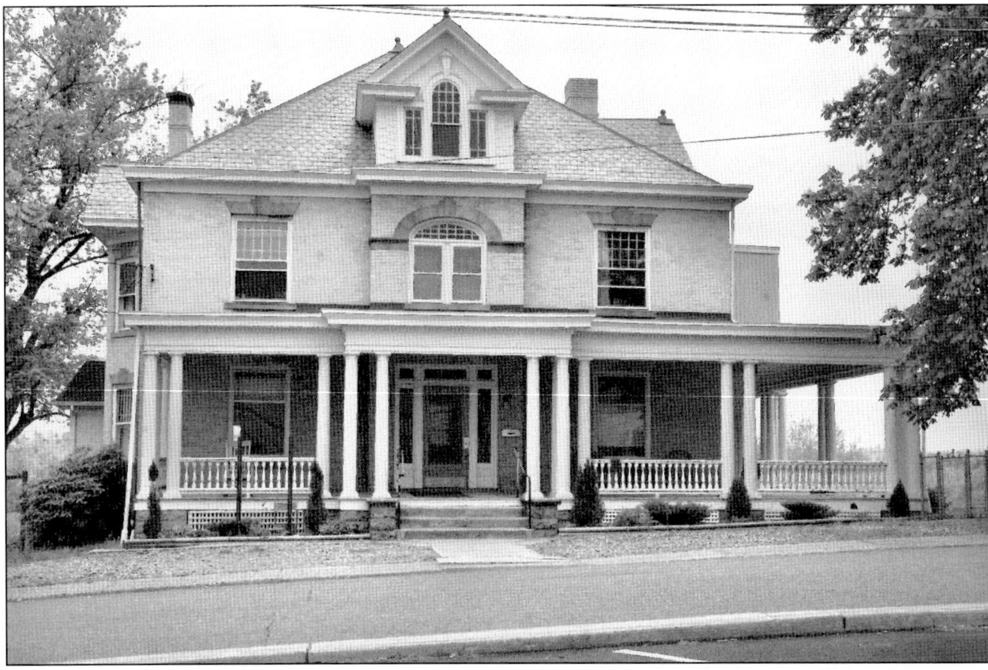

This was the residence of Newton Wilkinson on Newton Street, which runs off South Virginia Avenue in Bridgeport. It is today owned by Heritage Christian School, which is located across the street in the former Bridgeport High School building. (Courtesy of Dick Duez.)

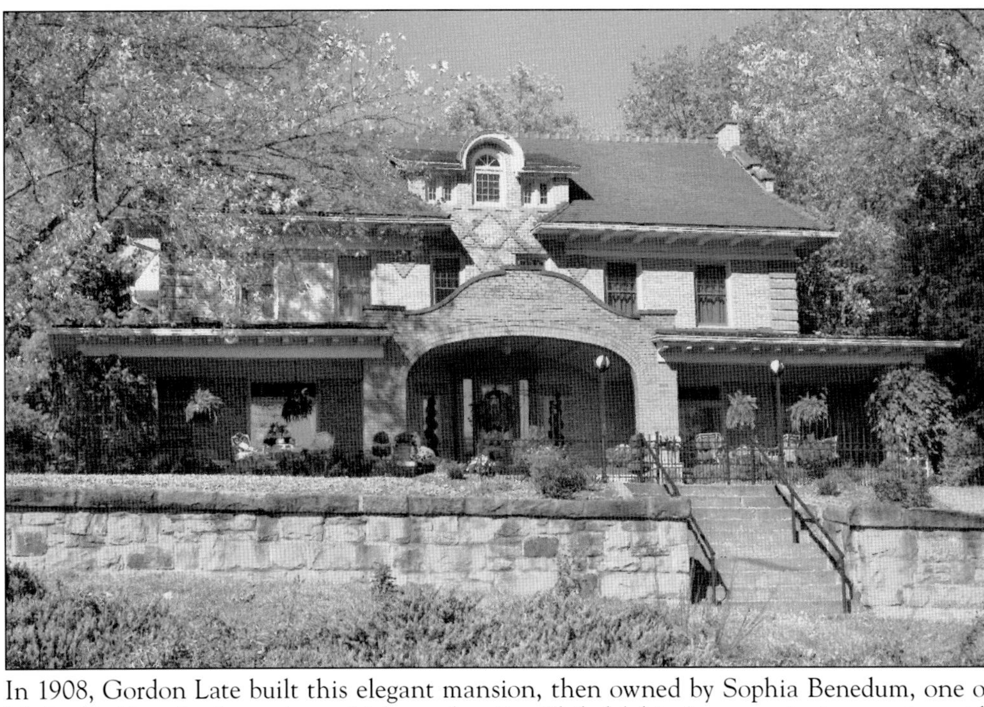

In 1908, Gordon Late built this elegant mansion, then owned by Sophia Benedum, one of Michael L. Benedum's two sisters. It's located on East Philadelphia Avenue at its intersection with Worthington Drive. It is today occupied by Dr. Robert Hess. (Courtesy of Dick Duez.)

The side of the J.C. Johnson house is shown looking eastward. The photograph was taken one winter day in about 1880, with Johnson's wife and pet dog in the foreground. This side of the house faces Virginia Avenue. (Courtesy of Dick Duez.)

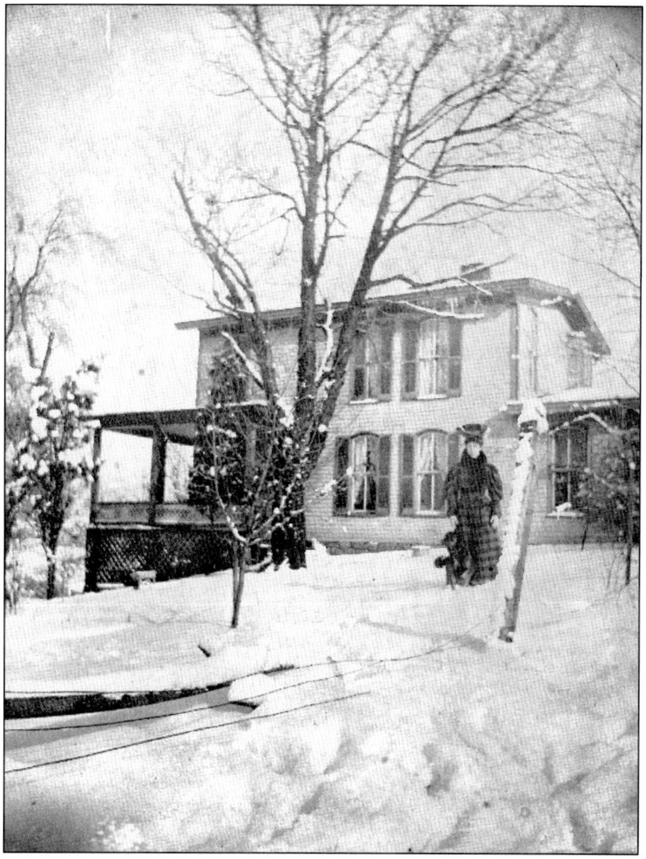

Directly behind the J. C. Johnson house were these slave quarters. The building was demolished in 1988. It may have been a "starter" Johnson home. (Courtesy of Dick Duez.)

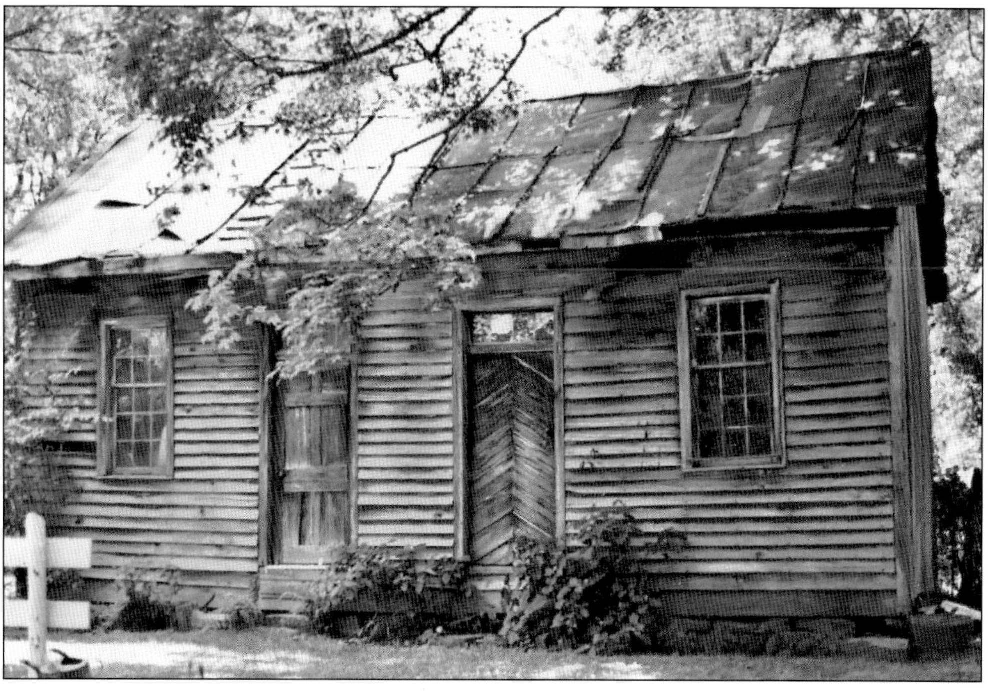

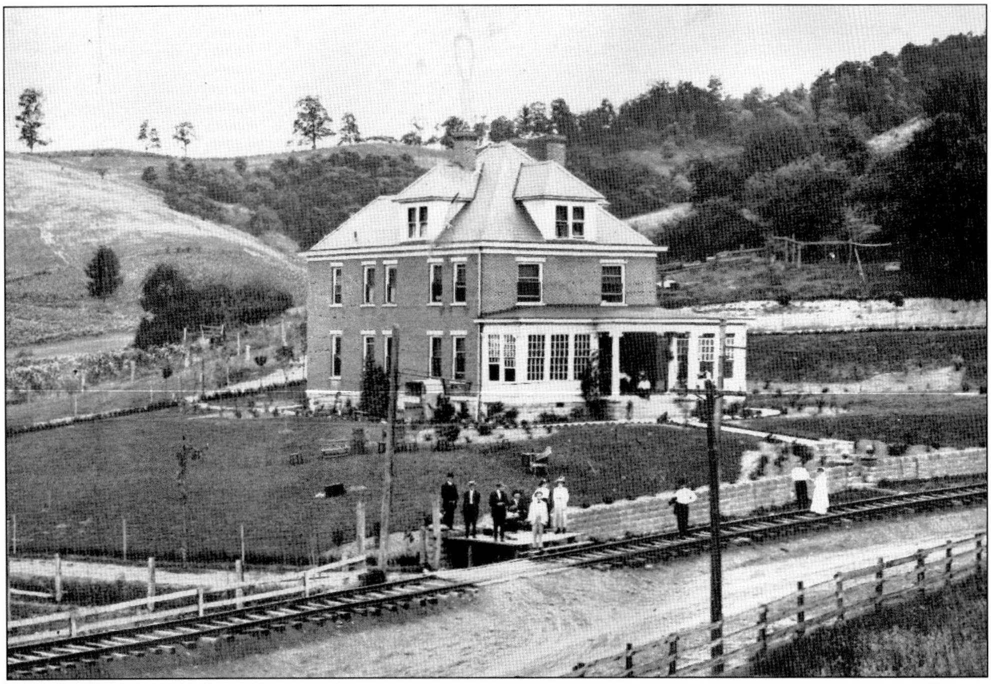

This was the J. B. Supler farmhouse, located on what today is State Route 58, the Anmoore Road. It would later become the Pieter Poth Holland Dairy Farm. The photograph was taken by Amon Studio of Clarksburg. (Courtesy of John Gissy.)

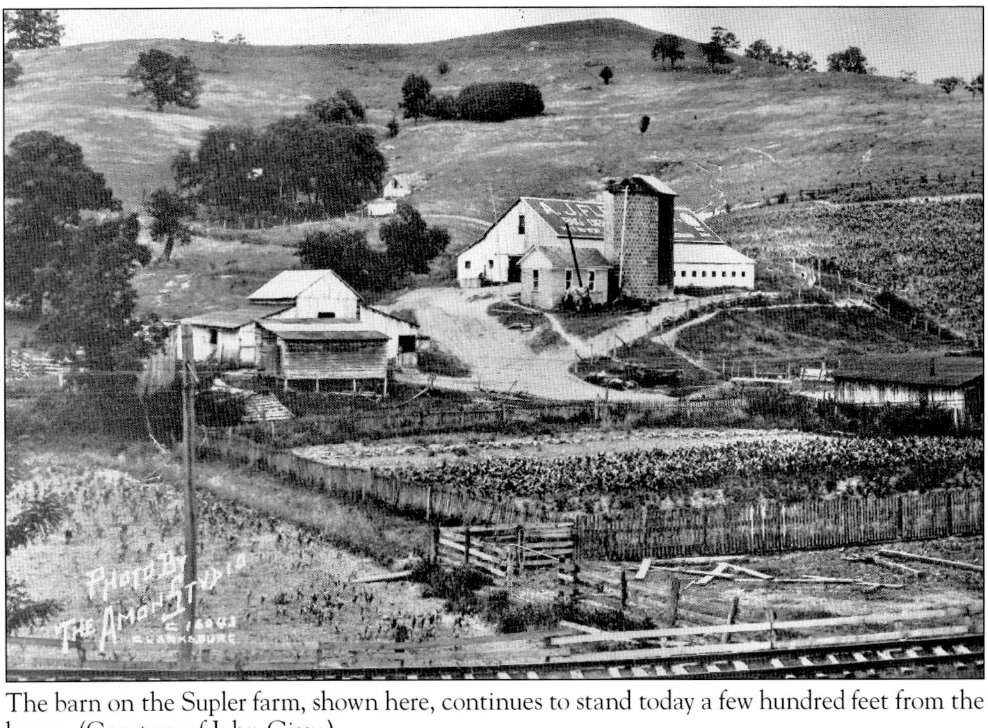

The barn on the Supler farm, shown here, continues to stand today a few hundred feet from the house. (Courtesy of John Gissy.)

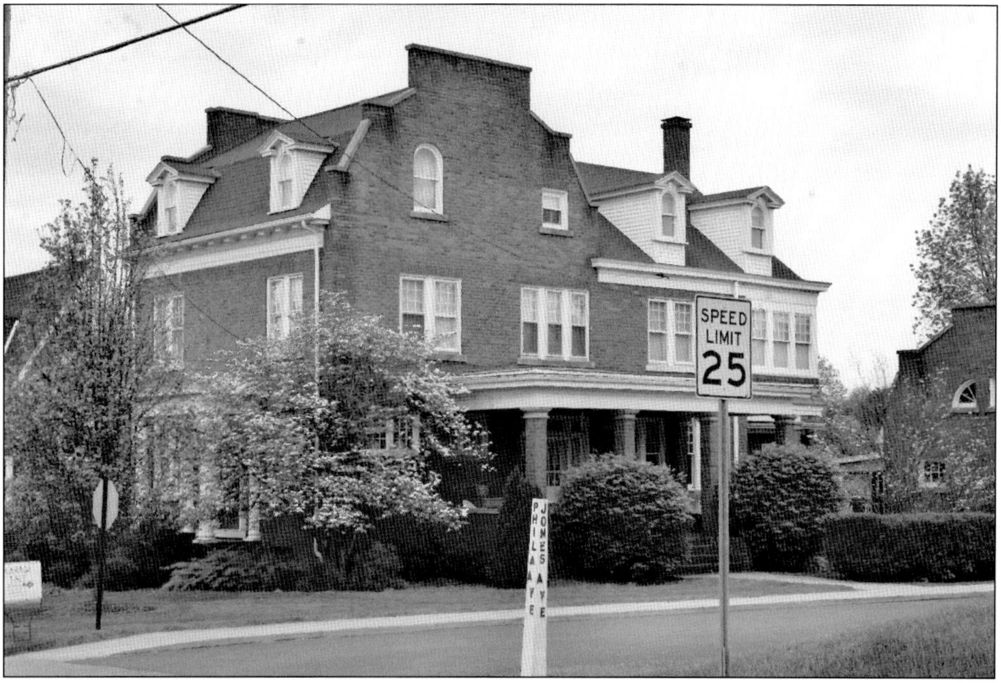

This smart, three-story brick residence, which was known as the Williams house, is today occupied by the Keith Gould family. It is on West Philadelphia Avenue at the corner of Jones Avenue. (Courtesy of Dick Duez.)

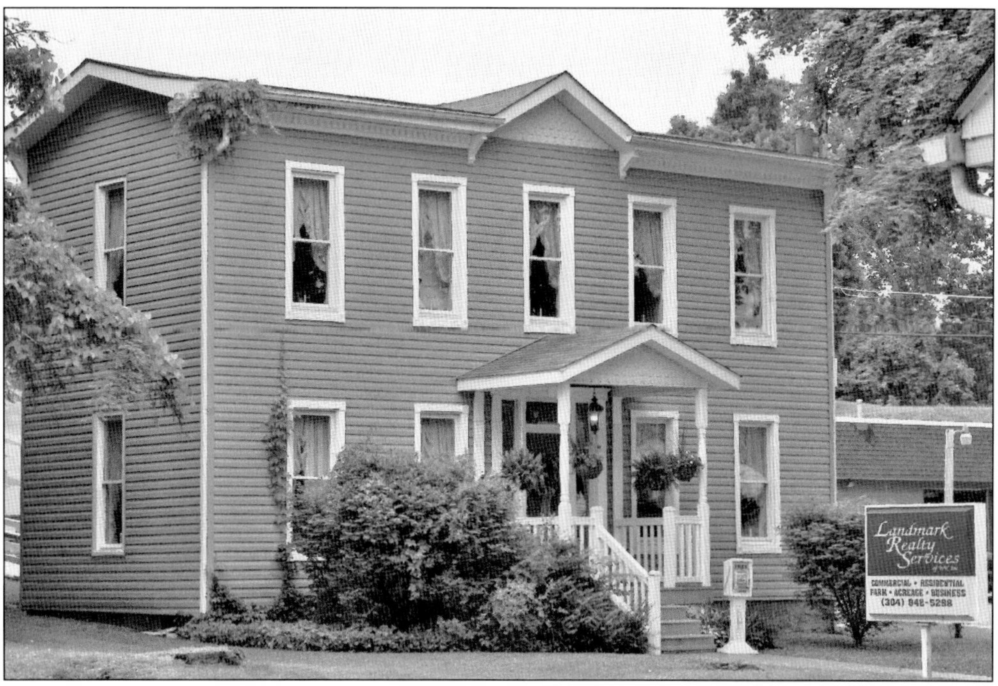

Today Landmark Realty Service occupies this attractive early Victorian structure, which is on East Main Street at the corner of Davis Street. (Courtesy of Dick Duez.)

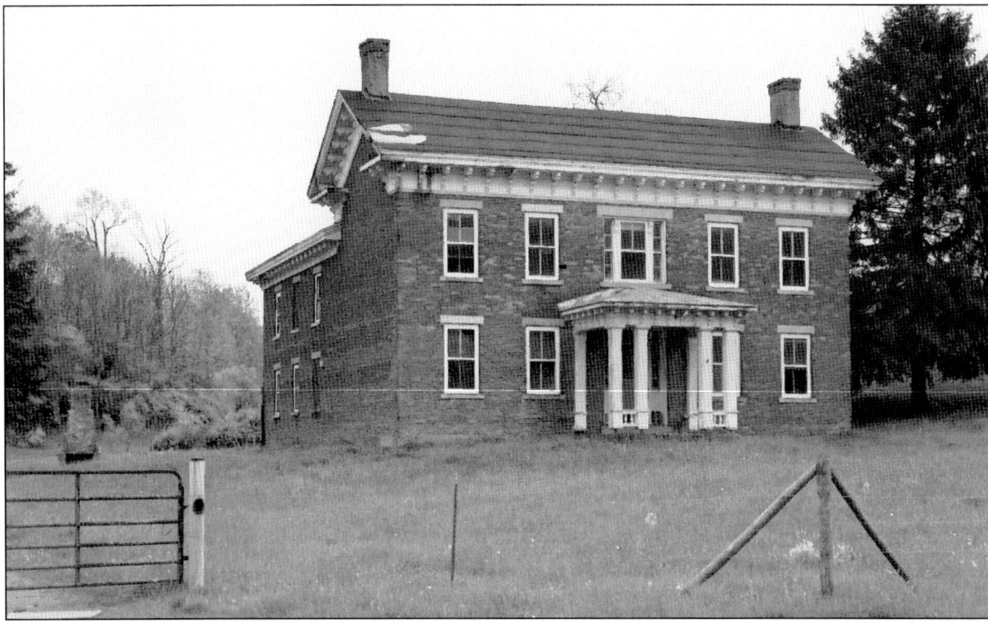

The Asa Gawthrop house is located along State Route 73 a few miles north of Bridgeport. (Courtesy of Dick Duez.)

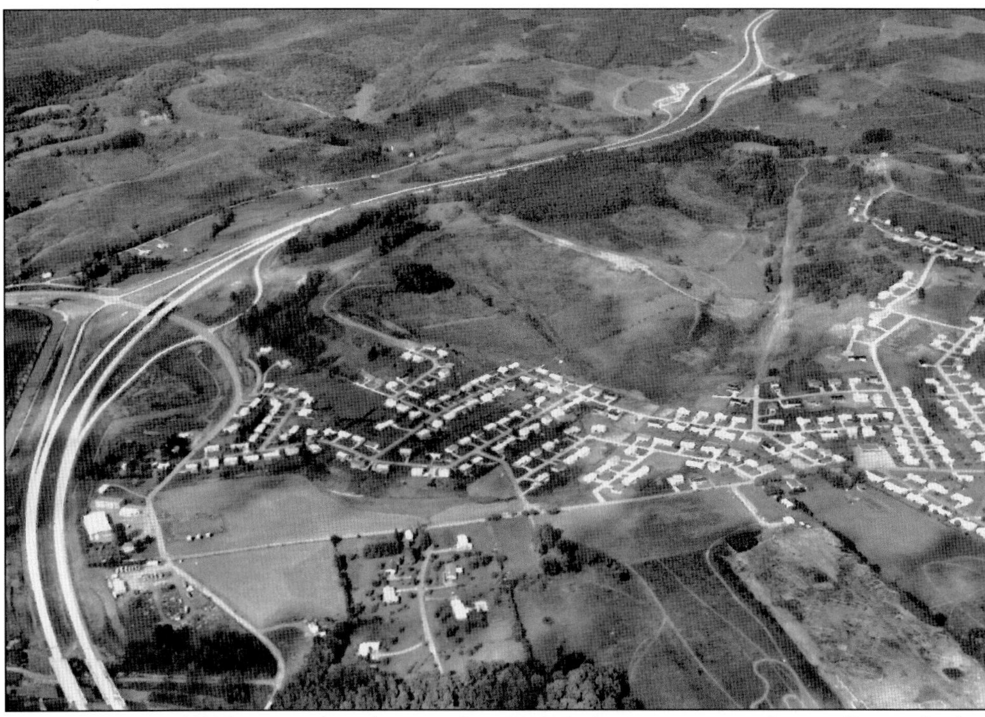

At left in this aerial photograph is the completed I-79 before it was opened to traffic, in the late 1960s or early 1970s. The housing development is Meadow Village, along Johnson Avenue. The barren area at upper left is where Meadowbrook Mall opened in 1982. Medbrook Urgent Care medical facility is now in the sharp curve on Johnson Avenue, where the new Lodgeville Road starts and extends to U.S. 50. Just north is Blake Center. (Courtesy of Dick Duez.)

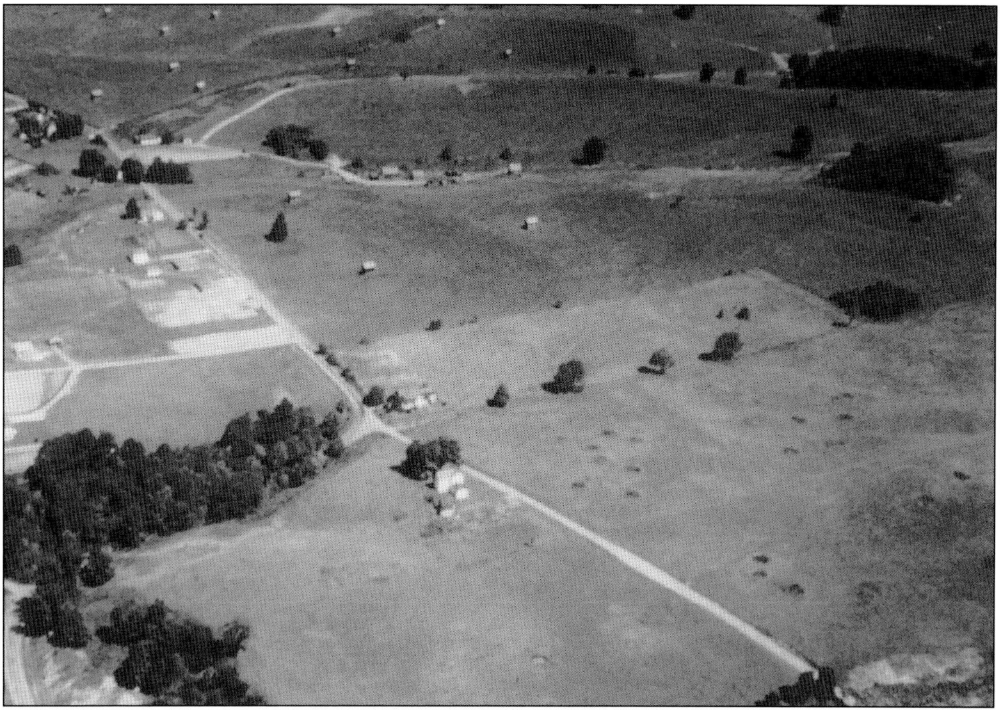

This aerial view shows the intersection of Johnson Avenue and Hall Street, seen in the middle of the photograph as it appeared c. 1955. Shown are numerous hay barns but virtually no houses. (Courtesy of Ray Blake.)

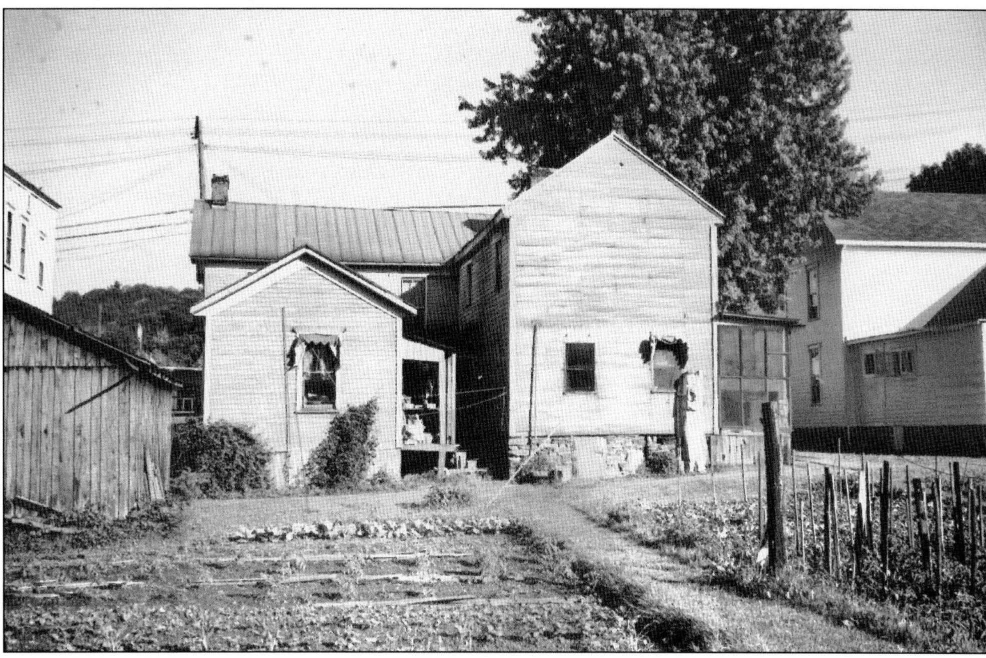

Looking south gives a back view of the Emanuel Benedum home, where Michael L. Benedum was born in 1869, including a small garden. The front of the house faced West Main Street. (Courtesy of Dick Duez.)

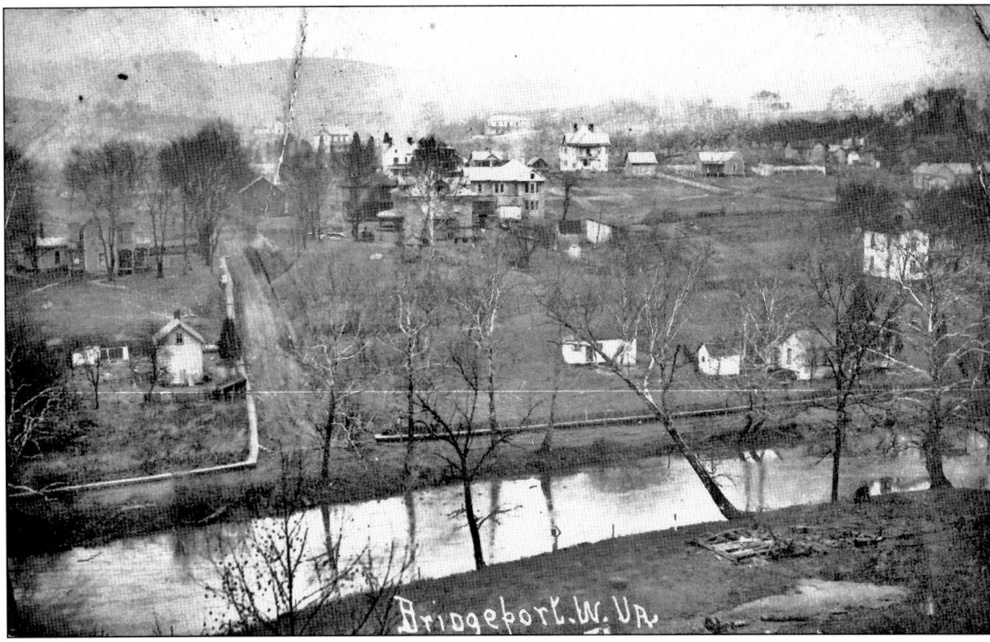

This section of Bridgeport was photographed in 1909. The Gov. Joseph Johnson house was among the cluster of houses in the center of the photograph. The large house at far left was the residence of Dr. William Late. The photograph was taken on a hillside behind what is Ace Hardware today. (Courtesy of Dick Duez.)

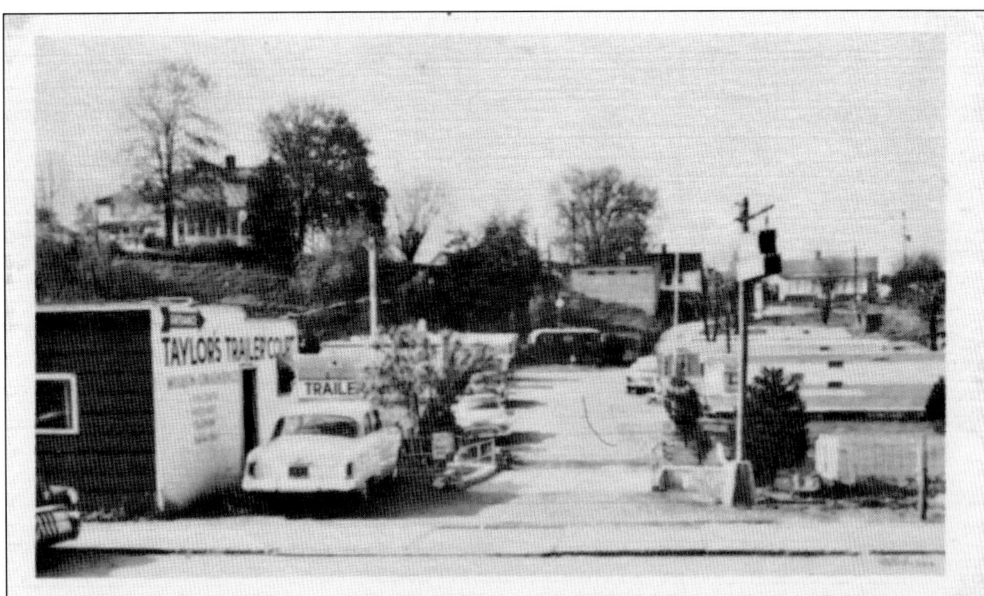

Taylor's Trailer Court, along East Main Street, was located next to Taylor's Restaurant. The Taylor family owned both businesses. (Courtesy of Dick Duez.)

Five

CHURCHES AND SCHOOLS

In 1974, the Simpson Creek Baptist Church observed its 200th birthday. Recognized as the oldest Baptist church in West Virginia by the West Virginia Baptist Convention, it has also been generally accepted as being the oldest Protestant church west of the Allegheny Mountains. In 1833, the old church at the cemetery was replaced with the "Old Brick Church," or the Simpson Creek Baptist Meeting House through the effort of members. Until the 1920s, it was located in the cemetery.

One of Michael Benedum's great ambitions was to erect a new Methodist church for Bridgeport. The cornerstone for it was laid on July 22, 1951, and by October 25, 1953, dedication ceremonies were held for a beautiful new building.

In 1933, Fr. Charles Carroll was given the All Saints Catholic Church Parish. The Catholic Church acquired a Methodist church on Main Street and dedicated in May 1954. St. Barnabas Episcopal Church also had groundbreaking ceremonies in June 1968.

In the 1850s, there were five schools in the Bridgeport area. After the Civil War, a public school was established in a one room log cabin on Worthington Drive. A few years later, a stone building replaced the log cabin on the site of the current Simpson Grade School. In 1909, a brick building was built on the site to house Bridgeport High School, and it eventually became a grade school. A new high school was built on Newton Avenue.

Overcrowding became a problem in the late 1940s. In September 1950, another grade school was built on Johnson Avenue. Bridgeport Union High School moved into a brick building on Johnson Avenue in the fall of 1964.

More than 30 years later, Bridgeport Junior High School became Bridgeport Middle School, and it, too, is located on Johnson Avenue.

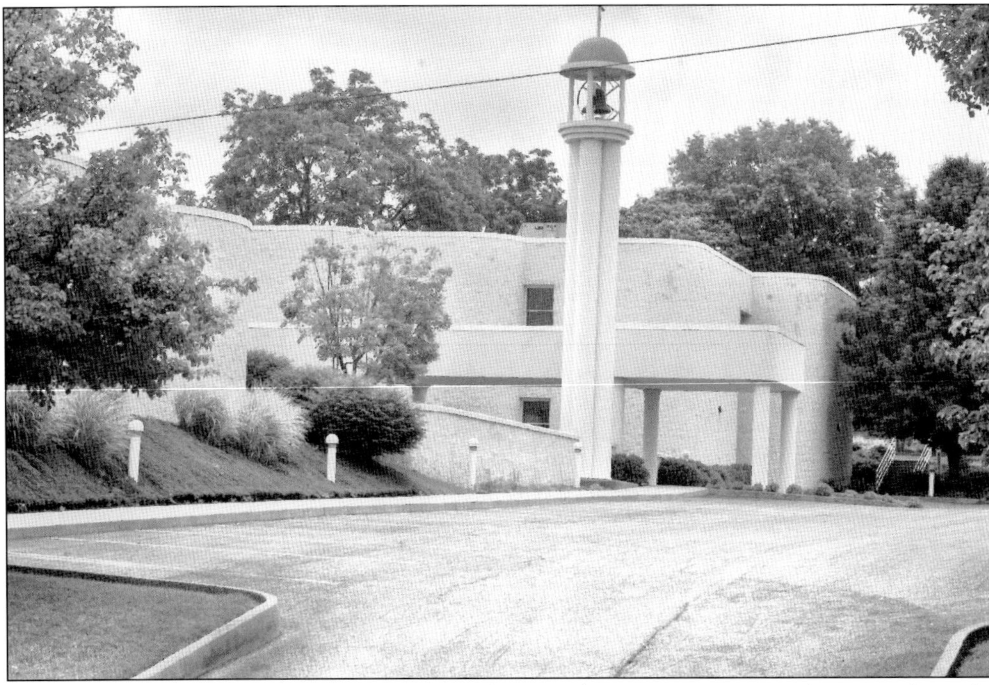

This new, modern, All Saints Catholic Church in Bridgeport is just across the street from the former All Saints building. (Courtesy of Dick Duez.)

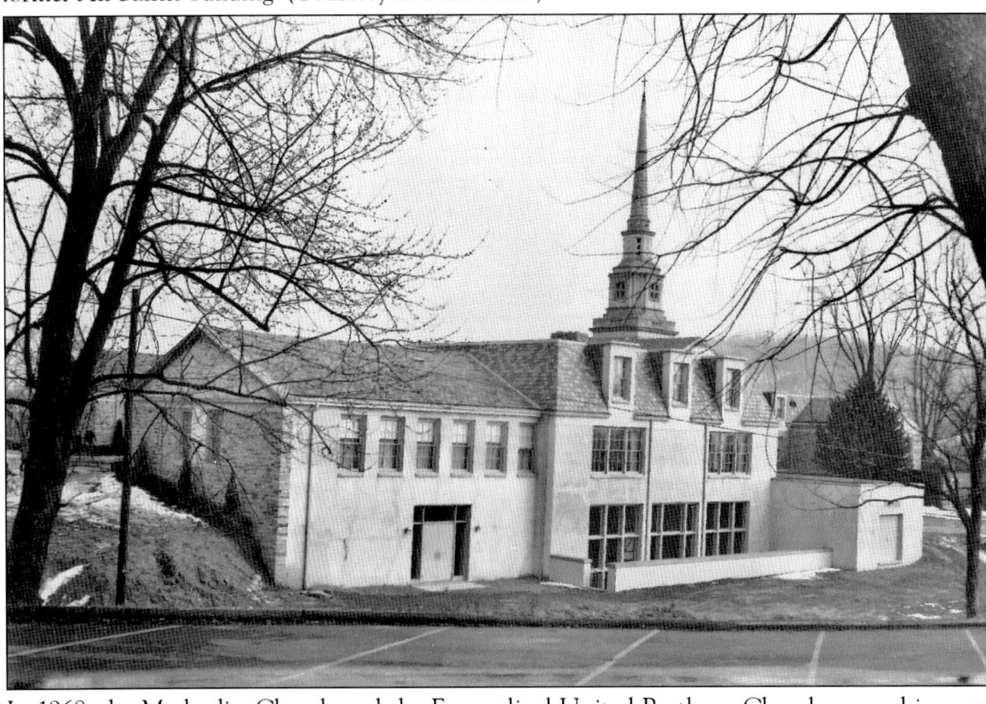

In 1968, the Methodist Church and the Evangelical United Brethren Church merged in most parts of the United States, thus the Bridgeport Methodist Church, the back of which is shown, became the Bridgeport United Methodists Church. Rev. Steven E. Dorsey was still pastor of the church in 2007. (From author's collection.)

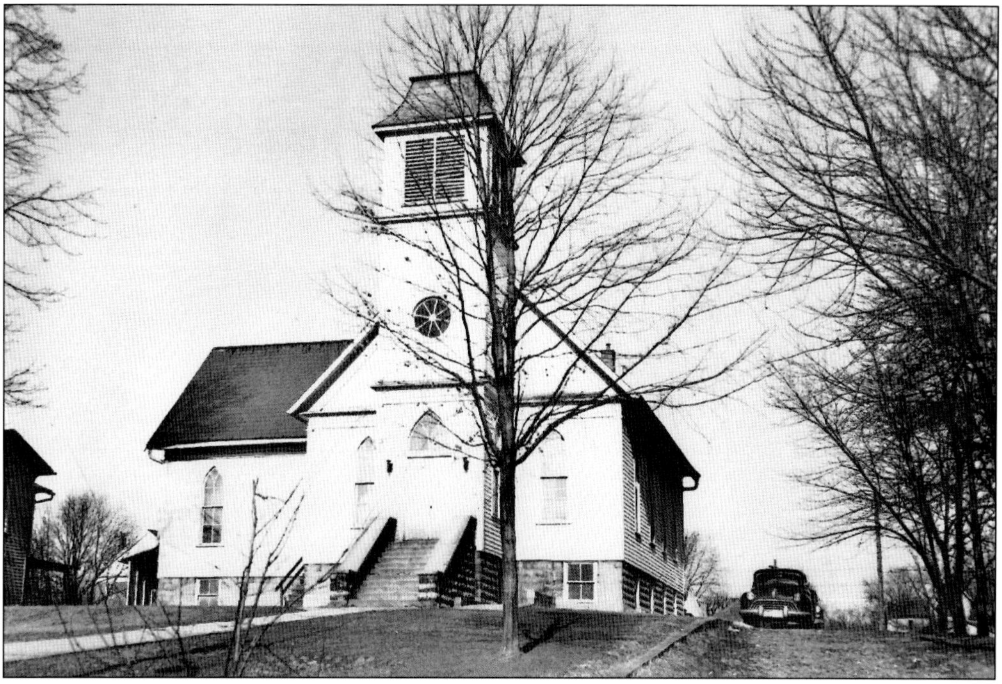

The Bridgeport Methodist Episcopal Church on Mechanic Street is pictured before plans were made to build a new church on Worthington Drive. Michael L. Benedum had attended the above church in 1871, but it was one of his great ambitions to build a new Methodist church for Bridgeport. The cornerstone for the new church was laid on July 22, 1951. (Courtesy of Dick Duez.)

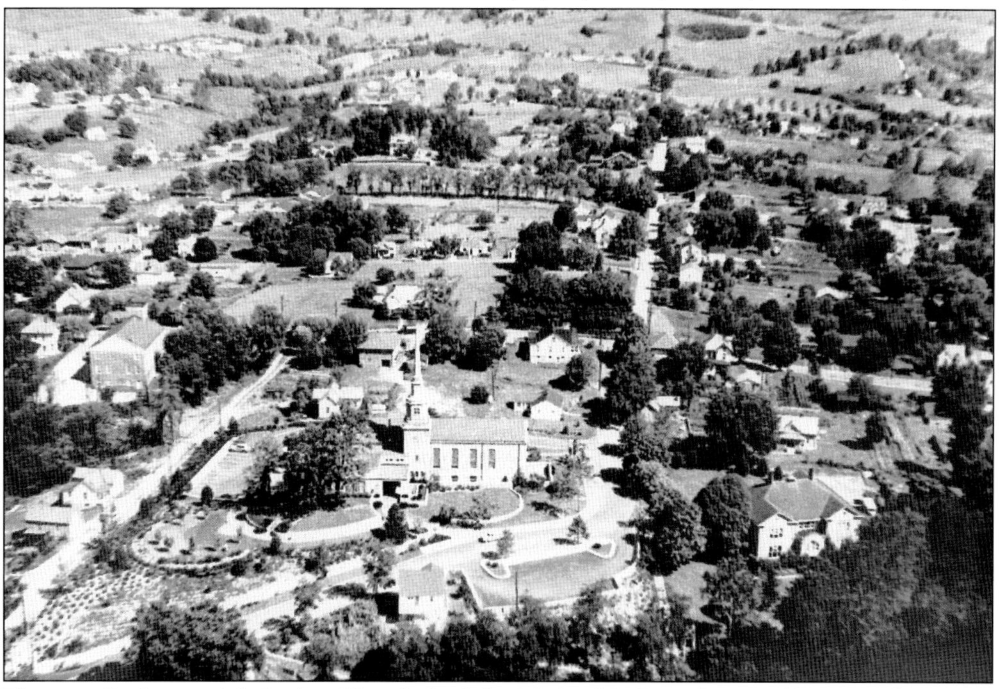

The new Bridgeport Methodist Church, built by Michael L. Benedum in the 1950s, dominates this aerial view of the city looking north. (Courtesy of Dick Duez.)

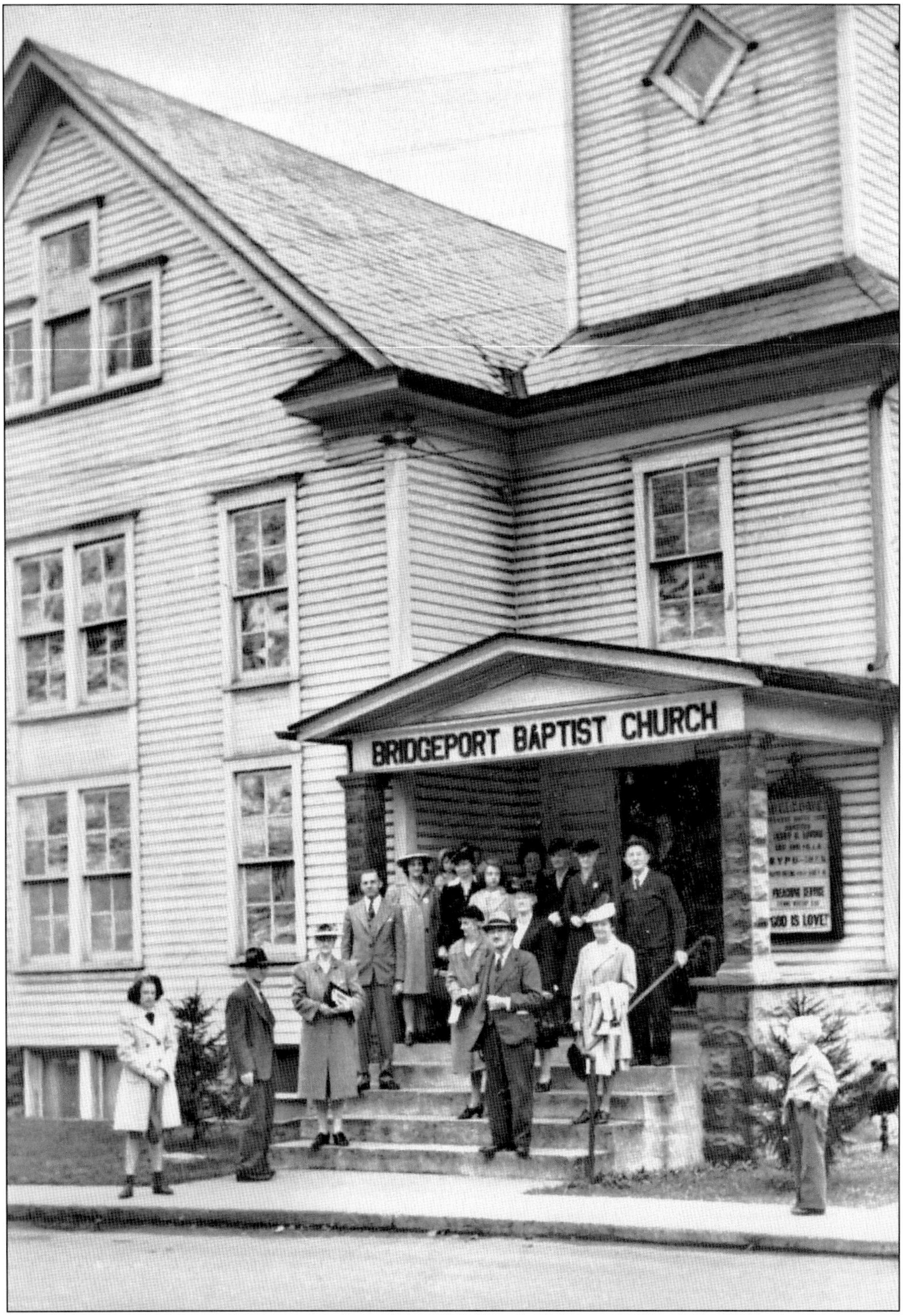

This group of members is seen in front of the wooden Bridgeport Baptist Church when it was located on East Main Street. The building formerly was part of the Sandusky Mill. (Courtesy of Dick Duez.)

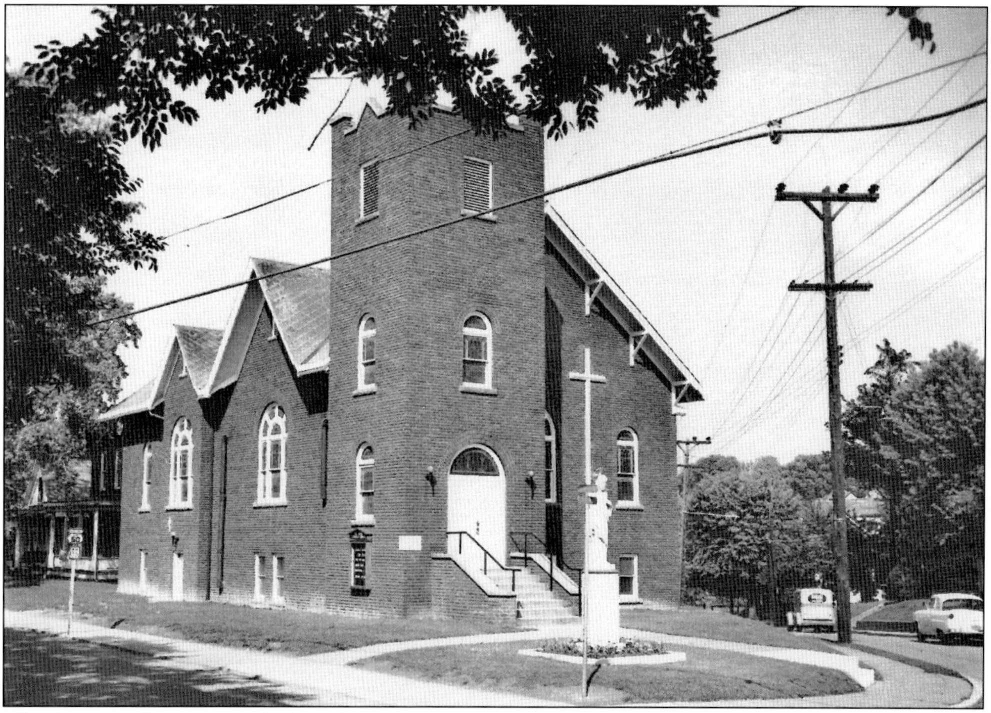

The former All Saints Catholic Church, on East Main Street at the corner of Philadelphia Avenue, was previously a Methodist Episcopal church. It was dedicated as a catholic church in 1954. Fr. Charles Carroll served as pastor of the church as early as 1933 and remained in the post until the early 1980s. It was demolished in the early to mid-1990s. (Courtesy of Dick Duez.)

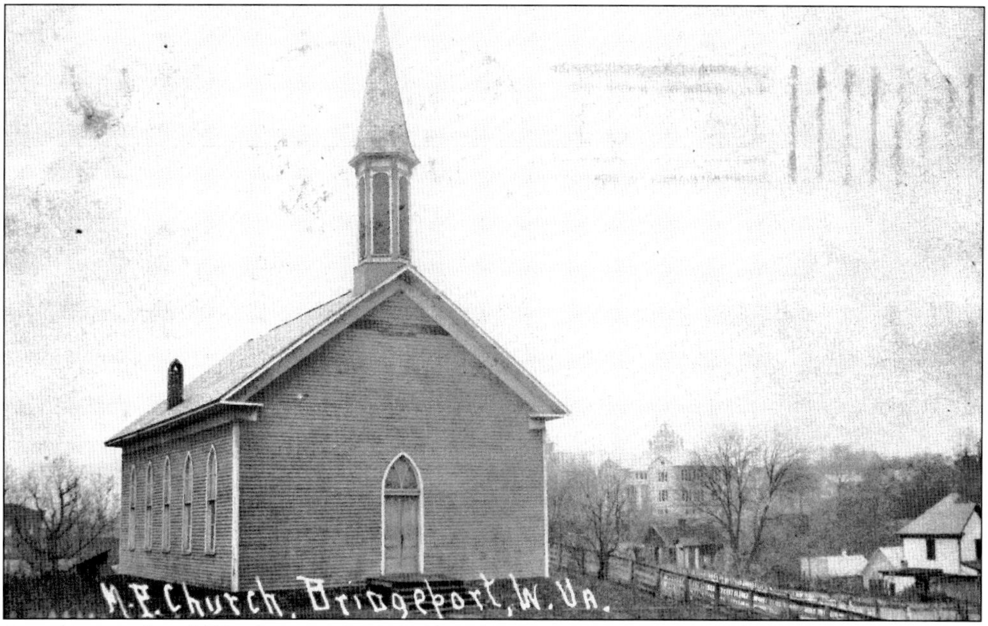

Seen here is the old Bridgeport A.M.E. Church on Davis Street in Bridgeport. In background, at right, is the old Bridgeport High School, now Simpson Elementary School. (Courtesy of Dick Duez.)

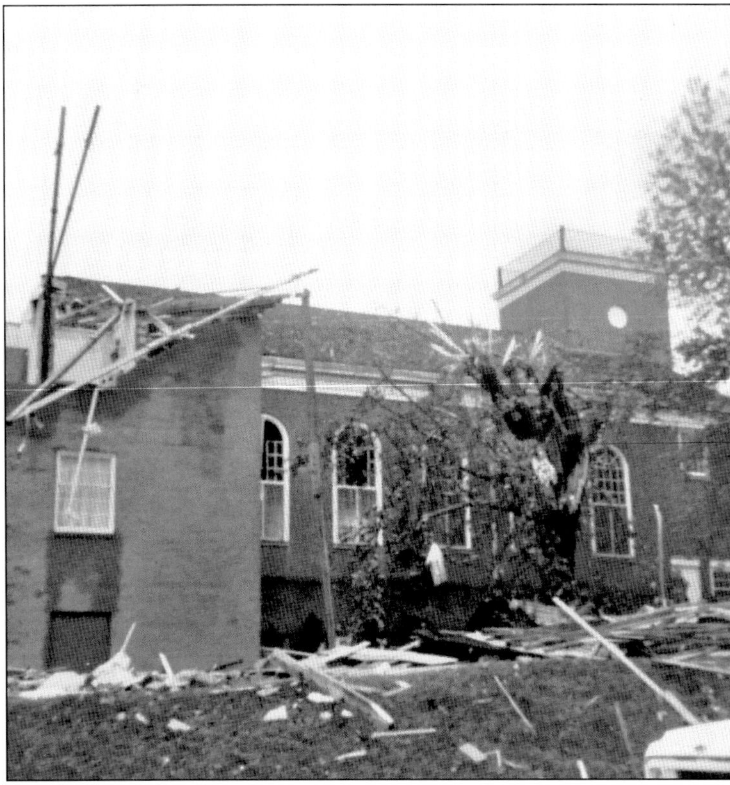

Simpson Creek Baptist Church sustained considerable damage because of a tornado that struck one evening in August 1970. (Courtesy of Dick Duez.)

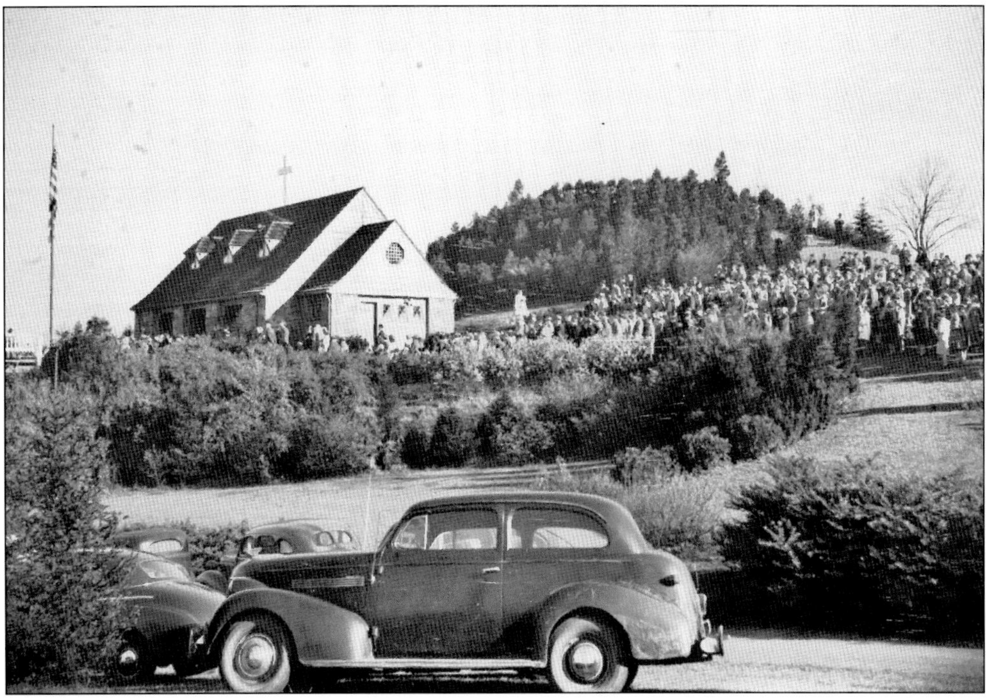

Easter services were held in 1946 at the church building in the Bridgeport Cemetery. (Courtesy of Dick Duez.)

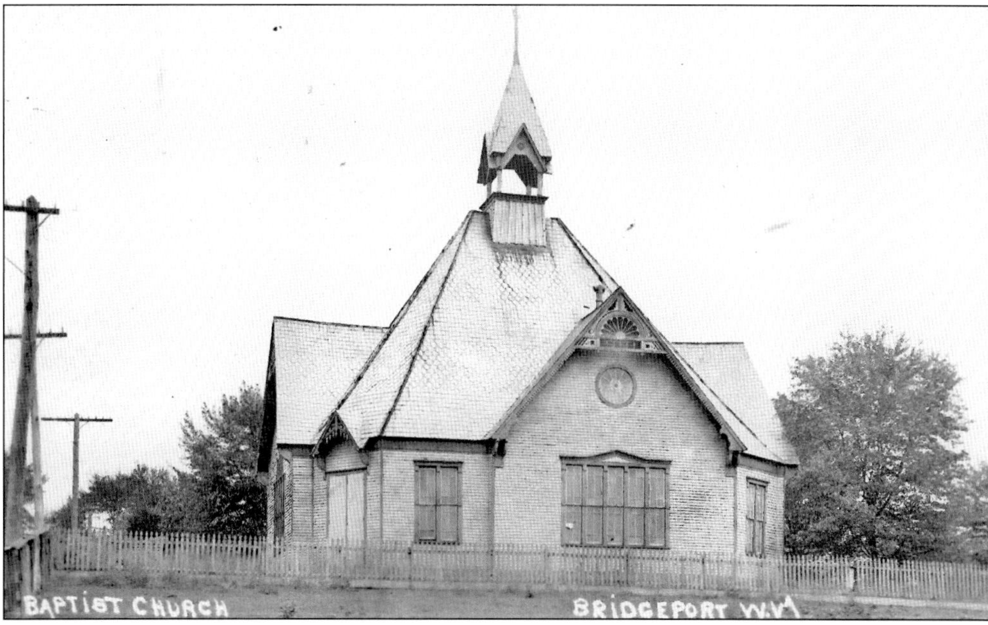

Looking east, the Simpson Creek Baptist Church on East Philadelphia Avenue is seen here. It is said to be the oldest Baptist church west of the Allegheny Mountains. The third of four Simpson Creek Baptist Church buildings is seen in this 1908 photograph. (Courtesy of Dick Duez.)

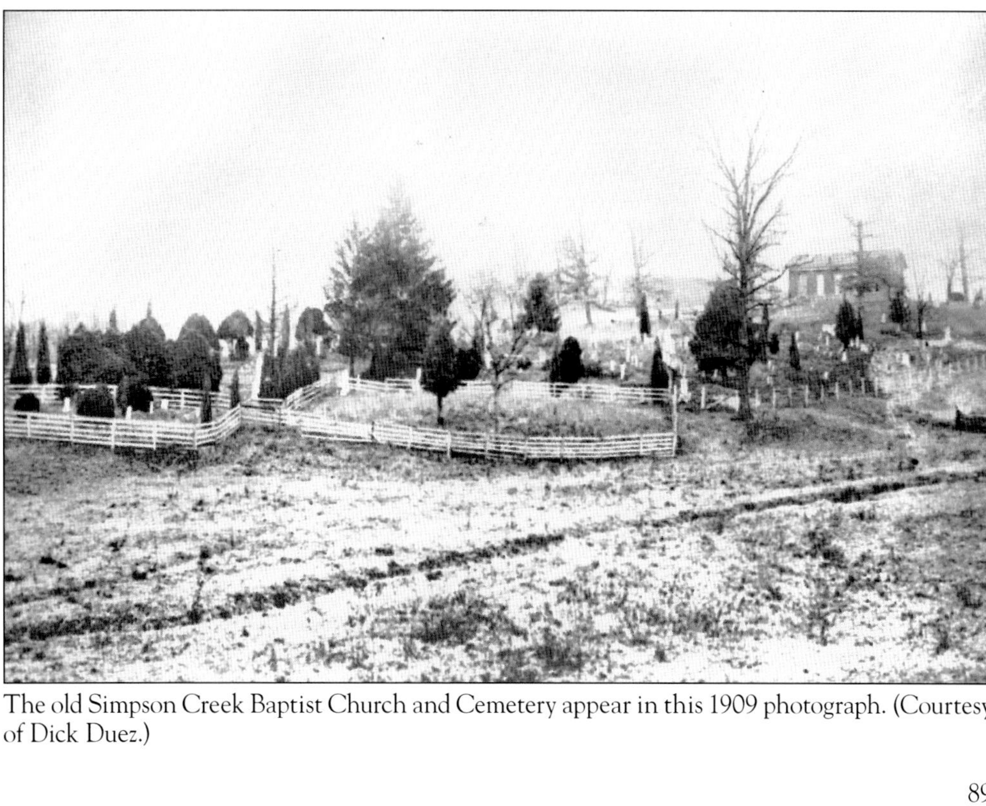

The old Simpson Creek Baptist Church and Cemetery appear in this 1909 photograph. (Courtesy of Dick Duez.)

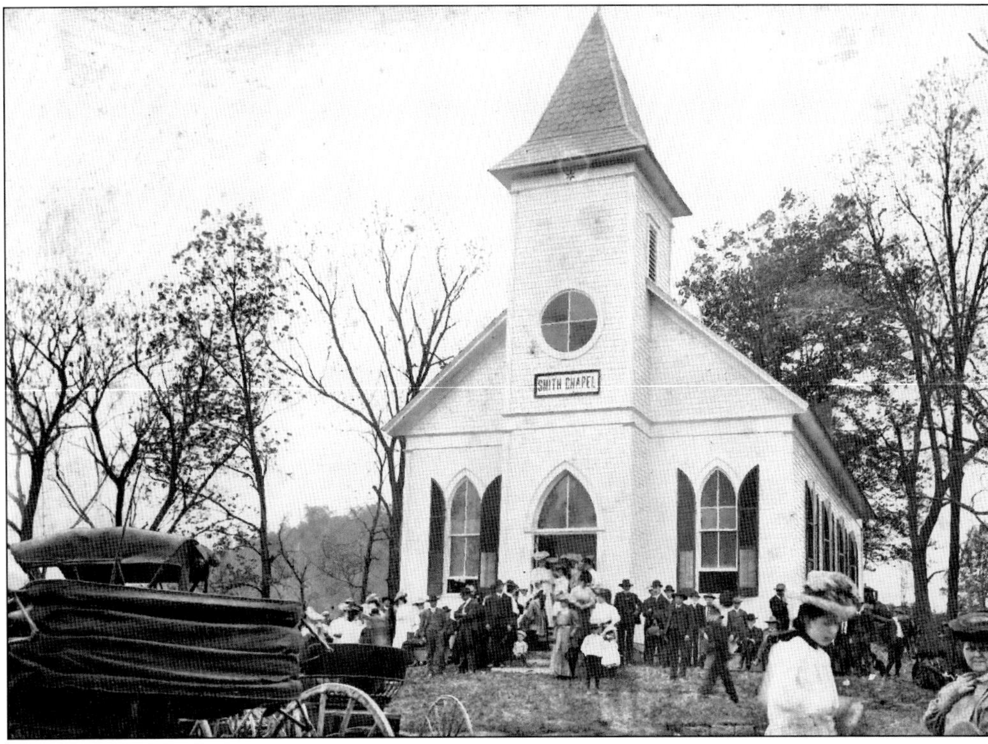

Smith Chapel, located about two miles north of Bridgeport, was being dedicated when this photograph was taken. Now the Smith Chapel United Methodist Church, it is located along County Route 24. (Courtesy of Dick Duez.)

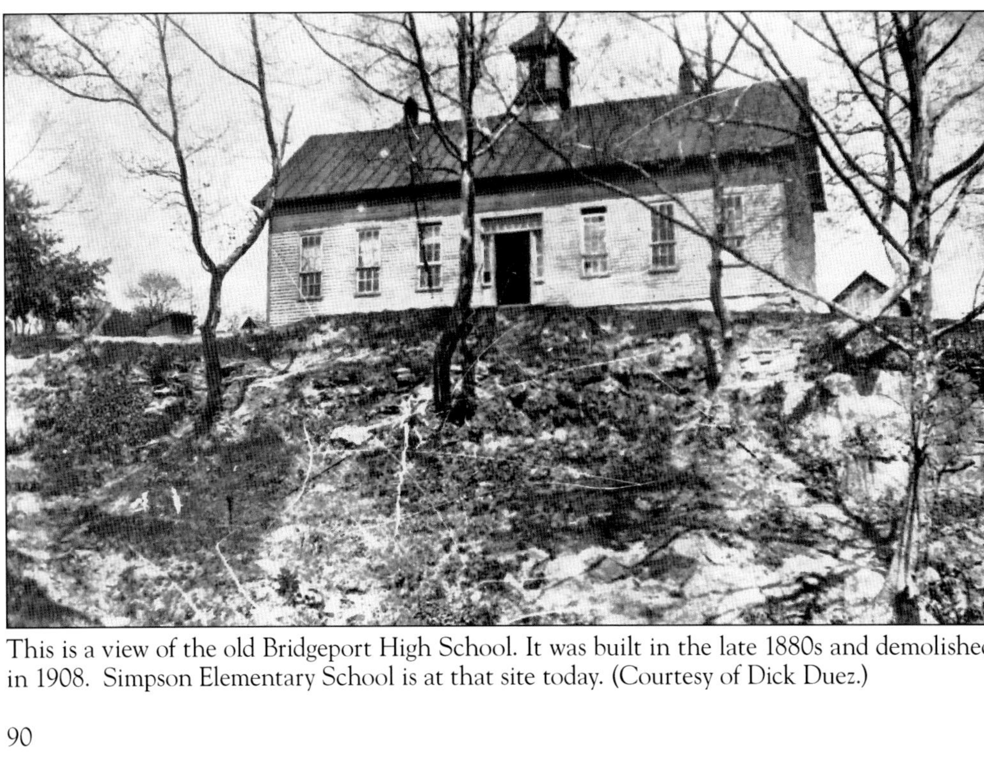

This is a view of the old Bridgeport High School. It was built in the late 1880s and demolished in 1908. Simpson Elementary School is at that site today. (Courtesy of Dick Duez.)

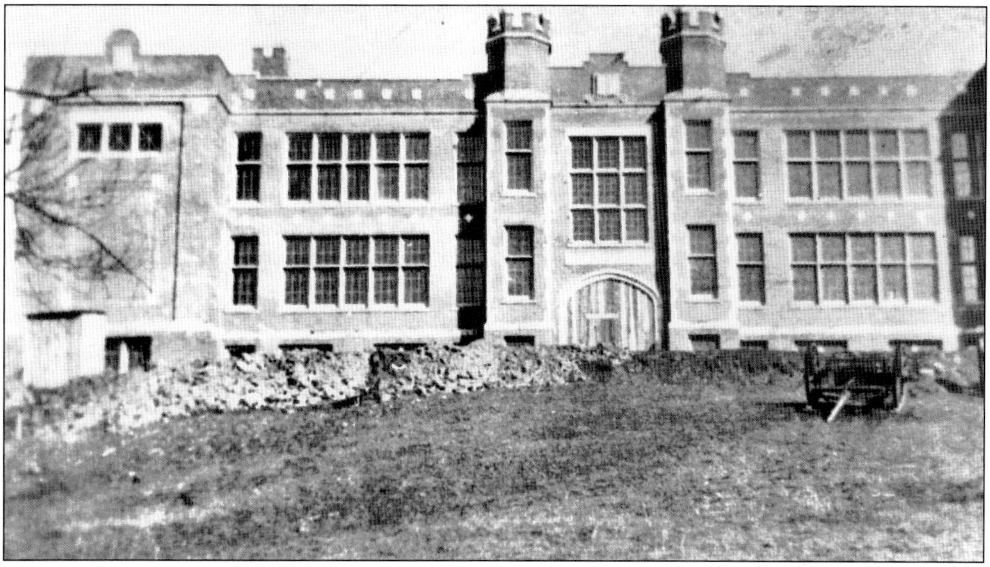

Construction of the old Bridgeport High School, at the top of Newton Street, is underway in this photograph. Today the building is owned by Heritage Christian School. (Courtesy of Dick Duez.)

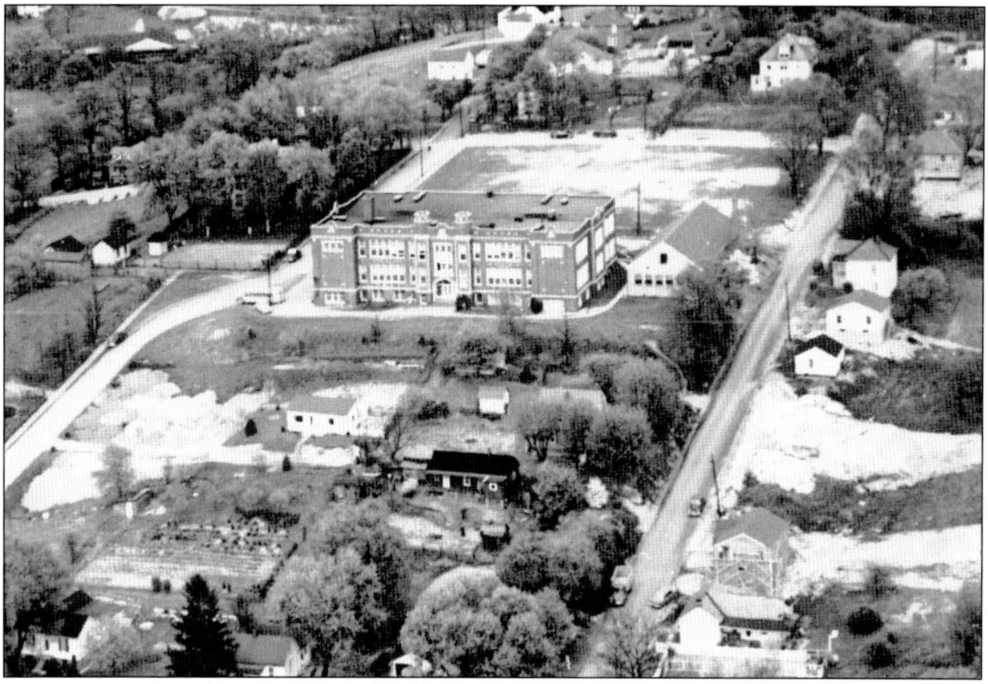

The completed Bridgeport High School between Newton and Foley Streets predominates this aerial photograph in earlier years. (Courtesy of Dick Duez.)

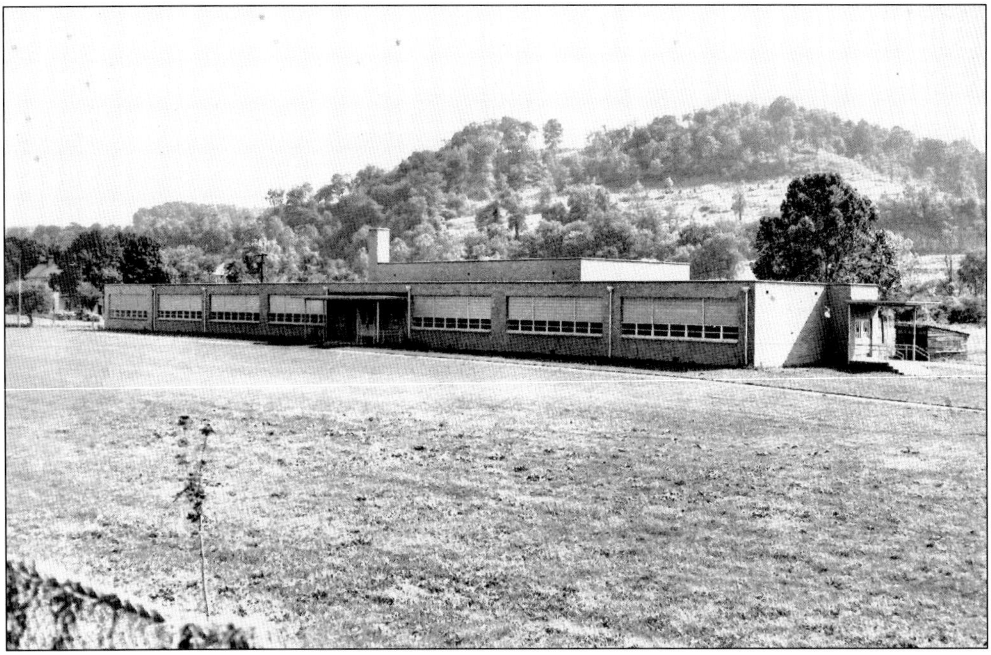

Johnson Elementary School is shown in 1960. It is located today just north of the new Bridgeport High School along Johnson Avenue in Bridgeport. (Courtesy of Dick Duez.)

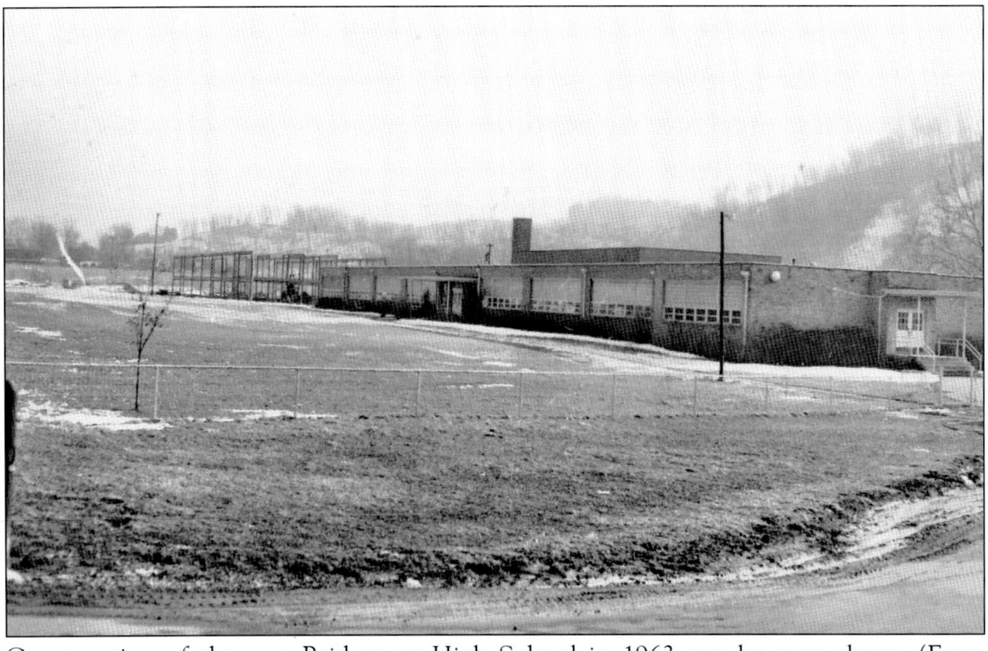

Construction of the new Bridgeport High School in 1963 can be seen above. (From author's collection.)

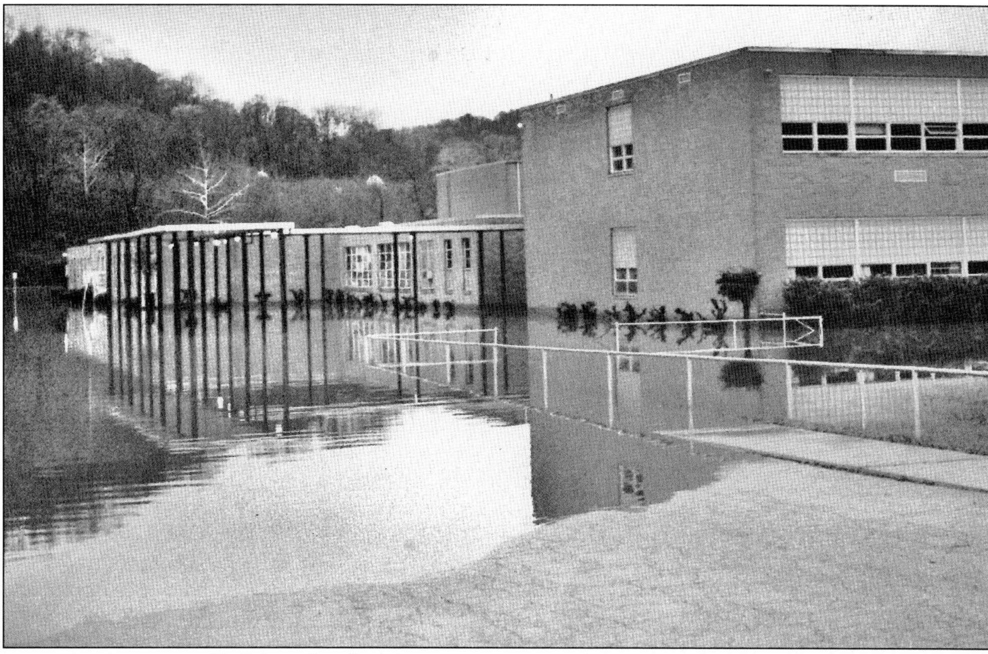

In 1985, what was called the "flood of the century" caused extensive damage to parts of Bridgeport High School, including the gymnasium floor. Note how the water crept up and surrounded the south end of the building. (Courtesy of Dick Duez.)

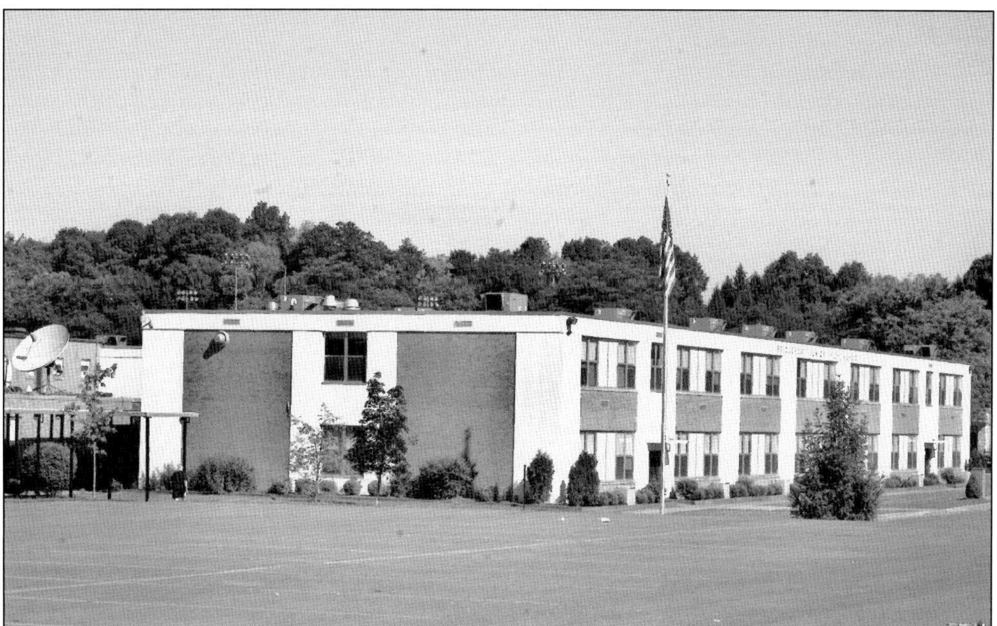

This is a recent view of Bridgeport High School, which has undergone extensive renovations. (Courtesy of Dick Duez.)

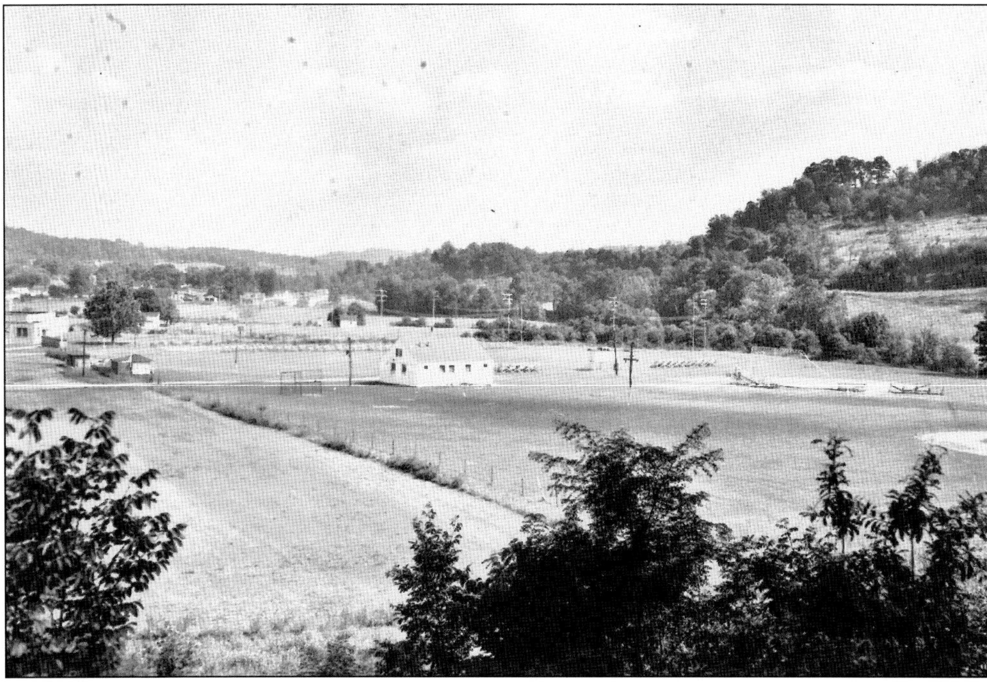

Photographed in the mid- to late 1950s is part of the Bridgeport High School athletic field. (From author's collection.)

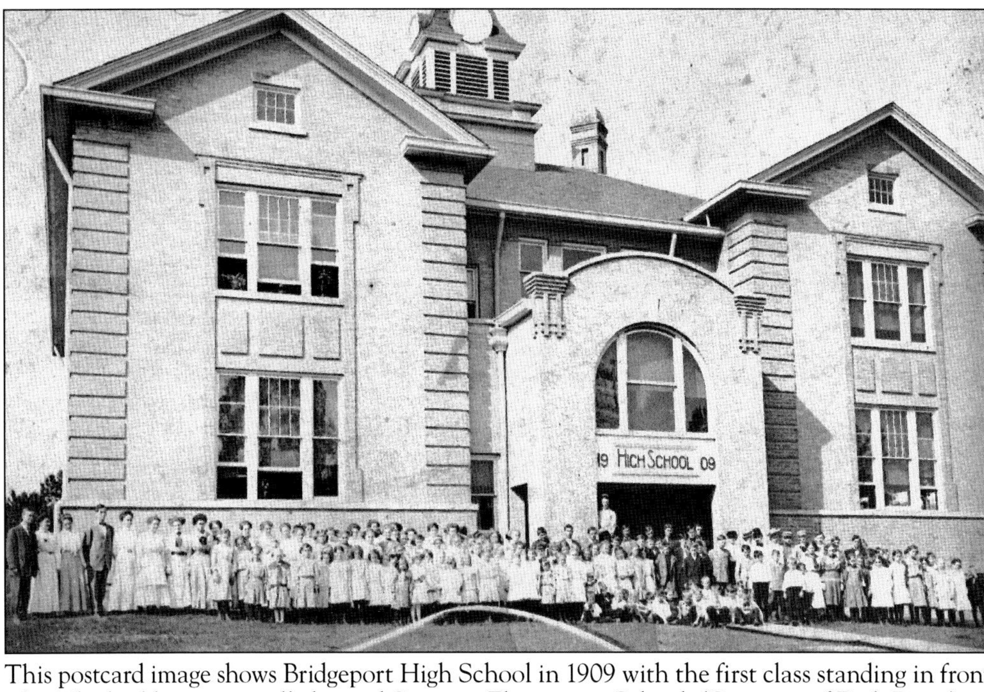

This postcard image shows Bridgeport High School in 1909 with the first class standing in front of it. The building eventually housed Simpson Elementary School. (Courtesy of Dick Duez.)

Six

Those Familiar Places

While earlier Bridgeport residents and others quite familiar with the city sometimes lamented the demolition of the buildings to which they were long accustomed over the years, others in more modern times have celebrated new sites, such as the new City Park behind Bridgeport High School, Compton Park in the northern part of the city, the modern bus stop area on West Main Street across from the Benedum Civic Center and the beautification of countless other locations.

There are plenty of sites that have claimed an indelible place in our memories after having been either removed or dramatically changed. No doubt there are buildings, stores, or other structures in Bridgeport that someone who hasn't been to town for 40 or even 30 years would be hard-pressed to recognize.

The images on the remaining pages run the gamut from very early to very modern times. Lots of improvements have been made in Bridgeport. Just a few of these have been the new athletic fields at Bridgeport High School, the new municipal building where Rish Equipment once was, the new Bridgeport firehouse, Medbrook Urgent Care, offices on Doctors Drive, and others.

There are old structures that have managed to elude the wrecker's ball, including the Bow Bridge, the building that housed the Millstone Restaurant and numerous other businesses, the Peshak and Utt Building, the railroad tracks, the buildings on Main Street between Virginia Avenue and the railroad crossing, the building that once housed the Pure Food Store, and others. And who could forget the Handy Shop, which is no more?

These images and several others are here to revive warm memories or arouse new hopes for tomorrow.

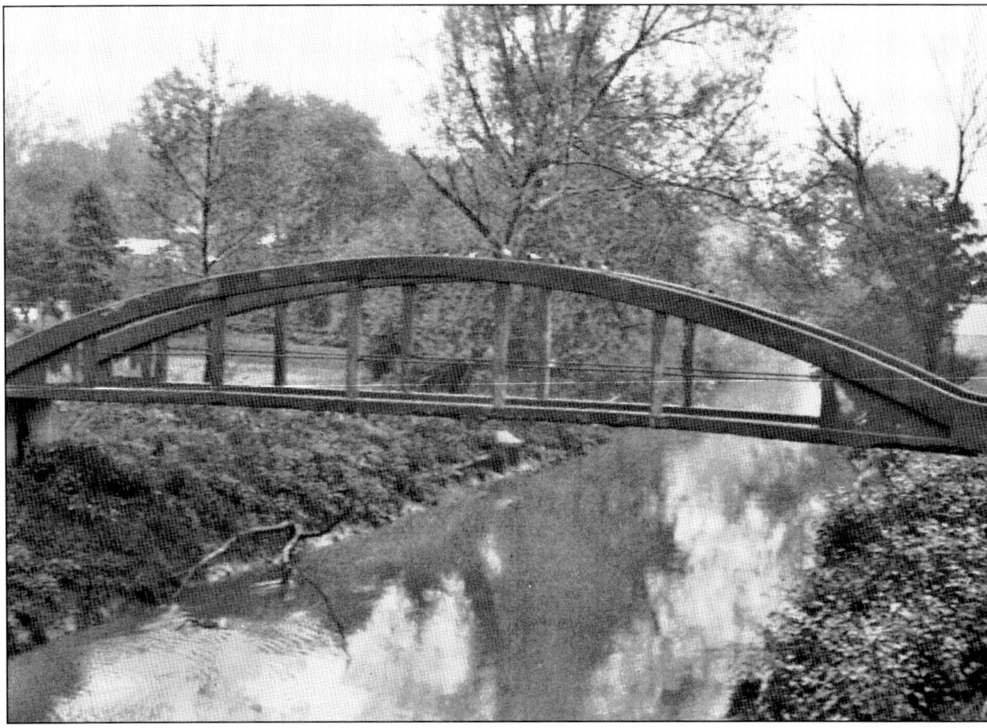

This 1961 photograph shows the famous Bow Bridge in Bridgeport, parallel to South Virginia Avenue. Built in 1924 to connect the Bridgeport Lamp Chimney Company with its warehouses, today it is a footbridge for people using the tennis and basketball courts. (Courtesy of Dick Duez.)

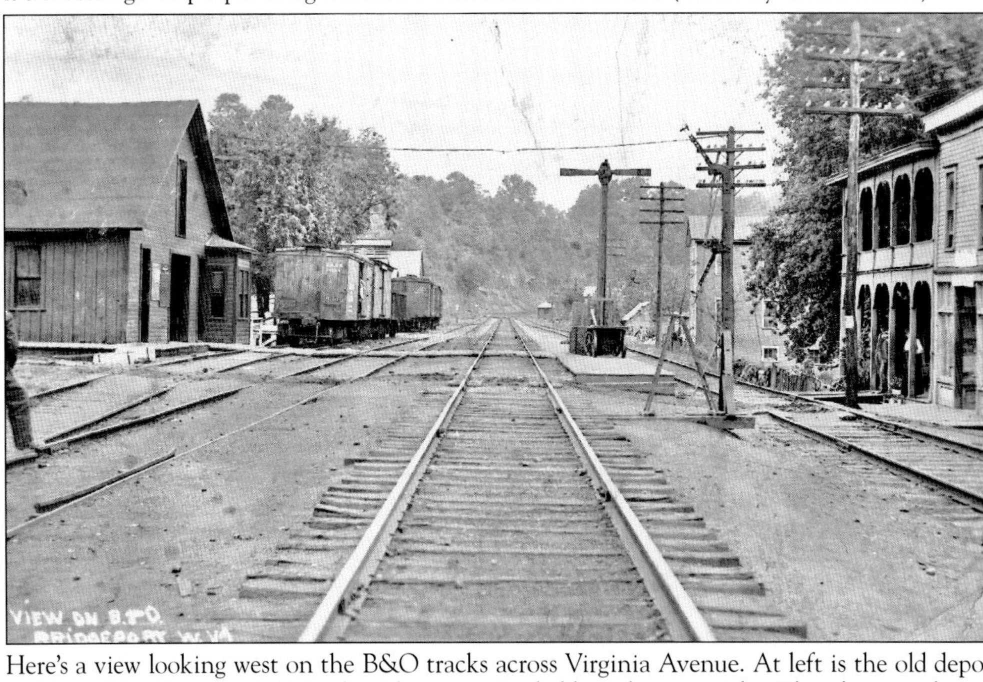

Here's a view looking west on the B&O tracks across Virginia Avenue. At left is the old depot building. The Commercial Hotel, with its unmistakable style, is at right. The photograph was taken in early 1900. (Courtesy of Dick Duez.)

The Fitzhugh Building, right, was located on West Main Street in Bridgeport. It housed the Knights of Pythias Hall in this 1910 photograph, taken just after completion of the Bridgeport Bank, barely visible at right. The main floor of the building was a general store. (Courtesy of Dick Duez.)

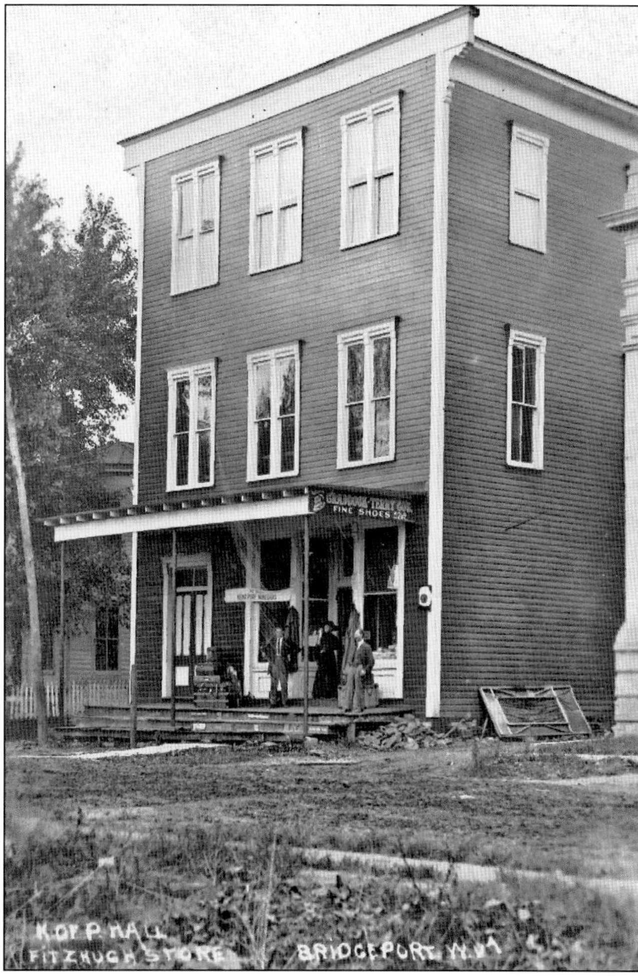

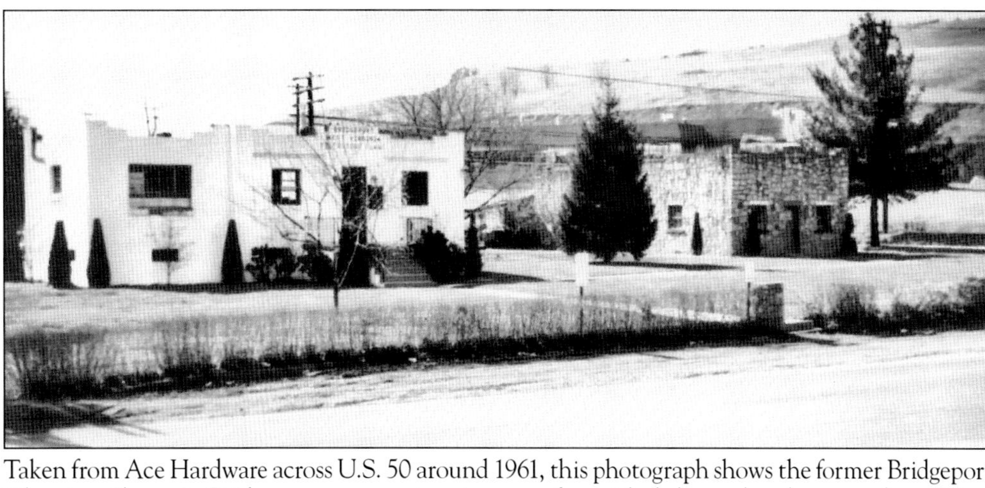

Taken from Ace Hardware across U.S. 50 around 1961, this photograph shows the former Bridgeport Filtration Plant. As Bridgeport now receives its water from Clarksburg, the plant was demolished in 2005. On the land at the top of the photograph today is Rosewood Development. (Courtesy of Dick Duez.)

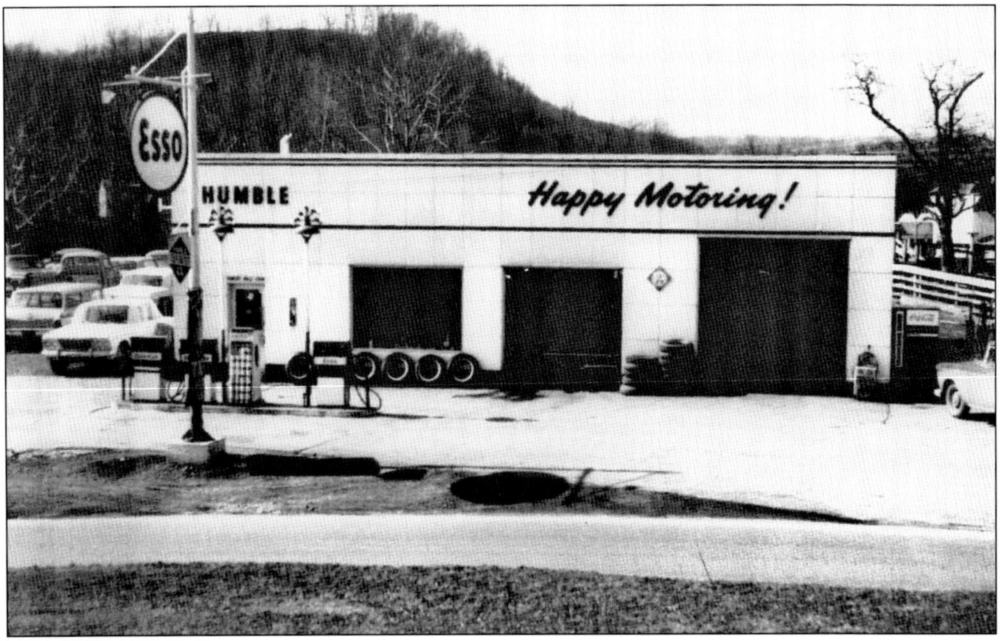

Dale Crim's Esso is pictured in 1962 from the William Johnson house property. The station was on West Main Street next to the Bridgeport Stockyards, seen at right. (Courtesy of Dick Duez.)

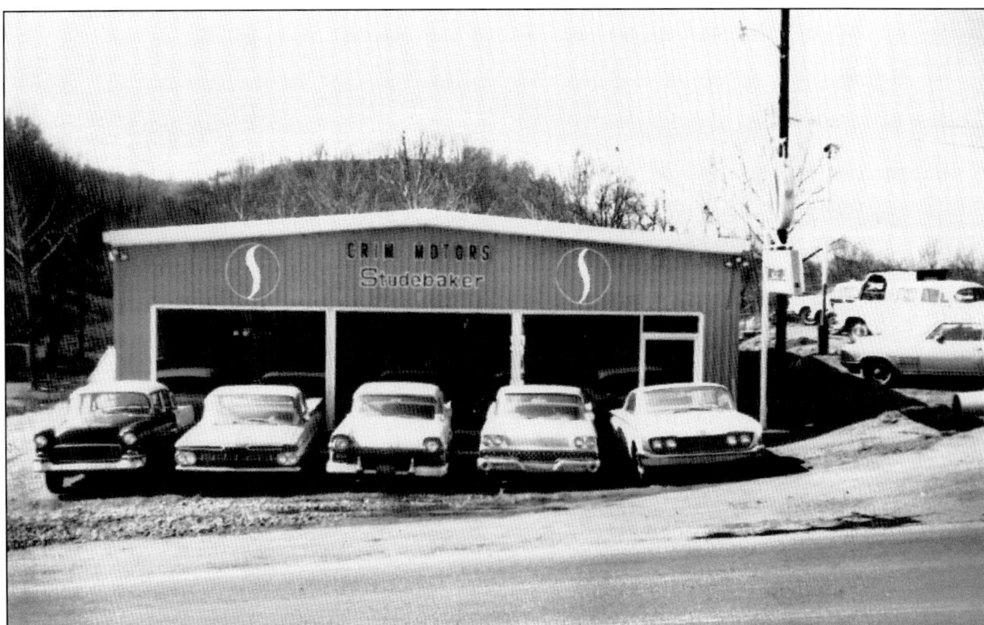

Crim Motors was the Studebaker dealership in Bridgeport in the late 1950s and early 1960s. It was next door to Dale Crim's Esso. (Courtesy of Dick Duez.)

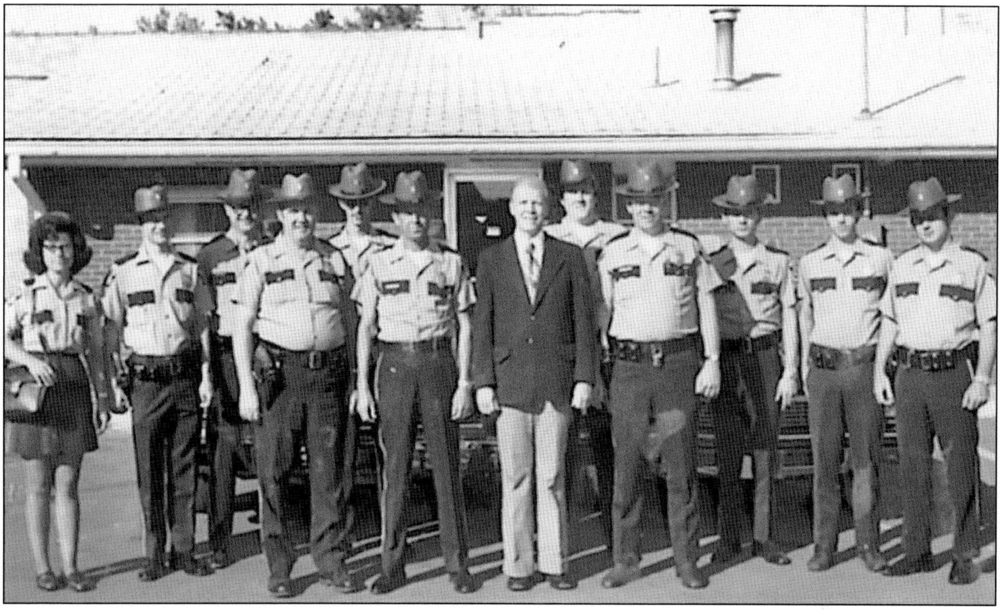

This mid-1960s photograph shows the Bridgeport Police Department with then-mayor Carl E. Furbee Jr. at center. From left to right are Sylvia Trippett, David Cox, Ervin Hull, William Allender, James Hotsinpiller, Chief John Diamond, Mayor Furbee, Clarence Sigley, Don Trippett, Steve Alfred, George Davis, and Ray Collins.

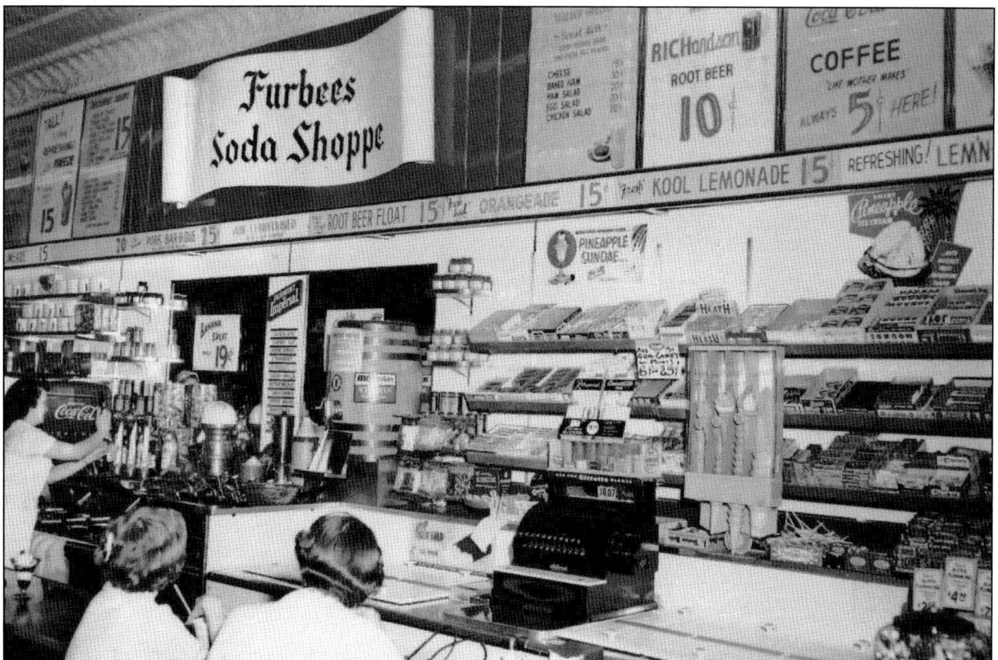

Furbee's Soda Shoppe was an old familiar place inside Furbee's Drug Store, where many people were served every day. In this 1962 image, a wide assortment of candy can be seen on the wall. (Courtesy of Dick Duez.)

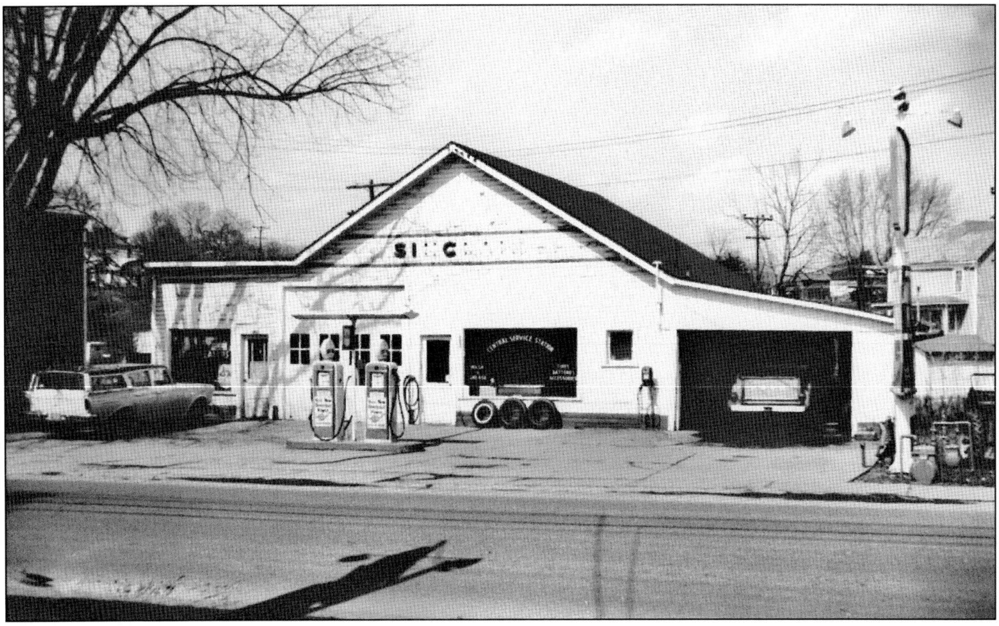

This is the Sinclair Central Service Station in 1962. It was located on East Main Street next to the Pure Food Store, now Shahady's Antiques. At left of the station site today is Hadorn Distributing Company. (Courtesy of Dick Duez.)

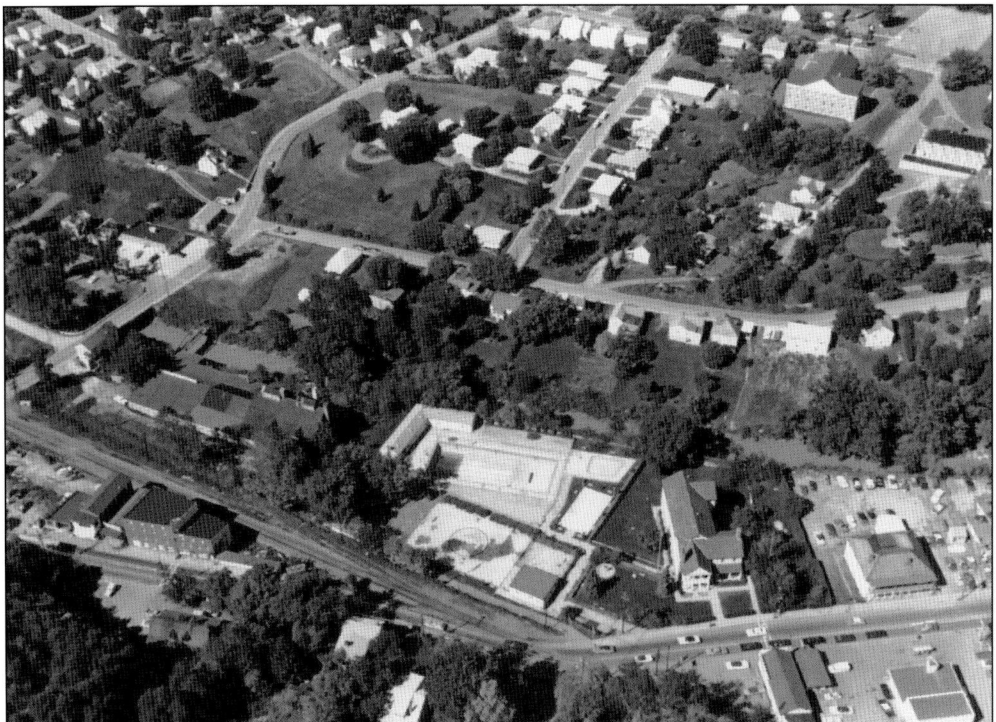

This 1973 aerial photograph overlooks Main Street (U.S. 50), near bottom, dominated by the Bridgeport Swimming Pool. Virginia Avenue is at left, with Worthington Drive nearly parallel to Main Street. (Courtesy of Dick Duez.)

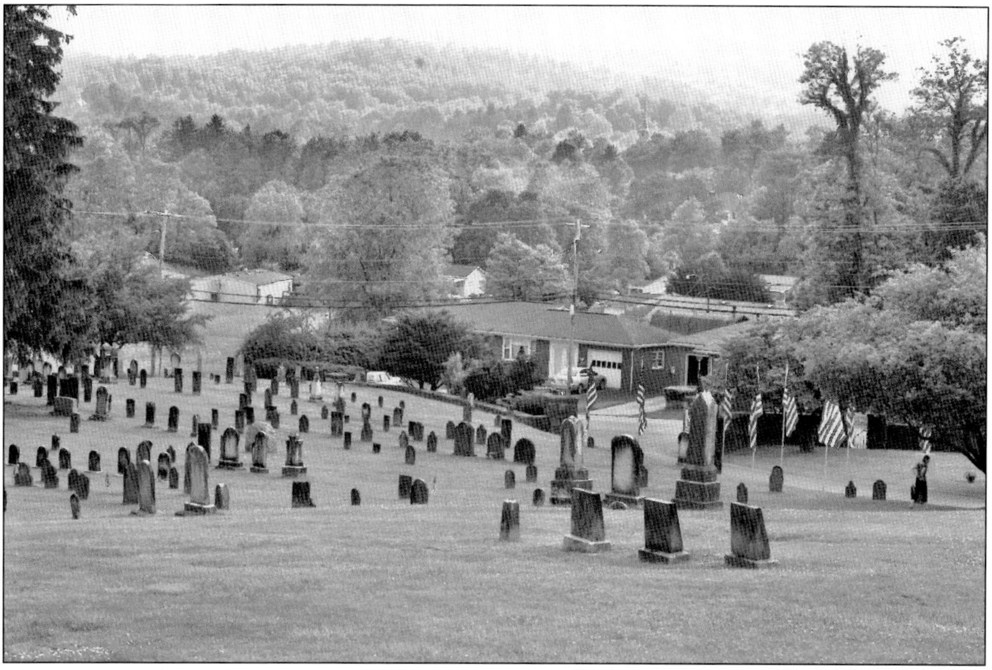

This is part of the old Baptist section, the oldest part of Bridgeport Cemetery, which is said to be the oldest cemetery in Harrison County. The photograph was taken from the site of the oldest Baptist church west of the Allegheny Mountains. (Courtesy of Dick Duez.)

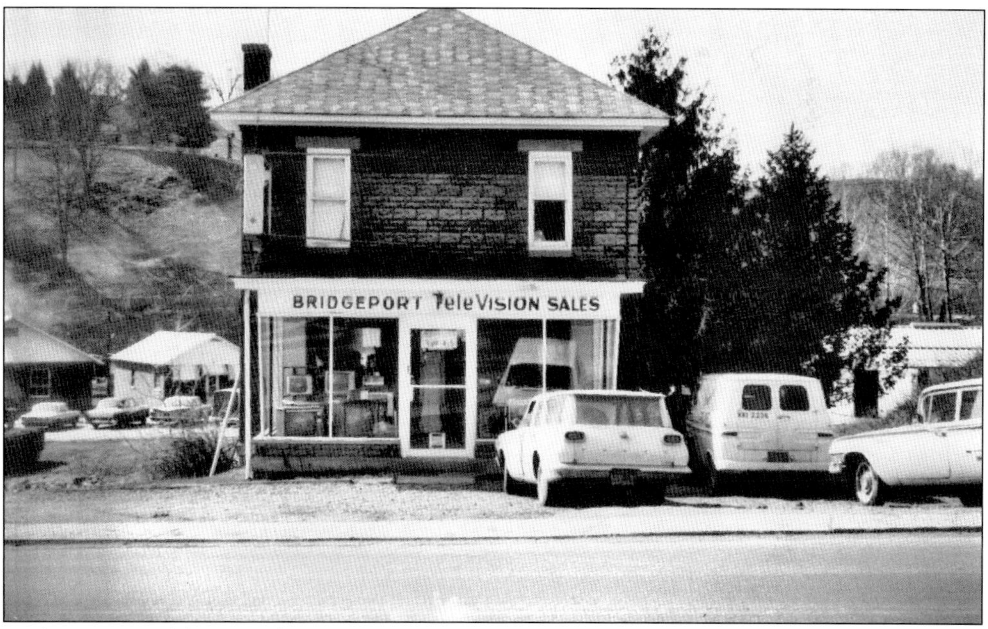

In the 1960s and for several years afterward, Bridgeport Television Sales was in business on West Main Street. It was owned and operated by Kenneth Strait. Note the old Hope Gas maintenance facility behind it at left. (Courtesy of Dick Duez.)

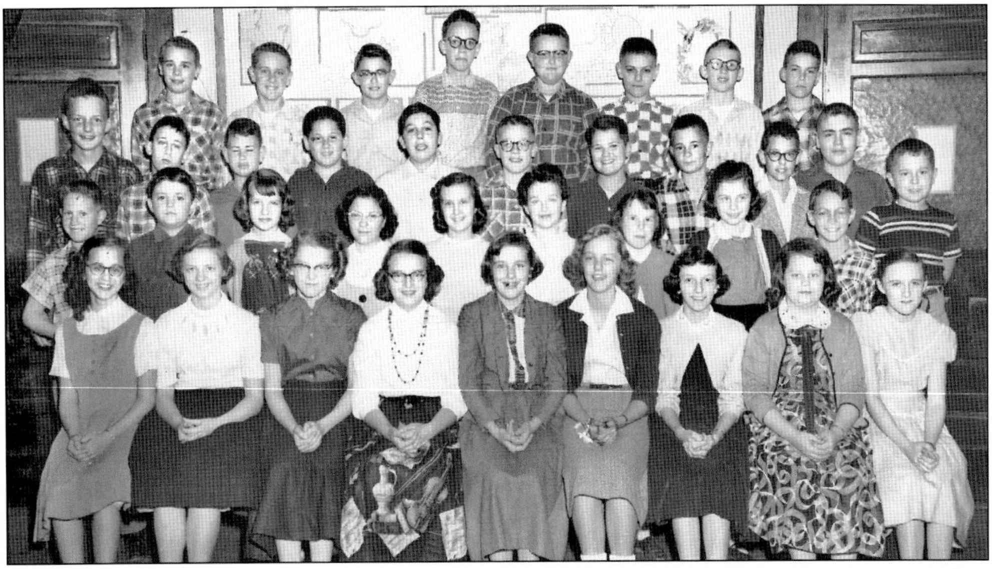

These are members of a sixth-grade class at the Simpson Elementary School in 1955. From left to right are (first row) Margaret Vassar, Frances Oldaker, Nancy Matteson, Carolyn Rogers, Jacqueline Root, Judith Smith, Judith Turbeville, Penny Snider, and Norma Lazzelle; (second row) unidentified, Ronald Bucy, unidentified, Geraldine Jones, Delores Alexander, unidentified, Barbara Campbell, Sue Wamsley, Richard Carrico, and Charles Loar; (third row) David Young, David Sanders, unidentified, Charles Fox, two unidentified students, John Sutton, James Strosnider, John Brannon, and Thomas Bowers; (fourth row) Dick Lynch, Everet Fenton, unidentified, James Trippett, Jeffrey Richards, Gene Compton, unidentified, and Eddie Tomes. (Courtesy of Norma Duez.)

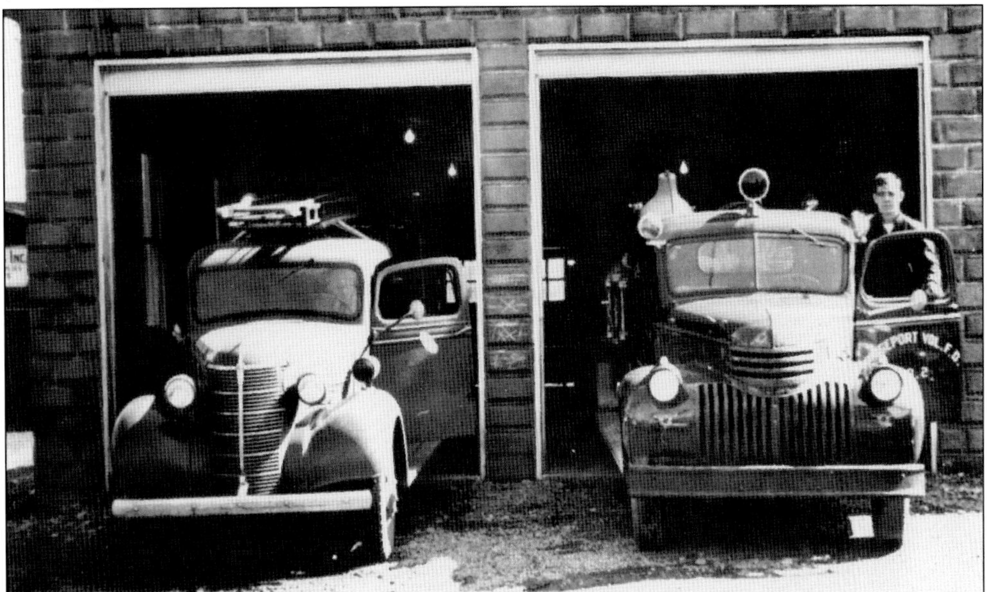

The old fire hall of the Bridgeport Volunteer Fire Department is pictured. The firefighter is not identified, but the trucks appear to be late 1940s or early 1950s models. Note the light bulbs hanging inside the station. (Courtesy of Dick Duez.)

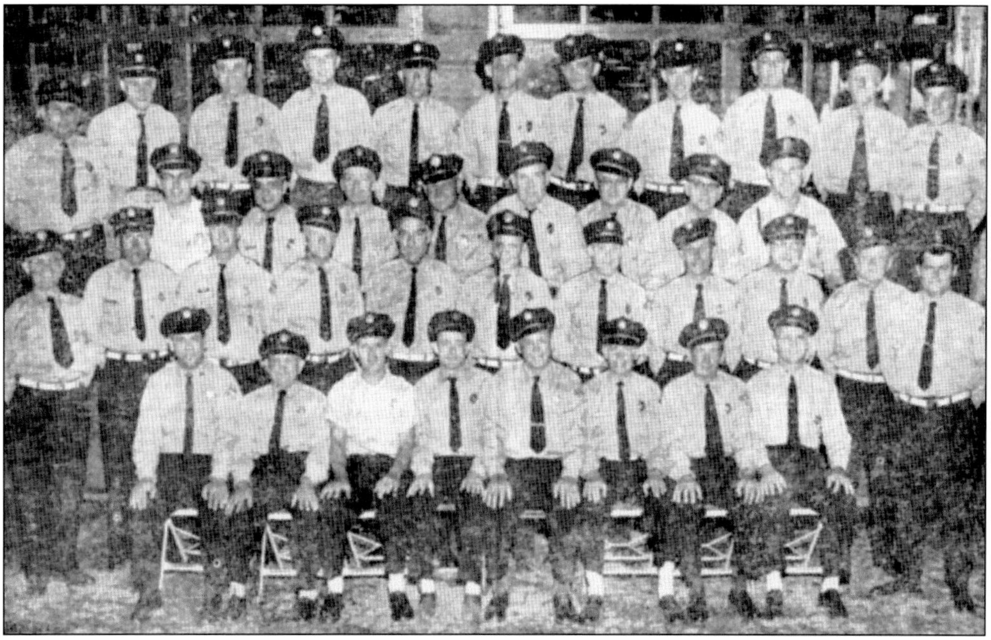

Members of the Bridgeport Volunteer Fire Department in 1962 are, from left to right, (first row) Fox, March, Chief of Police Clutter, Fire Chief Reed, President Wilson, Assistant Chief McCartney, Warder, and Buckhannon; (second row) Hart, Calfee, Stutler, T. Trippett, Wright, Kinney, McDaniels, Benedum, Rader, Lynch, and Steel; (third row) D. Trippett, Salvo, Skidmore, Worth, DeMoss, Campbell, Williams, and Allender, (fourth row) Pinti, McCallum, Daniels, Andrews, J. Diamond, Winters, Alfred, Ashcraft, Fishbaugh, T. Diamond, and Hess. (Courtesy of Phil Dye.)

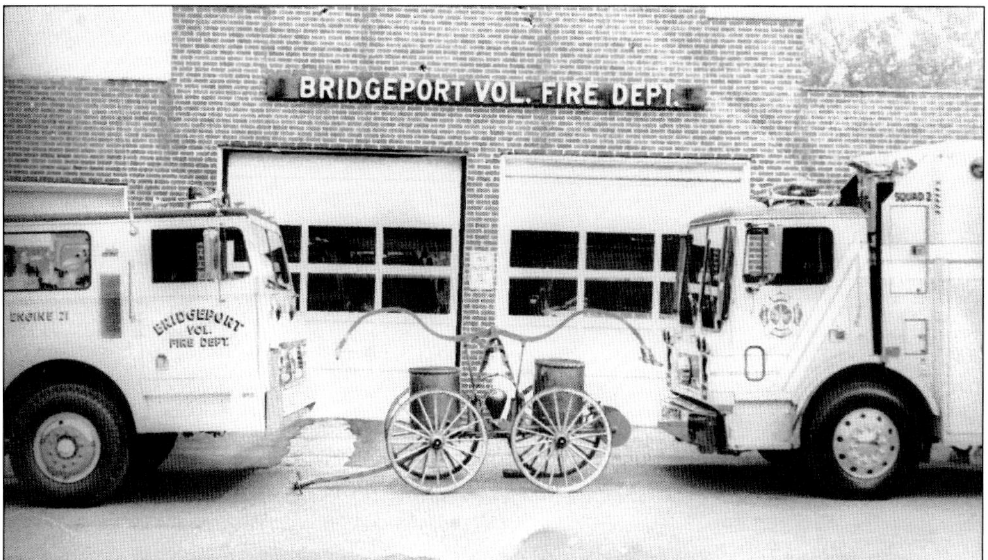

The Bridgeport Fire Department station is pictured after renovation around 1980. In the late 1970s, a tiny space in the fire station was used by Harrison County Fire Communications, which has grown tremendously and evolved into the Harrison-Taylor 911 Center in Nutter Fort. (Courtesy of Phil Dye.)

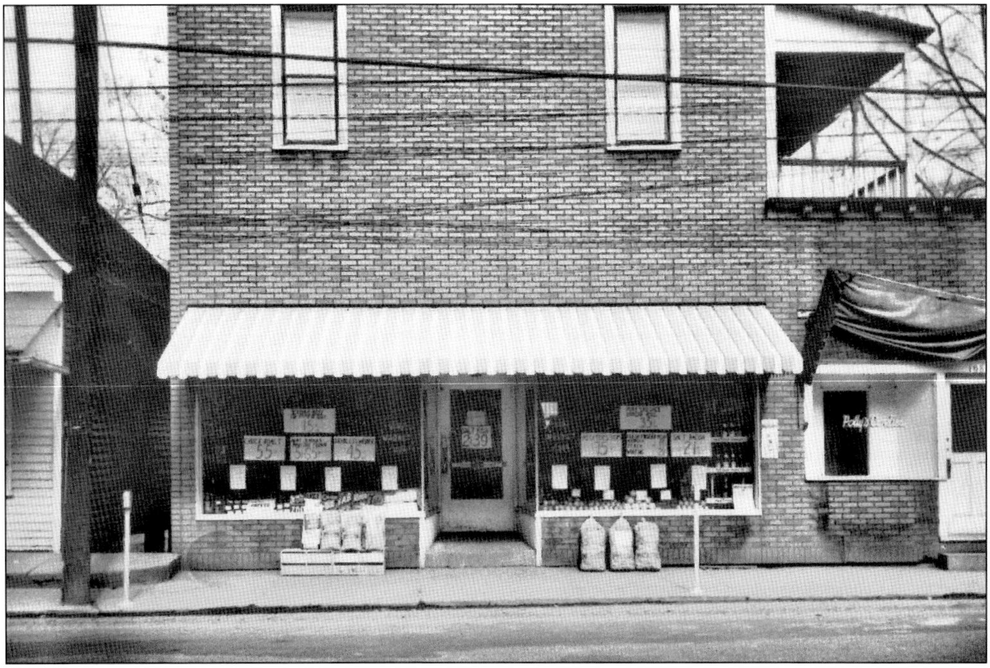

This grocery store building on East Main Street today is Mountain Heritage Coins. It was located across from the John Utt Building. (Courtesy of Dick Duez.)

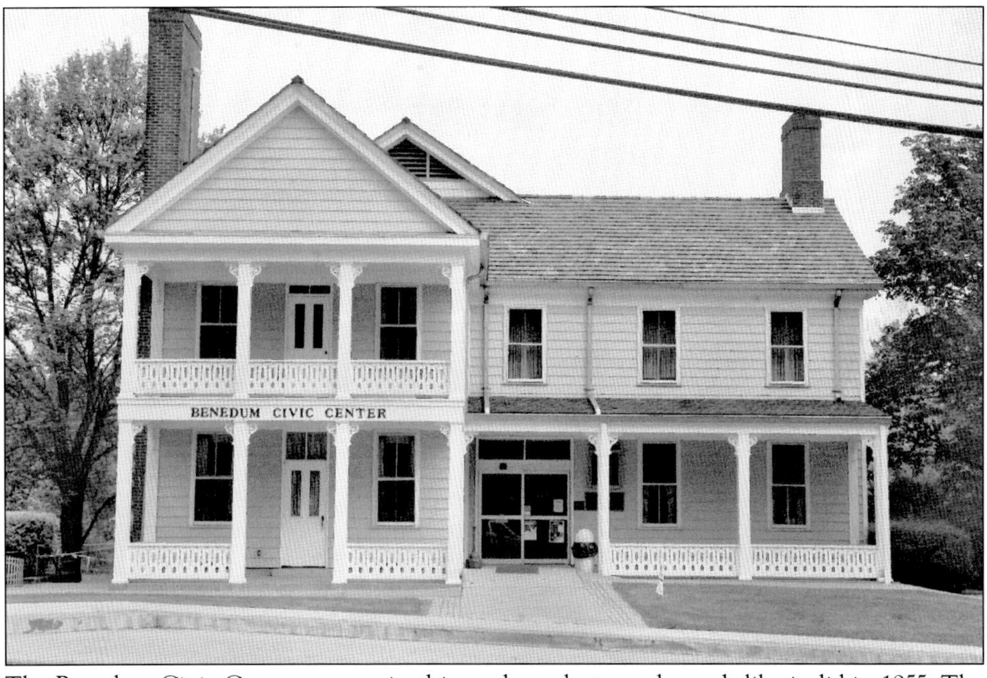

The Benedum Civic Center appears in this modern photograph much like it did in 1955. The center was dedicated on December 15, 1956. (Courtesy of Benedum Civic Center.)

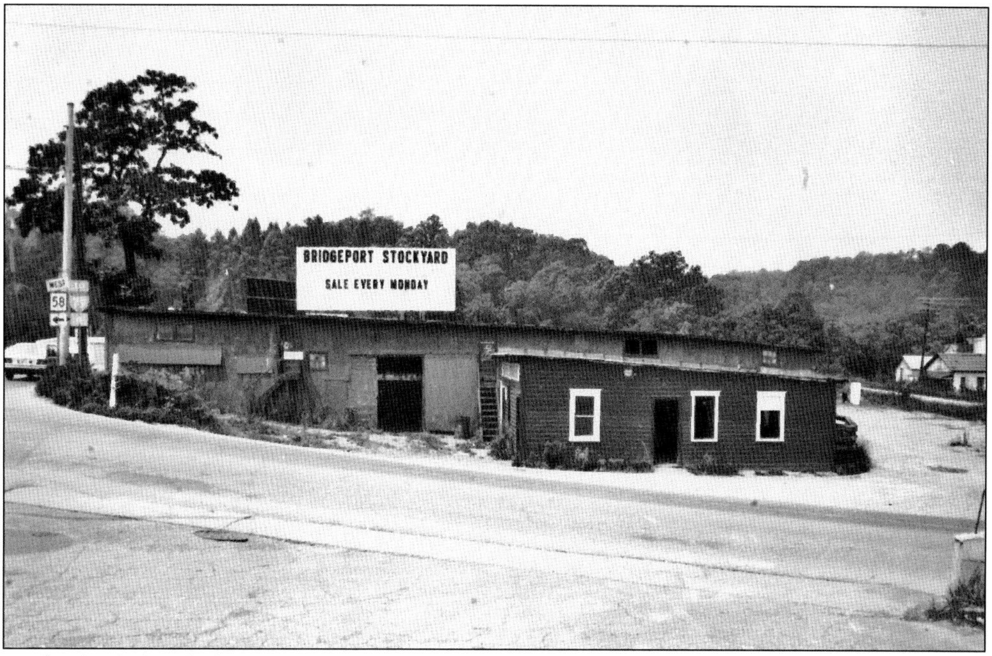

In the final days before it was demolished, the Bridgeport Stockyards building at West Main Street and Virginia Avenue was painted red. Located in that area today are Rite-Aid Discount Drugs and Bridgeport Physical Therapy. (Courtesy of Dick Duez.)

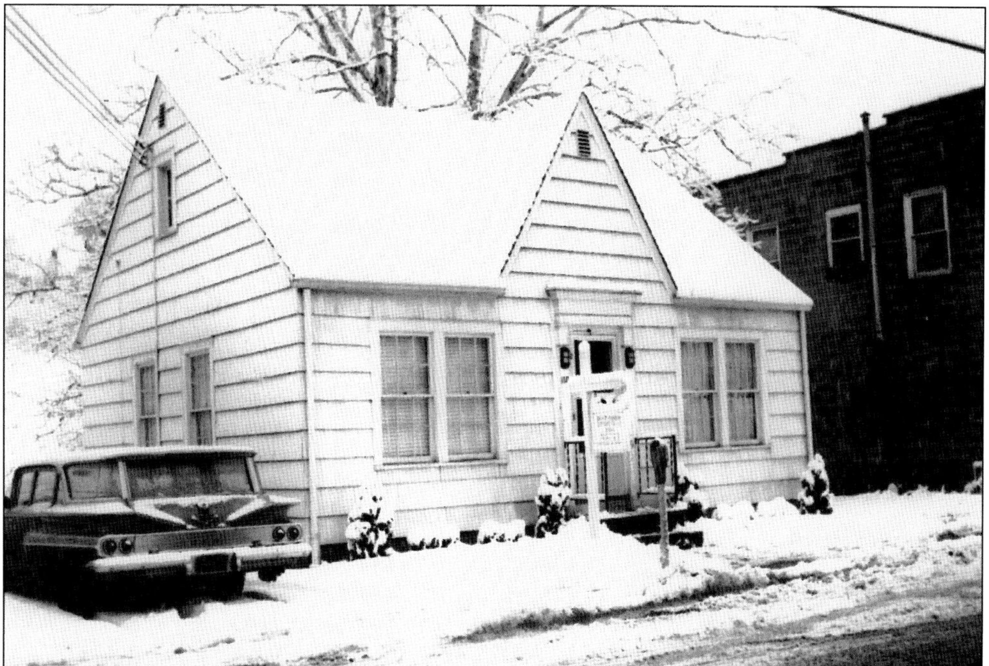

The small office building where Bridgeport optometrist Dr. Harry Murray practiced for years continues to exist. It is now occupied by Roger Murray, CPA. The building is on East Main Street east of the Center Street intersection. A 1960 Chevrolet station wagon can be seen in the parking spot. (Courtesy of Dick Duez.)

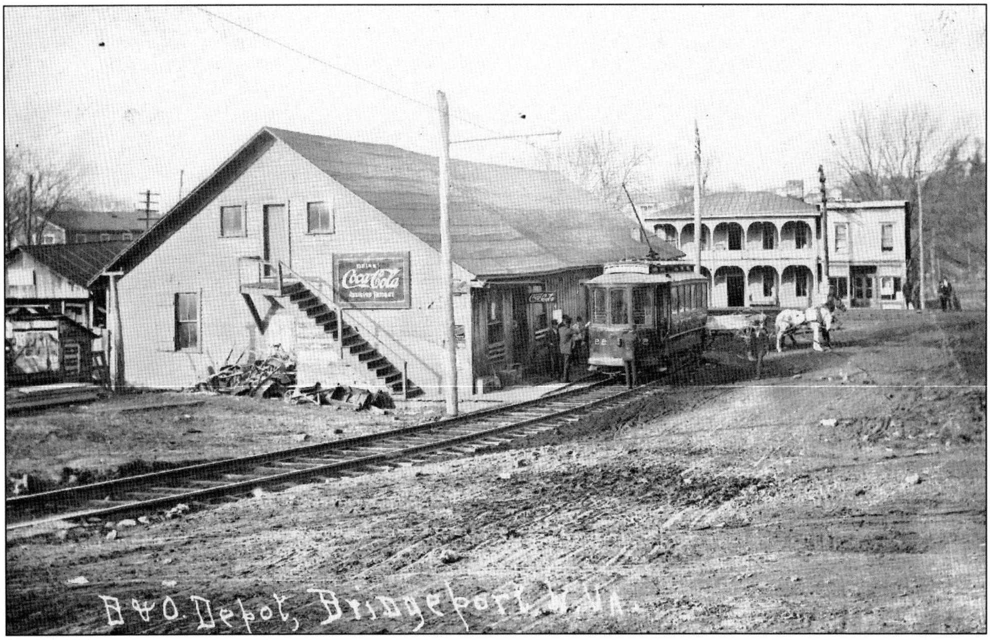

Bridgeport's B&O depot, built by William Johnson, is pictured in 1907. Also seen are streetcar tracks running to Anmoore and the railroad crossing on Virginia Avenue at the far right with the Commercial Hotel in the background. Today, behind the hotel site and not visible, is Dave Sanders' tavern and grill, known as Main Street Station (Courtesy of Dick Duez.)

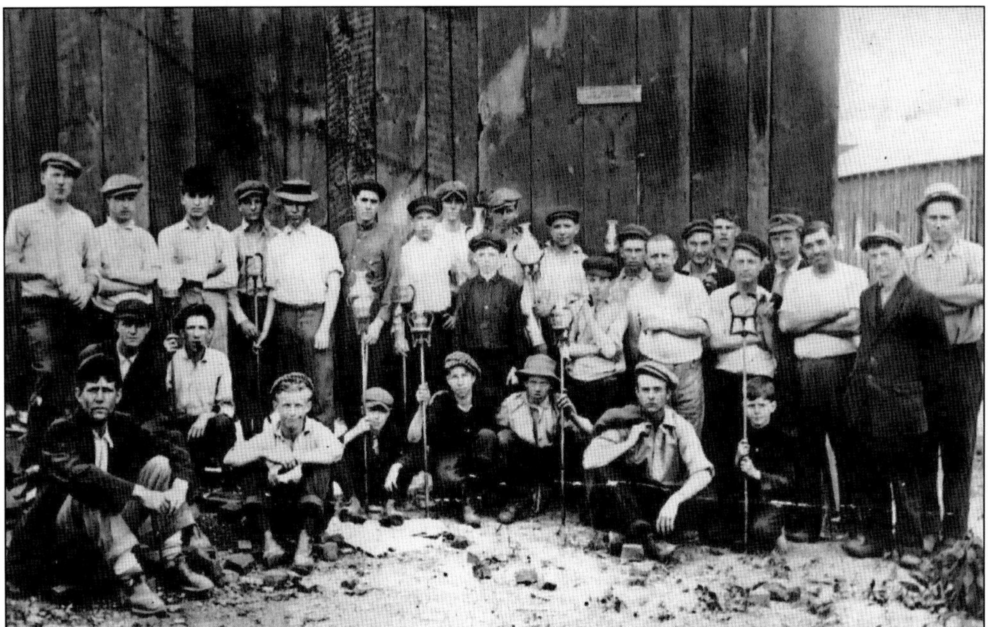

These "ware boys," photographed about around 1900 were employed by the Bridgeport Lamp Chimney Company, which was established in the city in 1904. Approximately 6,000 lamp chimneys were turned out per day. The chimneys were made from a heavy form of glass for oil lamps. (Bob Nichols.)

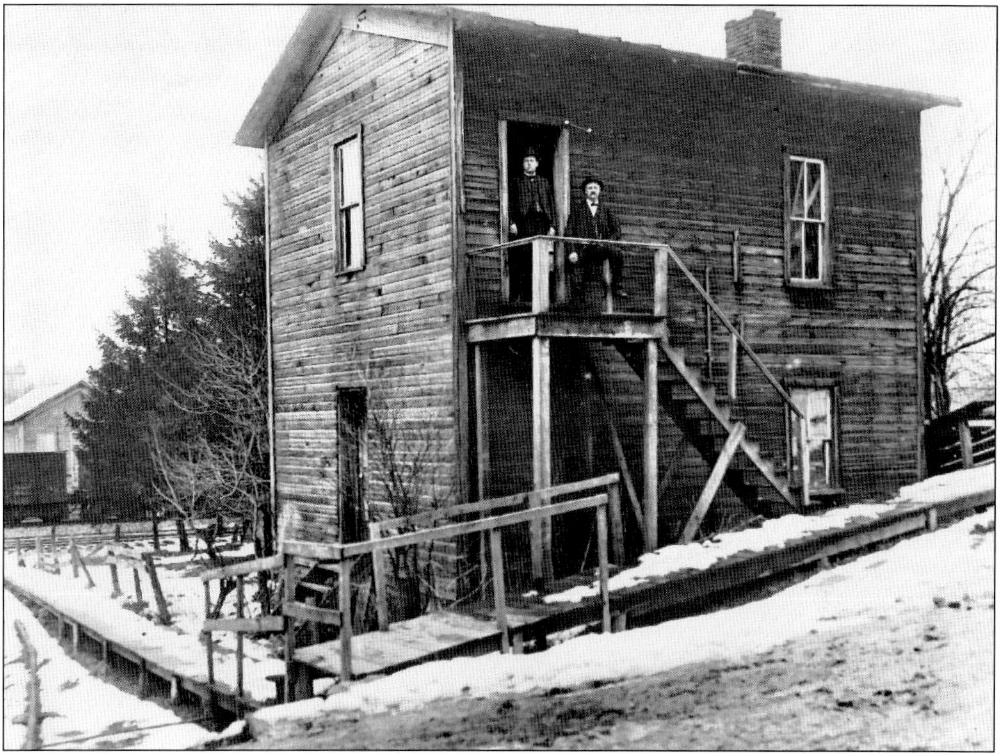

This was an office building on Main Street at the corner of Virginia Avenue. Beyond it, but mostly hidden by trees, was the Davisson house, which was built in 1791. (Courtesy of Dick Duez.)

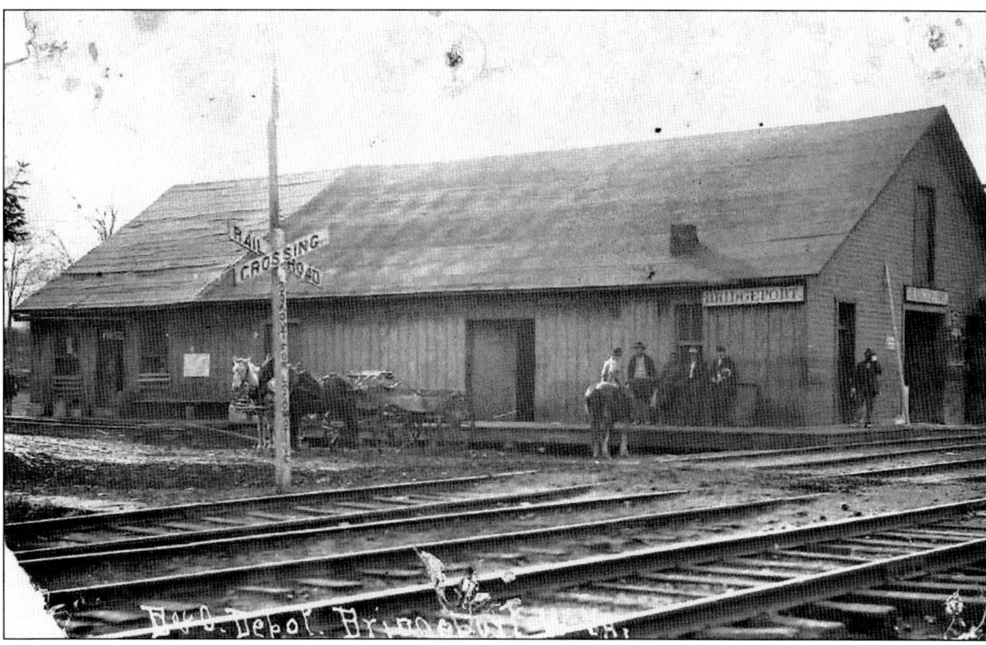

The old B&O depot appears above, looking west, in 1909. On the railroad crossing pole was written, "Look Out for Locomotive," a wise suggestion indeed. (Courtesy of Rose Davis.)

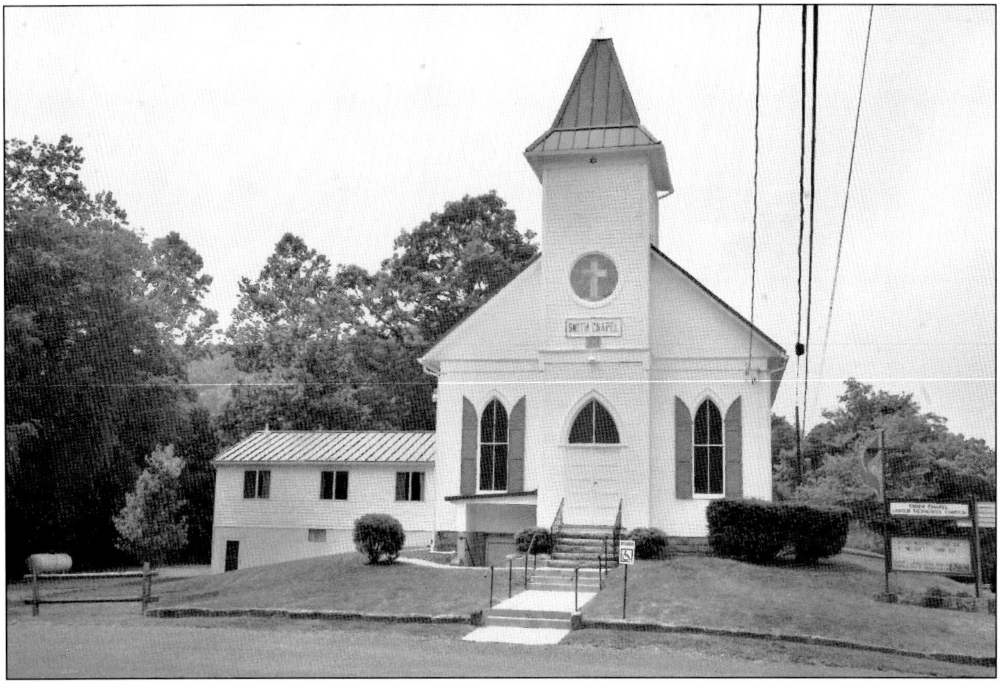

This is a late photograph of Smith Chapel, along Meadowbrook Road (County Route 24). Hardly any substantial changes could be seen from the time of its construction in 1906. (Courtesy of Dick Duez.)

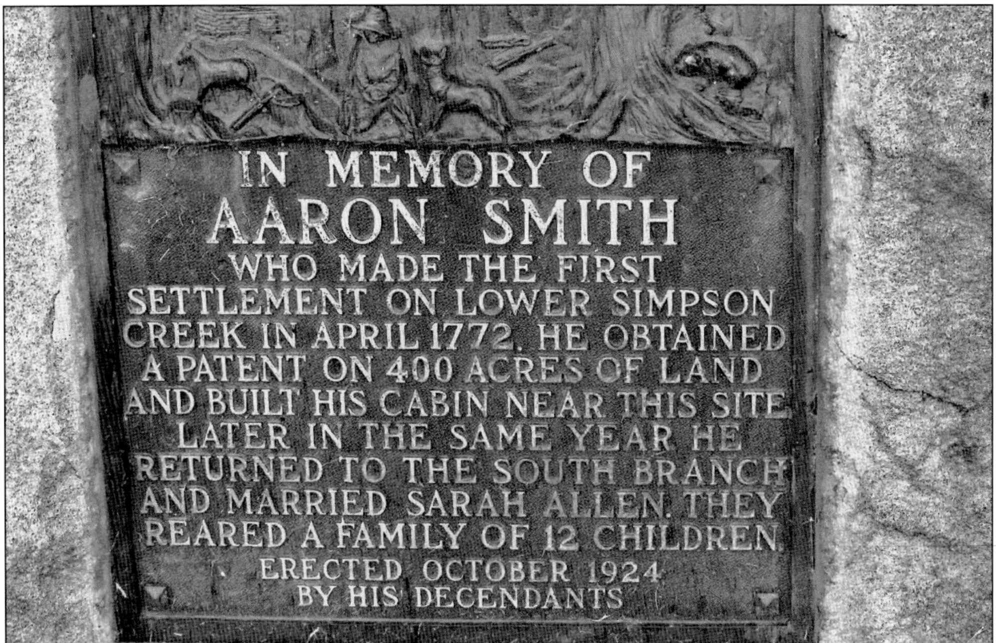

This marker pays tribute to the life of Aaron Smith, who, as the marker says, made the first settlement on Lower Simpson Creek in April 1772. It is less than a mile north of Smith Chapel and near the turnoff to the Pete Dye Golf Club. (Courtesy of Dick Duez.)

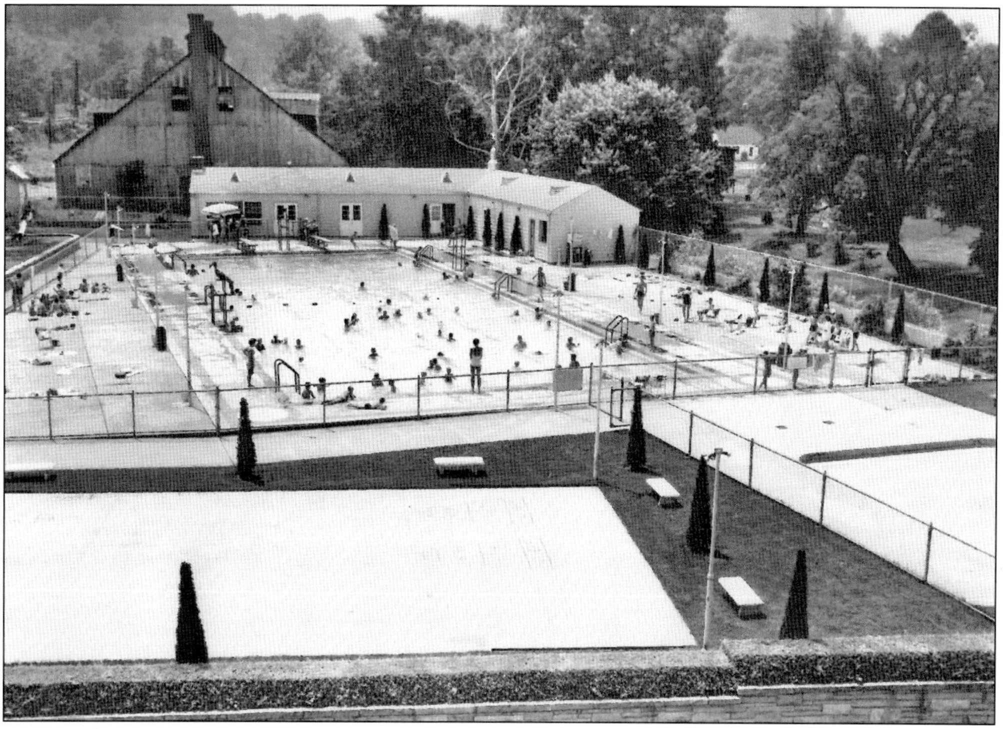

The Bridgeport Swimming Pool is pictured in 1962. (Courtesy of Dick Duez.)

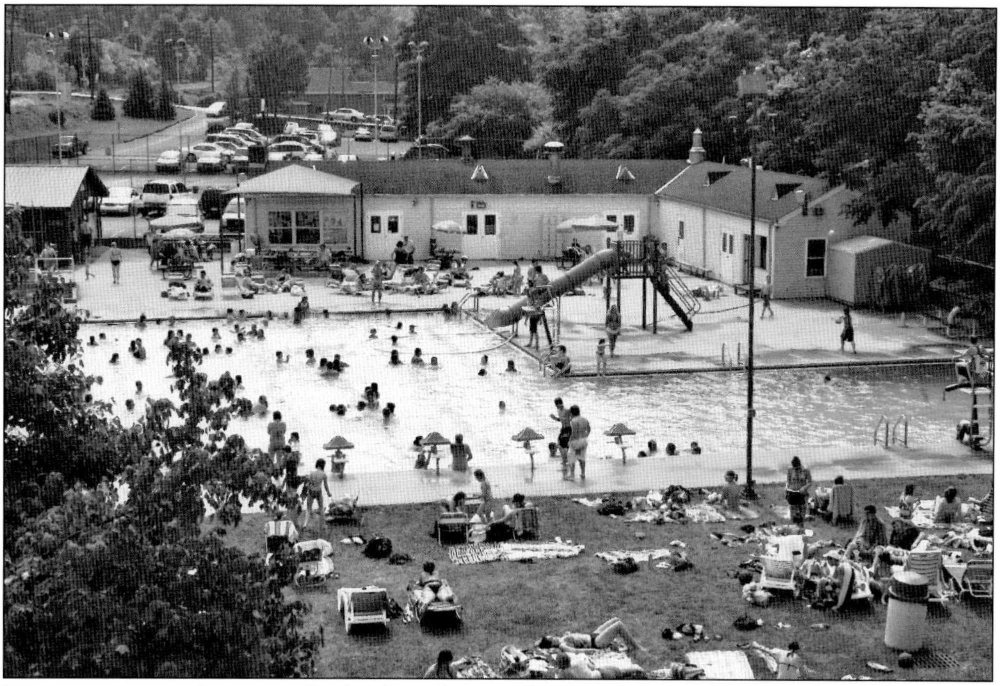

The swimming pool is pictured today from the same location. (Courtesy of Dick Duez, compliments of Benedum Civic Center.)

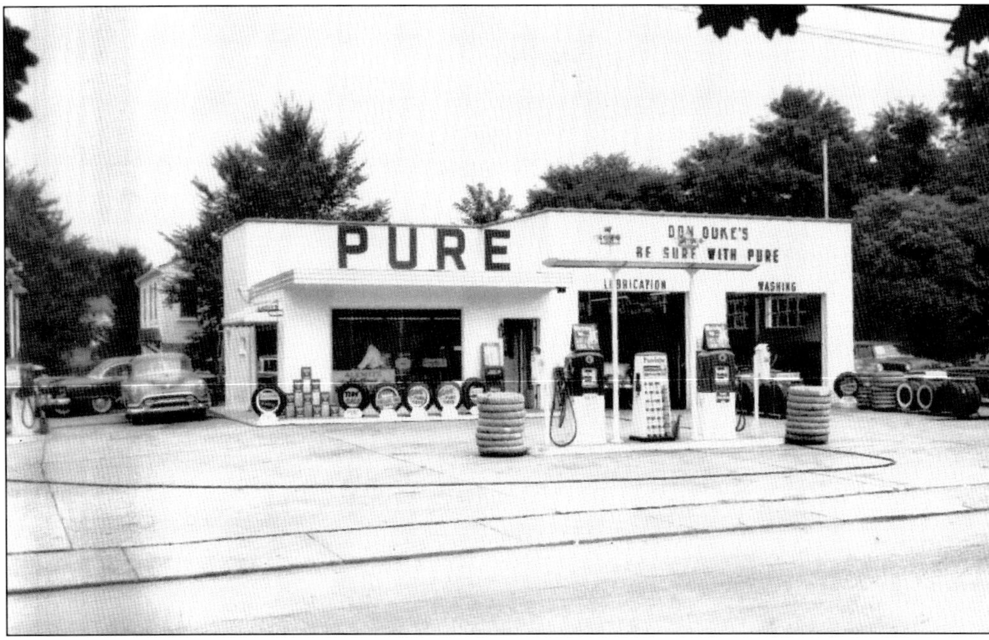

Don Duke's Pure service station was on East Main Street in Bridgeport at the corner of Pennsylvania Avenue in 1955. The Dairy Mart convenience store is located on the site today. (Courtesy of Dick Duez.)

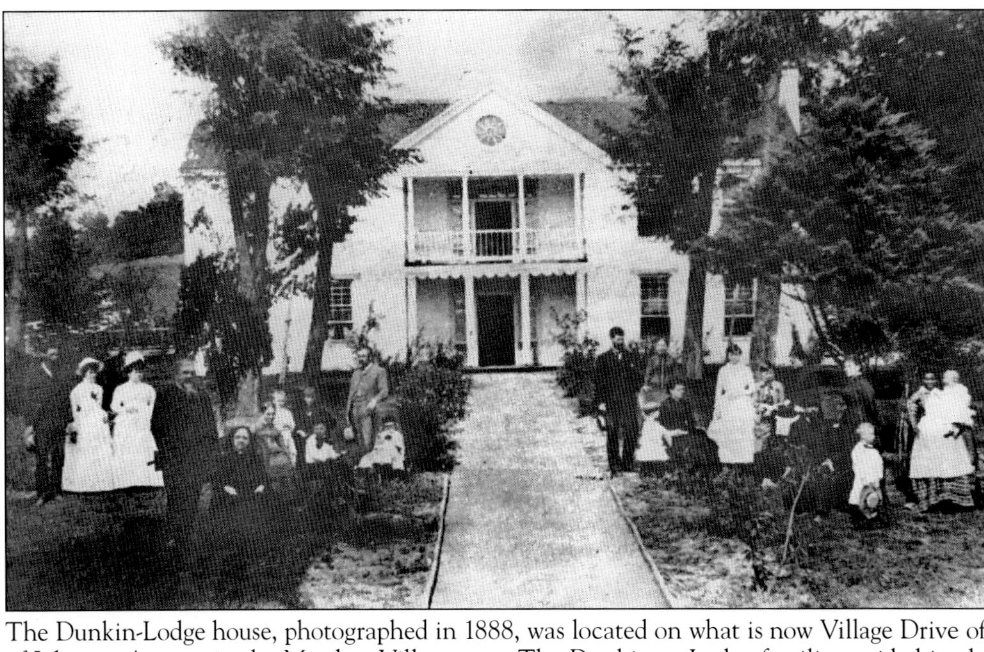

The Dunkin-Lodge house, photographed in 1888, was located on what is now Village Drive off of Johnson Avenue in the Meadow Village area. The Dunkin or Lodge families resided in the house at one time or another. (Courtesy of Ray Blake.)

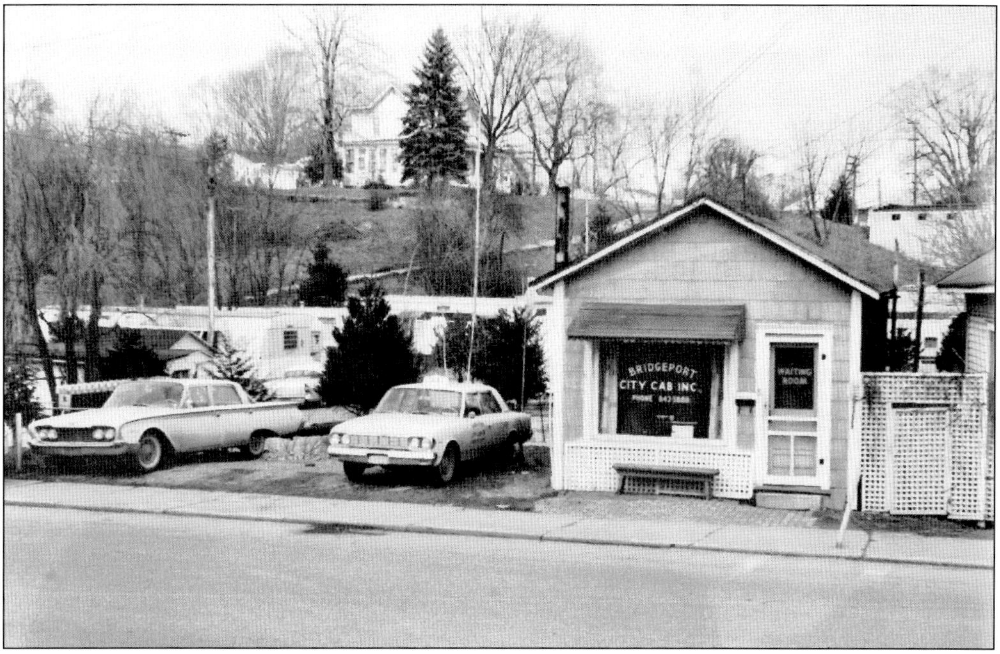

Bridgeport City Cab was in this small building, with Taylor's Trailer Court at left, looking north. The large house seen on the hill in the background was demolished earlier in 2007. (Courtesy of Dick Duez.)

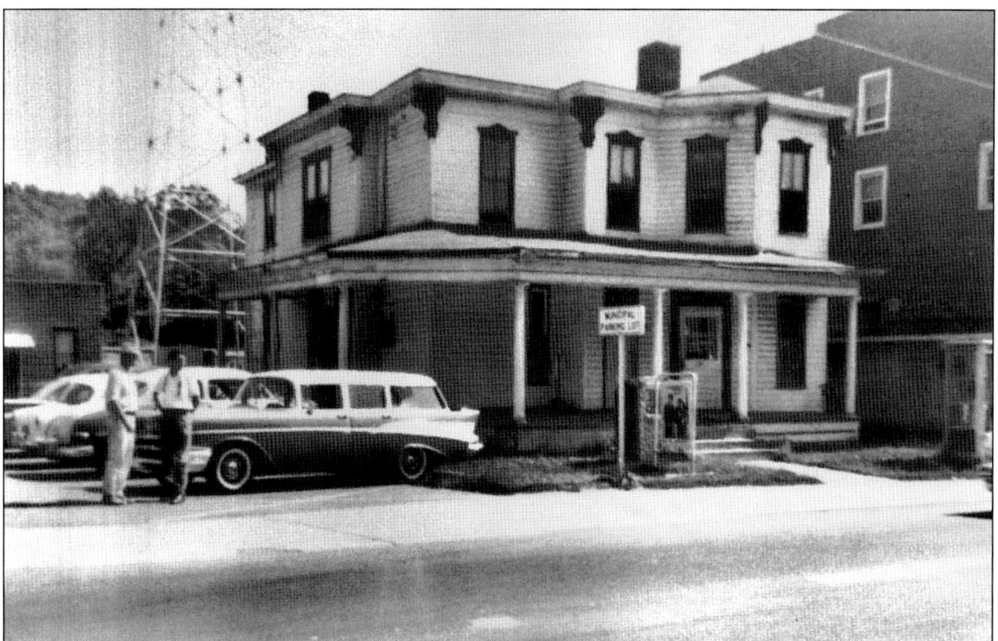

Here's a 1958 photograph of the municipal parking lot and the Bridgeport Municipal Building with the Fitzhugh Building at right. (Courtesy of Dick Duez.)

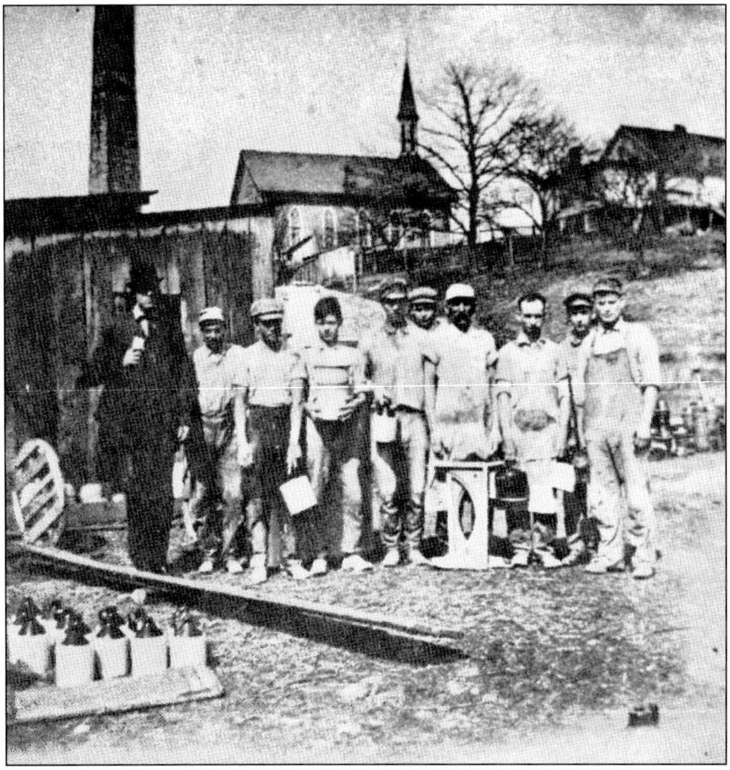

The workers at the old Bridgeport Pottery Factory are photographed in 1905. The Methodist Episcopal church, which is today a residence, can be seen in the background. The people in the photograph are not identified. (Courtesy of Dick Duez.)

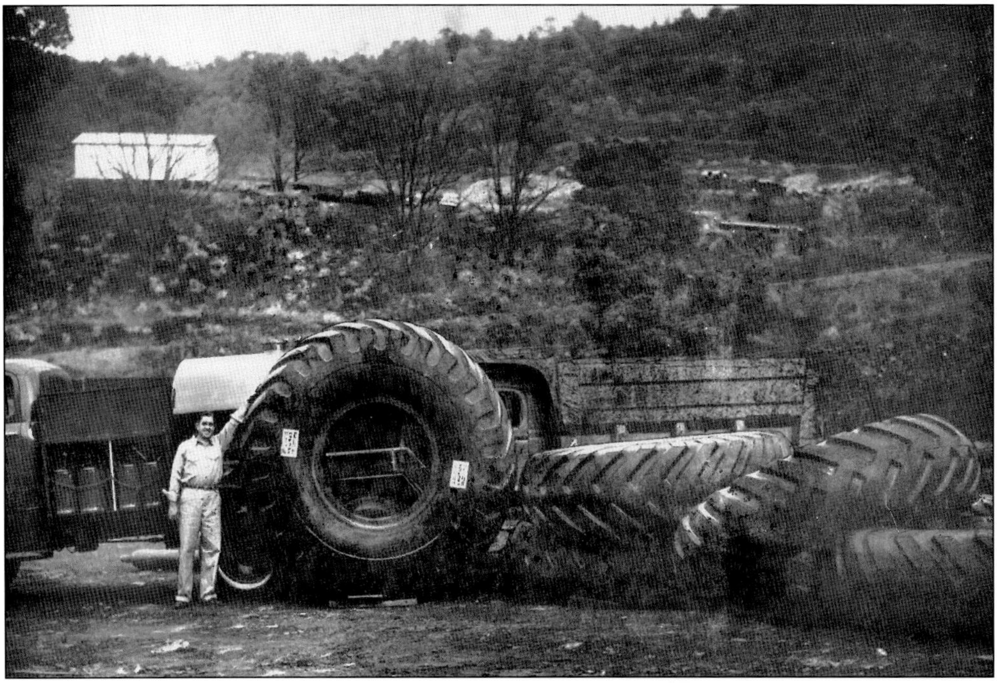

Charles E. "Jim" Compton, who was a prominent Bridgeport resident, was president of Grafton Coal when this 1944 photograph was taken. Here he stands beside some 30.00-40 tires from a mining front loader. (Courtesy of Dick Duez.)

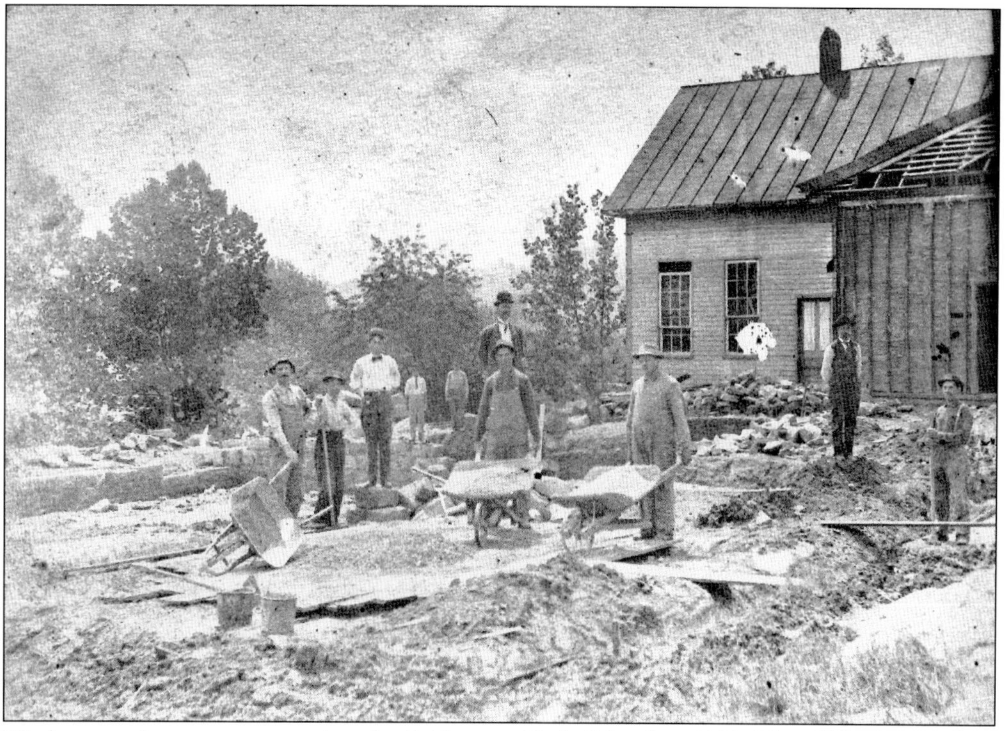

Workers can be seen constructing the Bridgeport High School in 1908. The old high school, at right, was about to be demolished. The high school would years later become Simpson Elementary School. (Courtesy of Don Higginbotham.)

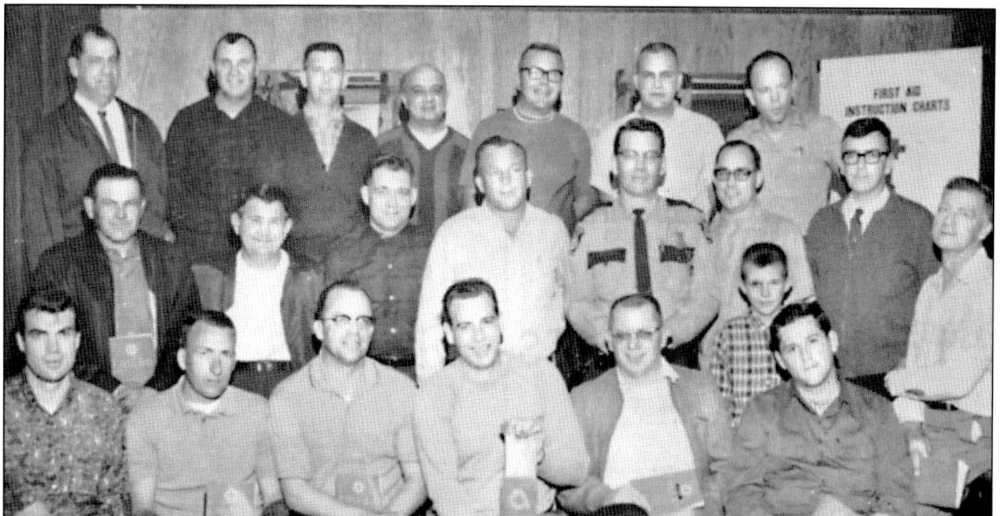

These firefighters completed an advanced course in first aid in 1968. Firefighters from left to right are (first row) William Mick, Bud Calfee, Ira Gherke, Bob Dunn, Tom Kinney, and Chuck Fox; (second row) Bob Worth, Chester March, Earl Findley, Chuck Wilson, Don Trippett, Dick Blackwell, George Harris, and instructor Francis Skidmore; (third row) Charles Fox, Bill Allender, Junior Fenton, Mike Salvio, Bob Rader, Tom Snider, and George Davis. (Courtesy of Phil Dye.)

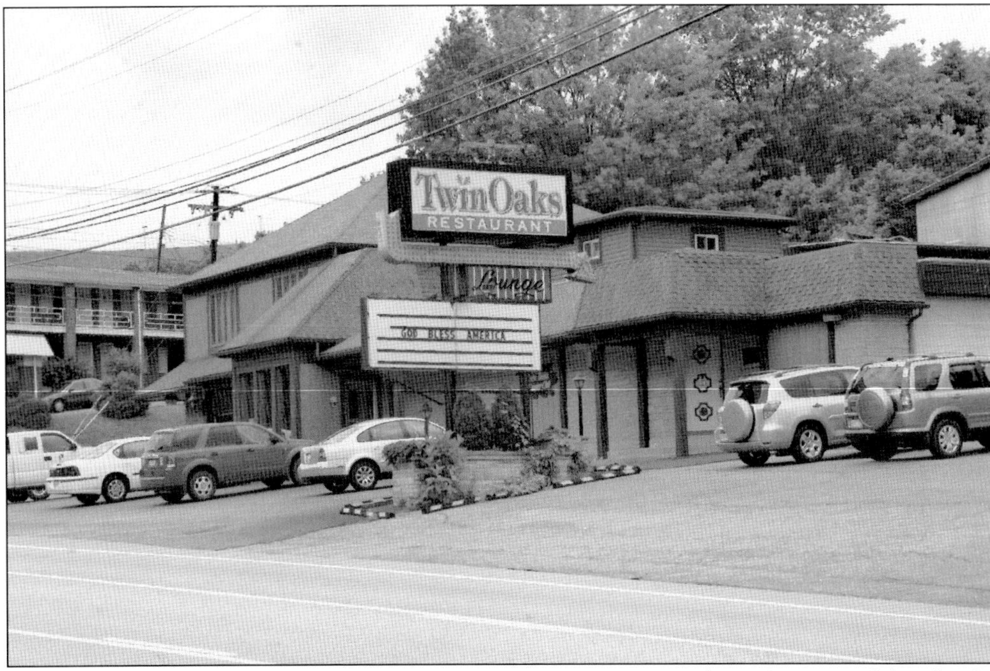

Twin Oaks, a famous family restaurant has been in business since the 1950s, owned first by the Shields family and more recently by the Ielapi family. It is located on U.S. 50 west of the center of town. Towne House East Motel can be seen in the background. (Courtesy of Dick Duez.)

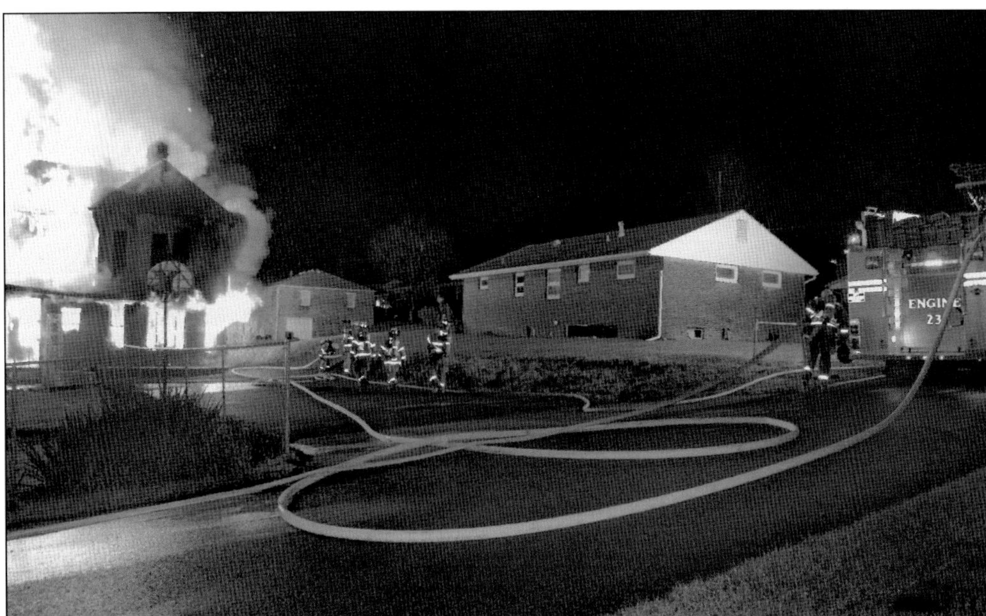

The Bridgeport Fire Department, assisted by firefighters from other stations, was kept busy the night of January 5, 2005, when the old Stout home, located on Holt Street in Bridgeport, was destroyed by fire. (Photograph taken by Dick Duez.)

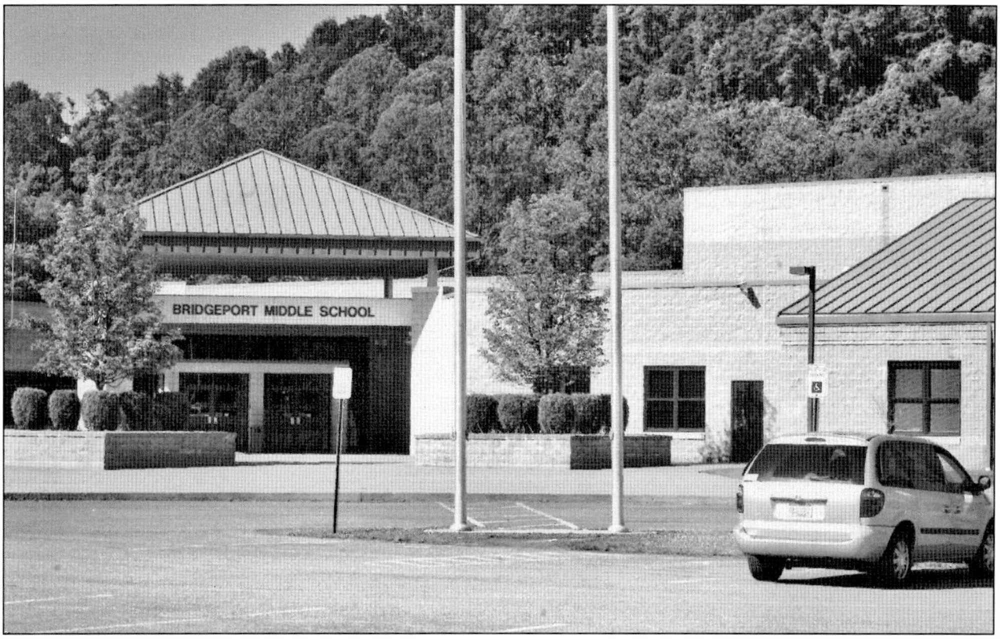

A familiar sight is the Bridgeport Middle School, located next to Bridgeport High School. (Courtesy of Dick Duez.)

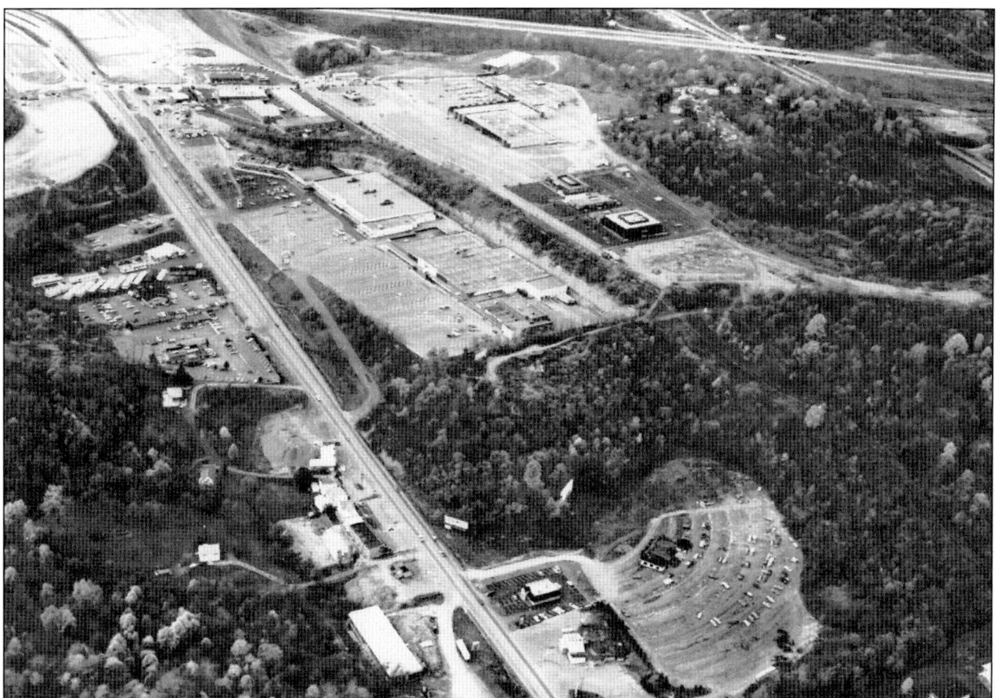

Bridgeport Hill, just west of Bridgeport, is seen in this early-1980s aerial photograph. At the right of the highway can be seen the Ellis Drive-in Theater, which later became a large Sunday flea market; Hill's and Terrace shopping plazas, and, at top center, Holiday Plaza. (From author's collection.)

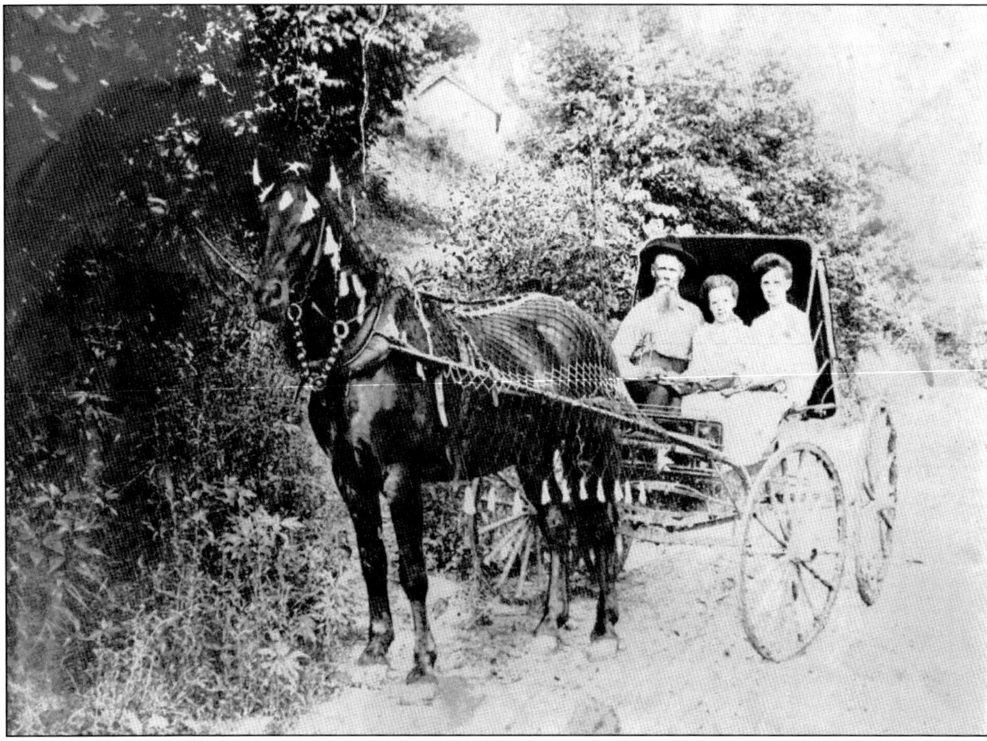

This horse-and-buggy scene from July 10, 1904, was taken near the corner of Main Street and Virginia Avenue in Bridgeport looking west. At the reins is Joseph Johnson Winters, with his nieces, Sadie Johnson Winters Dykstra (center) and Izie Winters Jones. (Courtesy of Roger Hardy.)

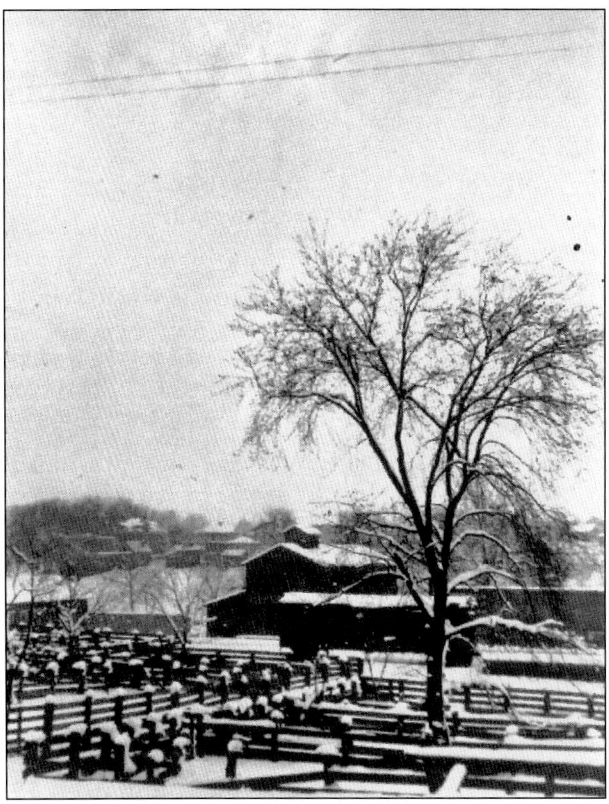

Photographed looking north in the winter of 1900 are the Bridgeport stock pens, with the Gov. Joseph Johnson house in the background at far left. (Courtesy of Roger Hardy.)

This H. N. and J. B. Sandusky three-gallon stoneware pot was made at the old Bridgeport Pottery on Davis Street. (Courtesy of Dick Duez.)

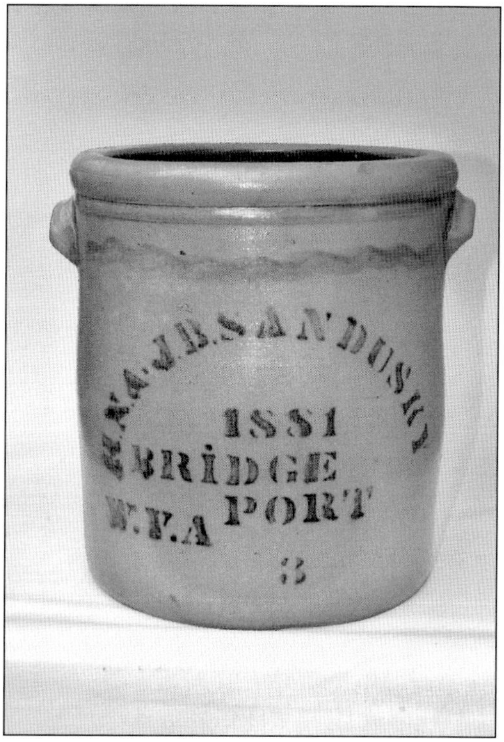

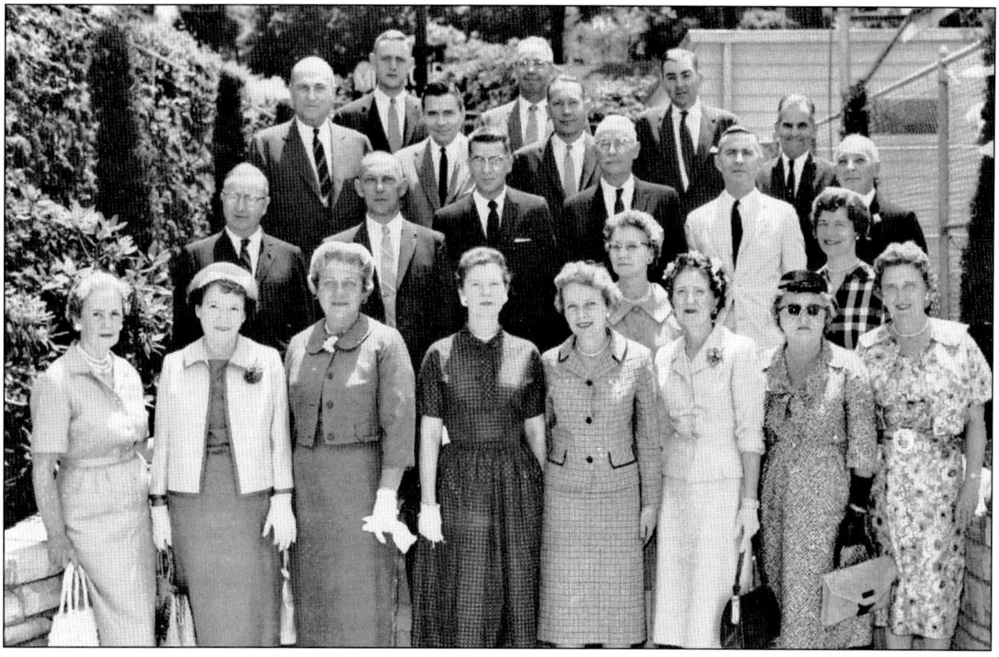

These folks are members of the Benedum Foundation trustees, including wives, friends, and other people of Bridgeport. From left to right are (first row) Mrs. R. L. Cutlip, two unidentified, Mrs. Byron Randolph, three unidentified, and Mrs. Margaret Merrells; (second row) David Johnson, two unidentified, and Mrs. Ross Linger; (third row) three unidentified and R. L. Cutlip; (fourth row) unidentified, Rev. Ross Linger, and Byron Randolph. (Courtesy of Benedum Civic Center.)

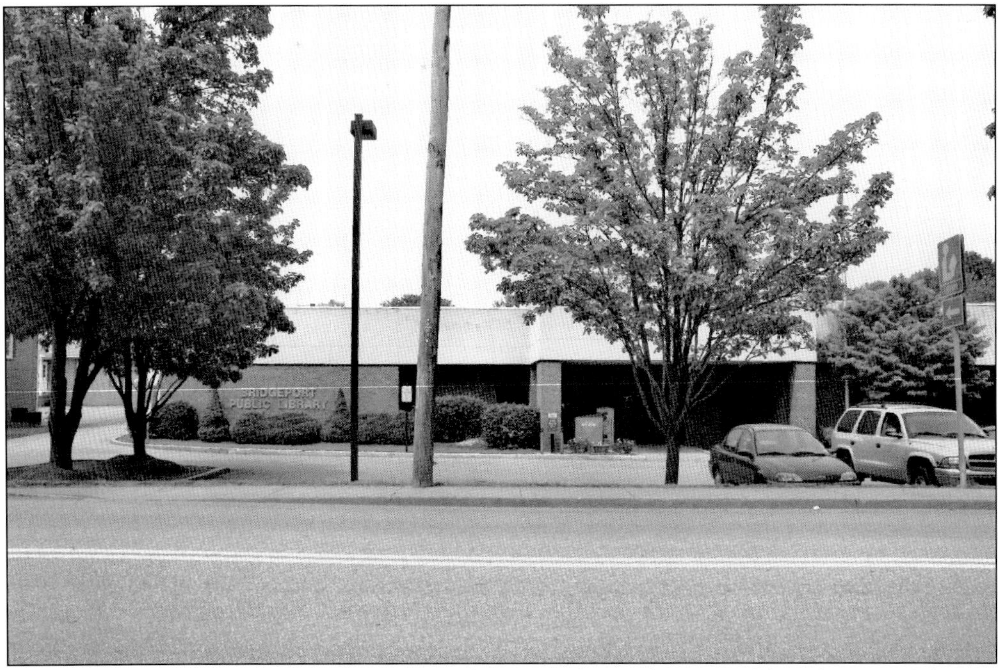

One of the more frequently visited places in the city is the Bridgeport Public Library on Johnson Avenue. (Courtesy of Dick Duez.)

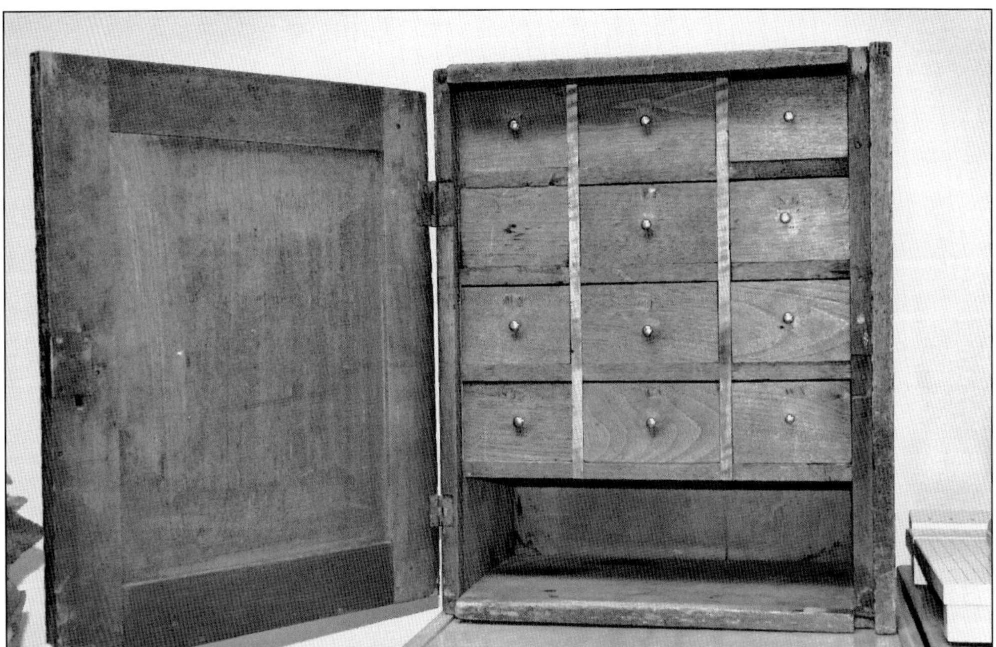
This was the first Bridgeport "post office" around 1850. It was a walnut chest with 12 alphabetized drawers. (Courtesy of Bridgeport Public Library.)

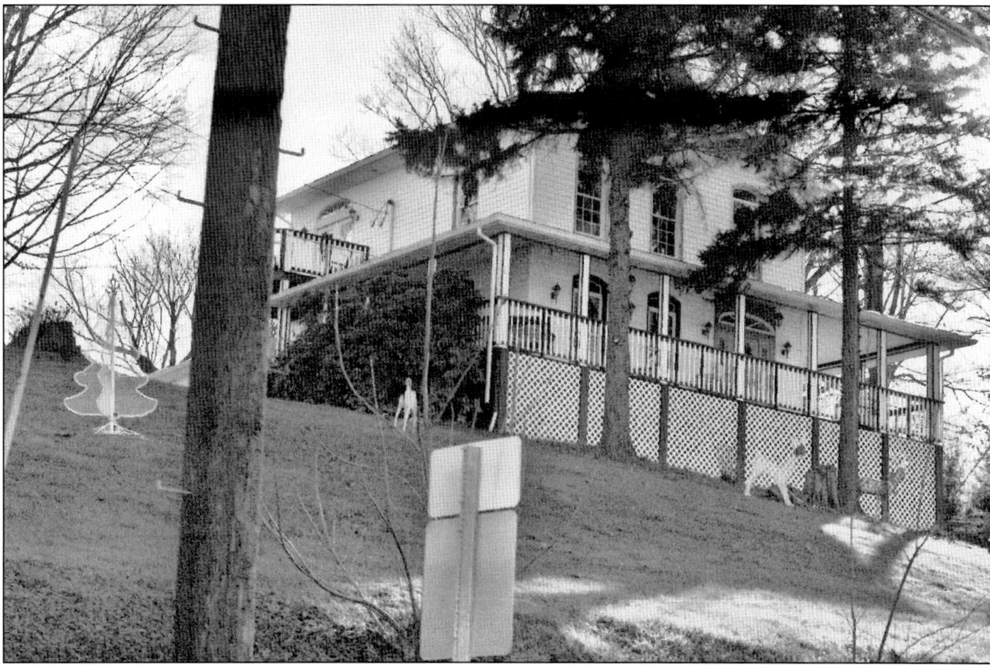

The original J. C. Johnson house, later the Patton house, stands on the hill above the corner of West Main Street and Virginia Avenue. It was restored in 2005 by Nancy Rush. (Courtesy of Dick Duez.)

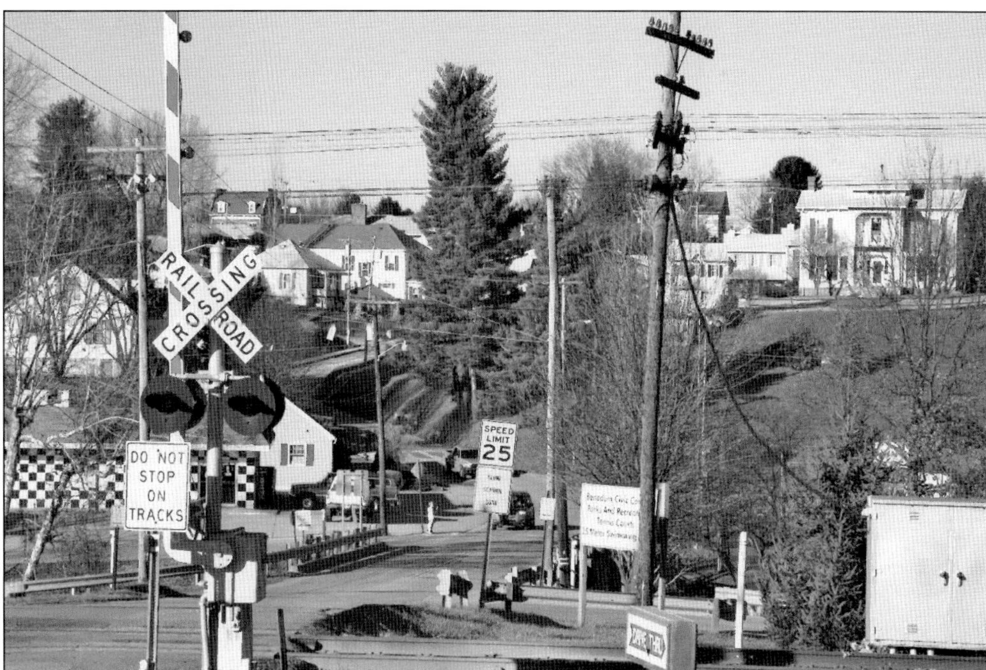

Here's a rather busy scene. It shows the railroad crossing at North Virginia Avenue. Venture Realty Company is the larger building at top right. (Courtesy of Dick Duez.)

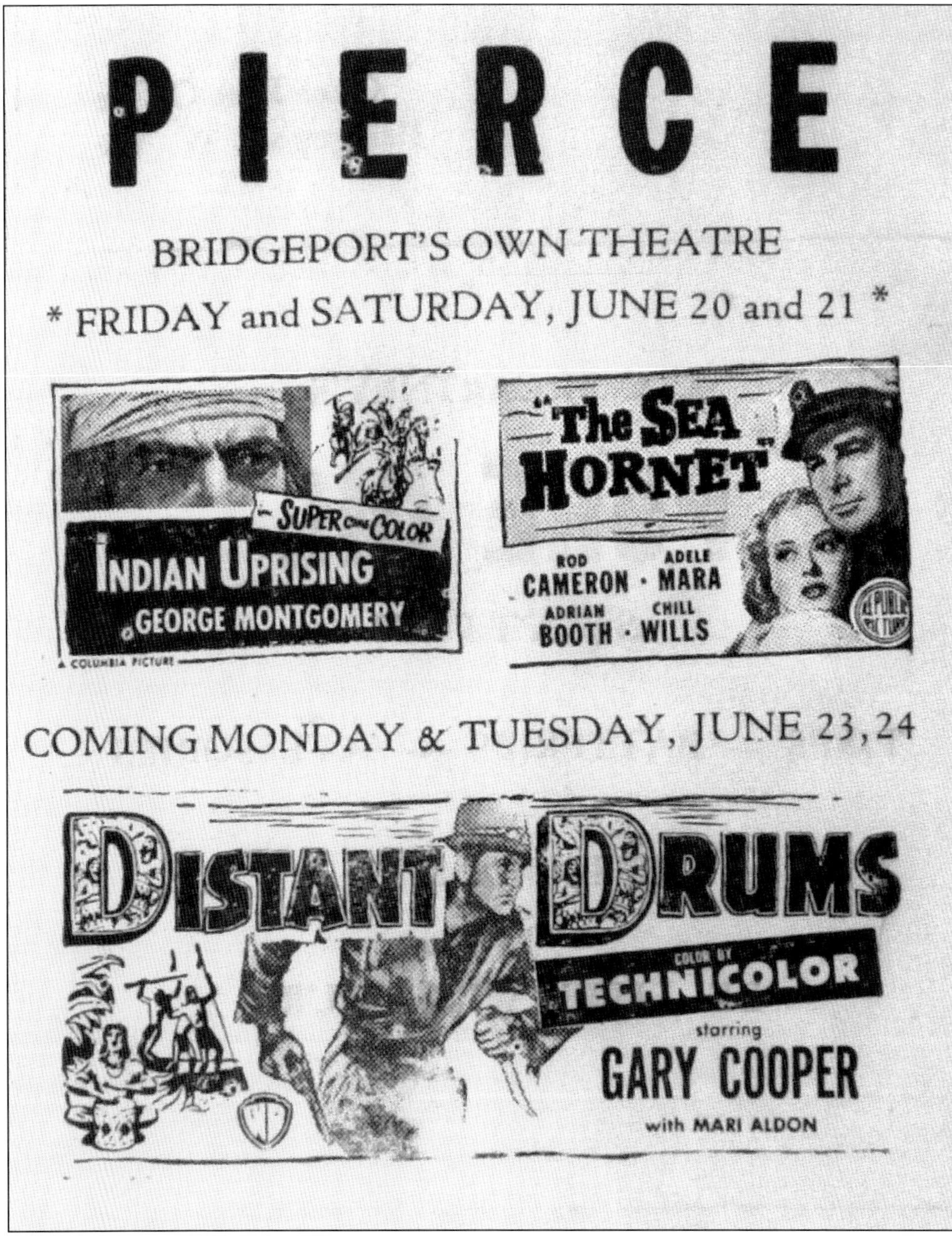

This is an advertisement for movies playing at the old Pierce Theatre, located in a building that would become the Pure Food Store on East Main Street in Bridgeport. They included *Indian Uprising* with George Montgomery, *The Sea Hornet* with Rod Cameron, and *Distant Drums* with Gary Cooper. The advertisement appeared in an old Bridgeport Fire Department souvenir program. (Courtesy of Fred Layman.)

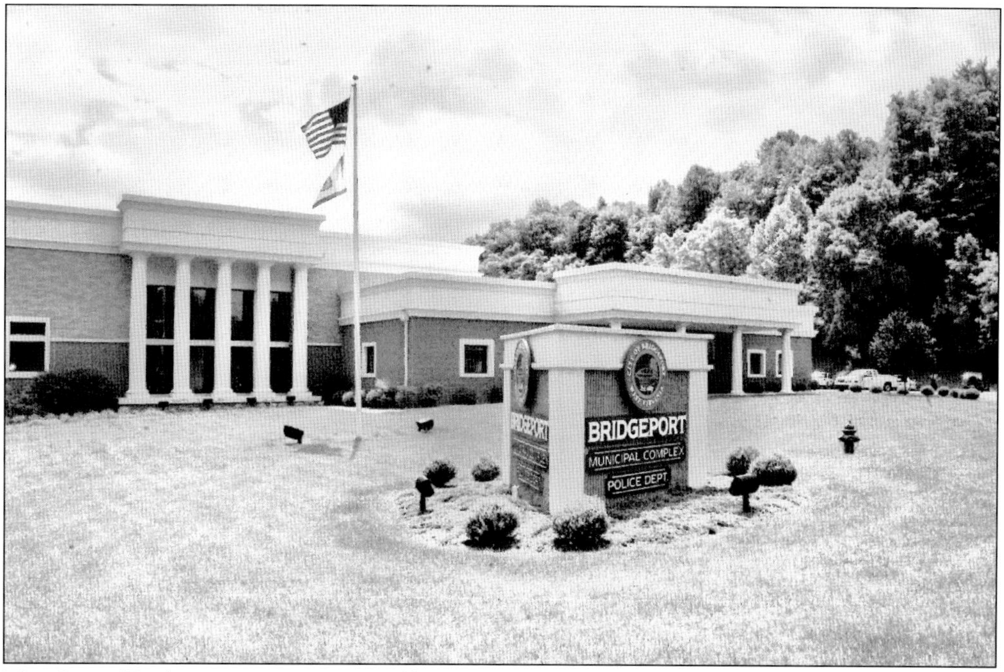

The City of Bridgeport's new municipal building is located on West Main Street, across from Ace Hardware. The building that housed the offices of Rish Equipment was renovated to become the new center of city business. (Courtesy of Dick Duez.)

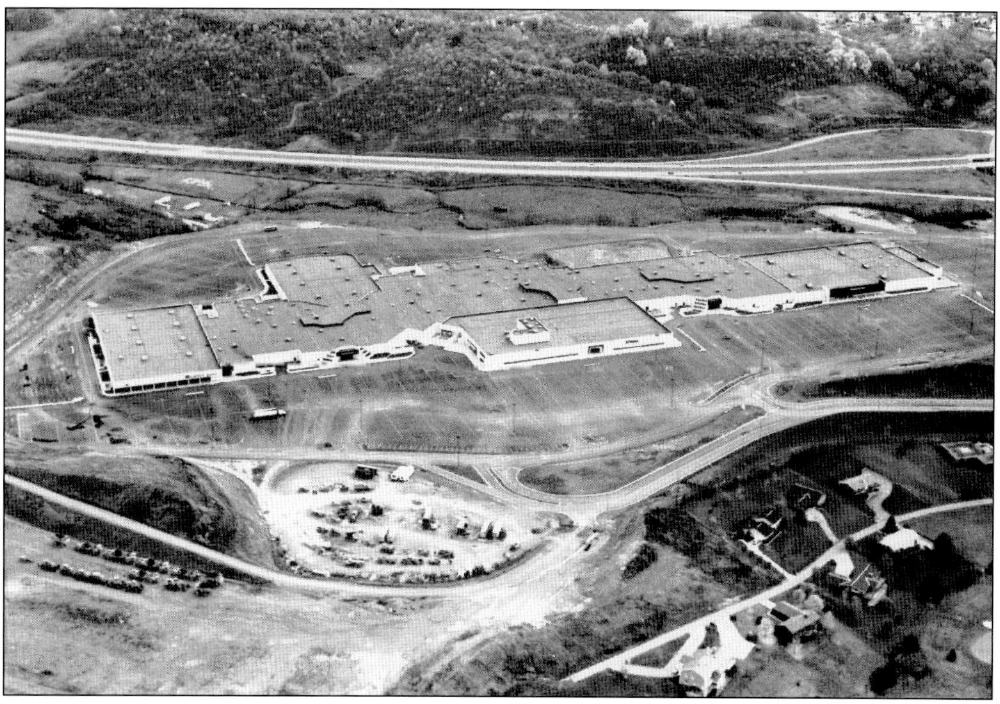

This 1982 aerial photograph shows construction nearly completed on the Meadowbrook Mall in Bridgeport. The section in front is the J. C. Penney store. The former Montgomery Ward store was at far right. I-79 can be seen near the top. (From author's collection.)

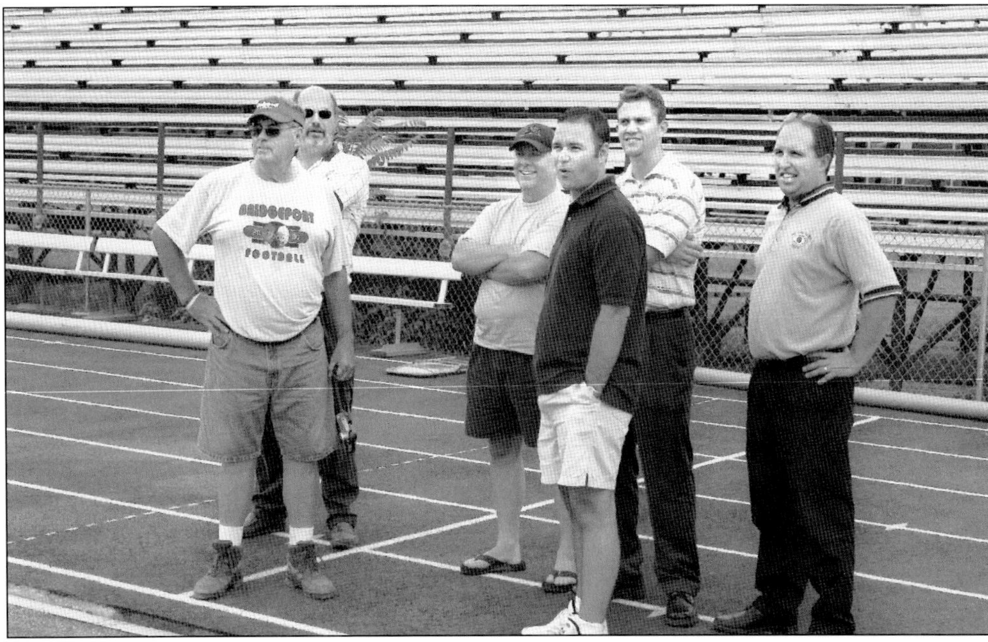

Some interested members of the community are pictured, with, from left to right, Walter Barth, Ron Vernon (behind Barth), Phil Nicewarner, Jeff Toquinto, Ryan Nicewarner, and Chris Cleghorn, all looking at the new turf for Wayne Jamison Field, Bridgeport High School's football stadium. (Courtesy of Dick Duez.)

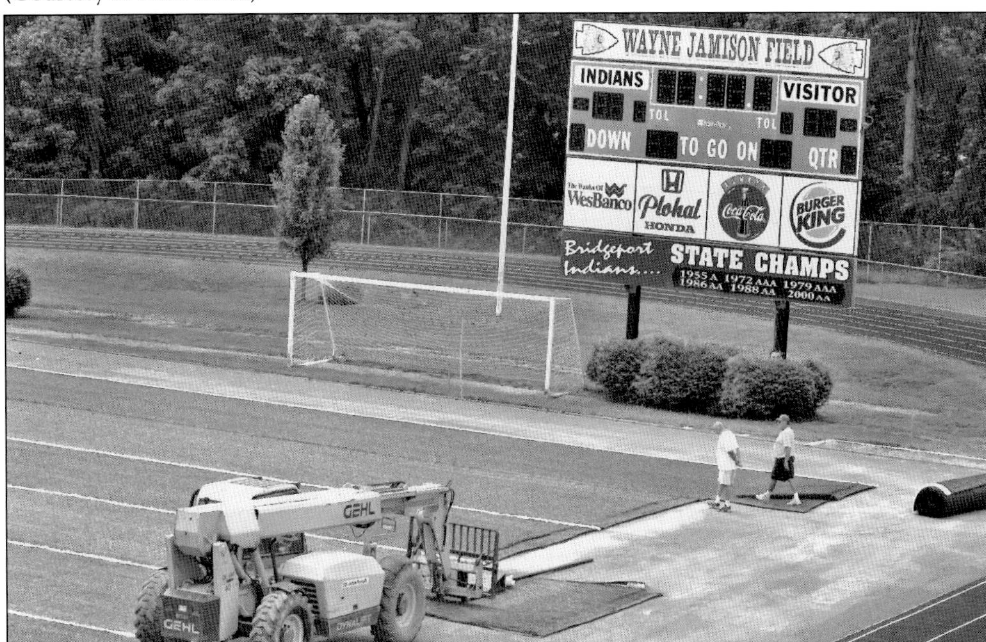

Final work is being done laying the turf at Wayne Jamison Field. Overseer Walter Barth can be seen at left. The new scoreboard bears the name of the field. The Bridgeport Indians have won numerous county scholastic football championships and some state titles. (Courtesy of Dick Duez.)

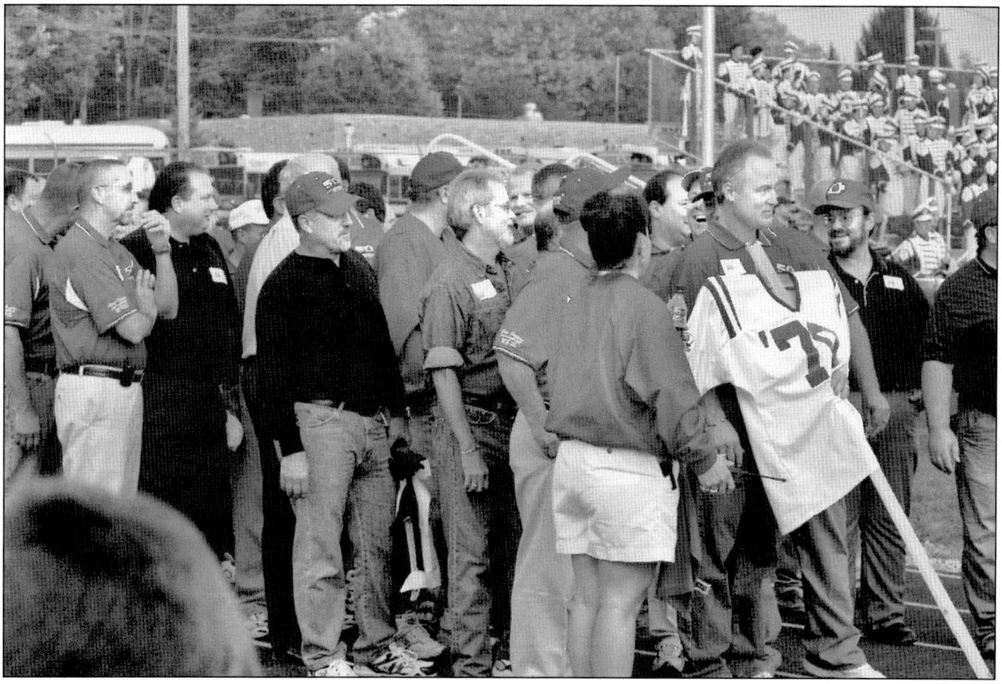

At the 50th anniversary celebration for Bridgeport High School football, these alumni and fans of Bridgeport High School football crowd around Steve Stout, holding up a jersey bearing the number 70 for the BHS players of the 1970s. Other decades were also represented at the celebration. Stout was regarded by some as the greatest football player to ever don a Bridgeport High School jersey. (Courtesy of Dick Duez.)

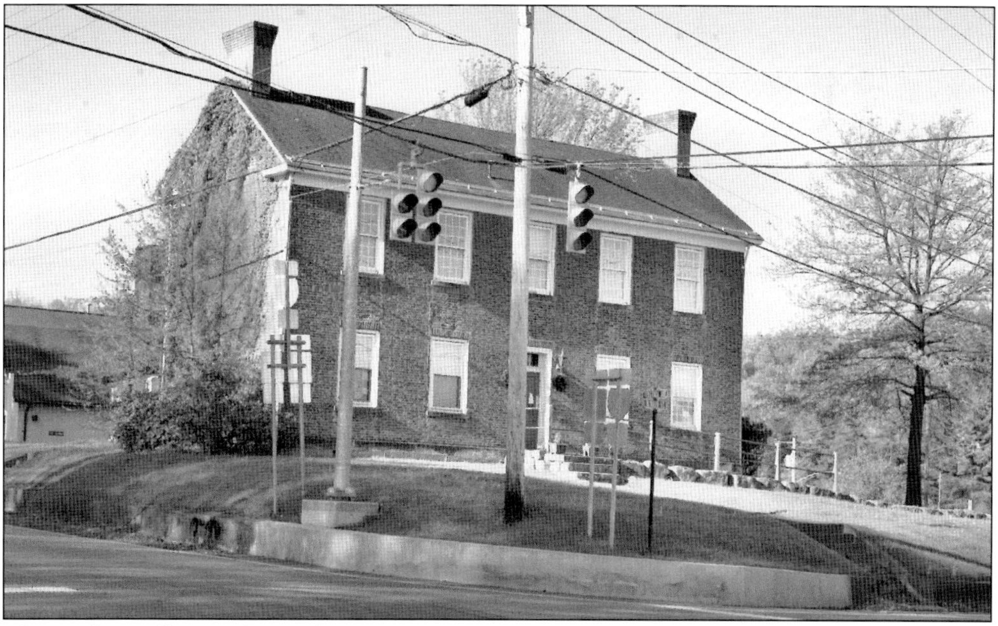

This is the William Johnson house as it appears today. It was built in 1840 on the southwest corner of the intersection of West Main Street and Virginia Avenue. It now houses a day-care center. (Courtesy of Dick Duez.)

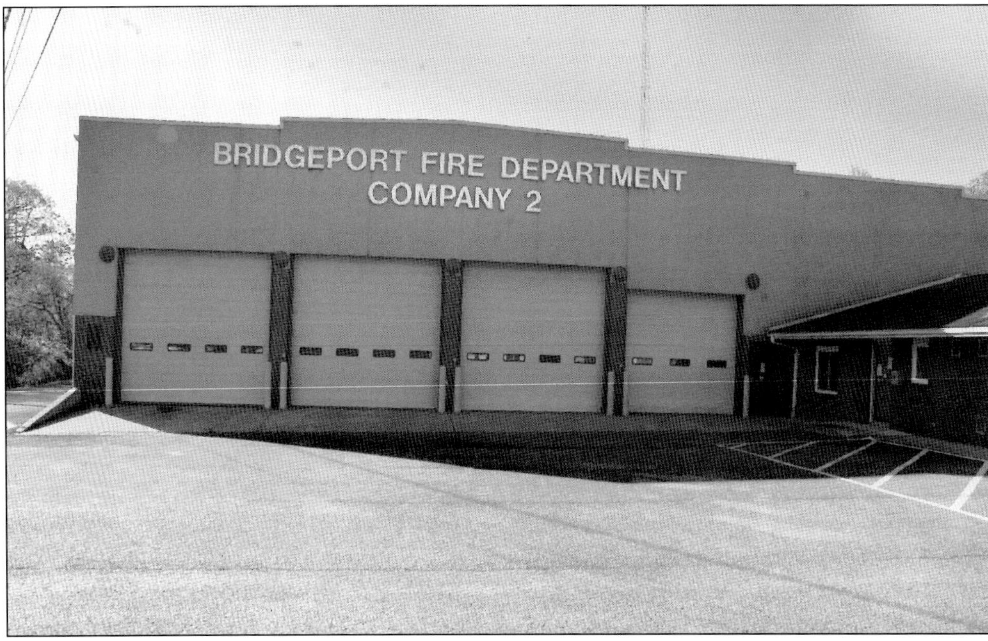

The City of Bridgeport and its residents can be proud of the newest look of the fire station. The former city building can be seen at right. (Courtesy of Dick Duez.)

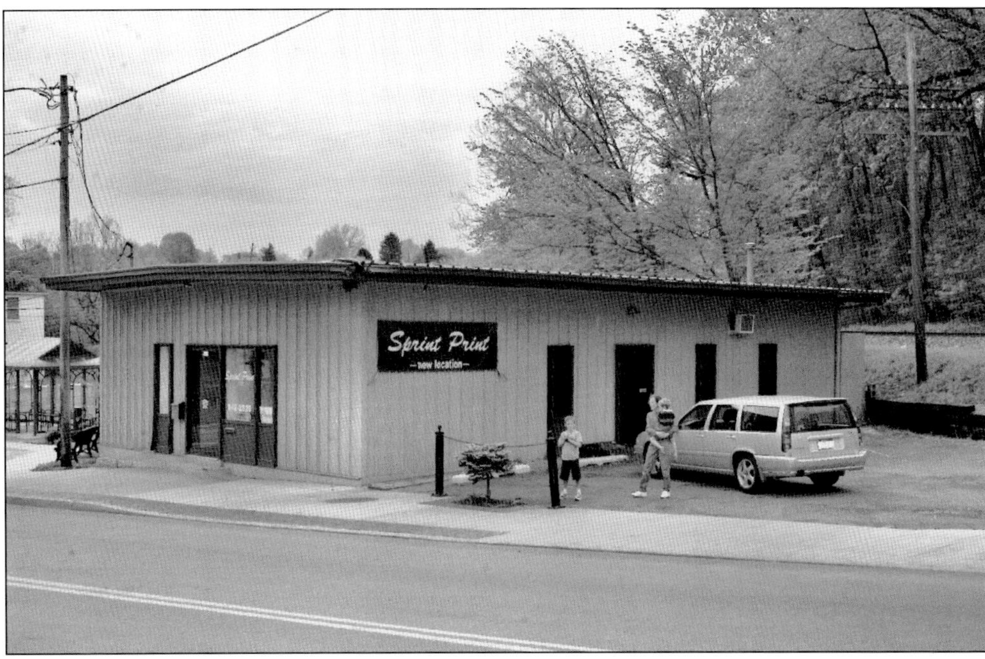

Once the Chevrolet dealership in Bridgeport and later the Handy Shop, this is the Sprint Print, across West Main Street from the Benedum Civic Center. (Courtesy of Dick Duez.)

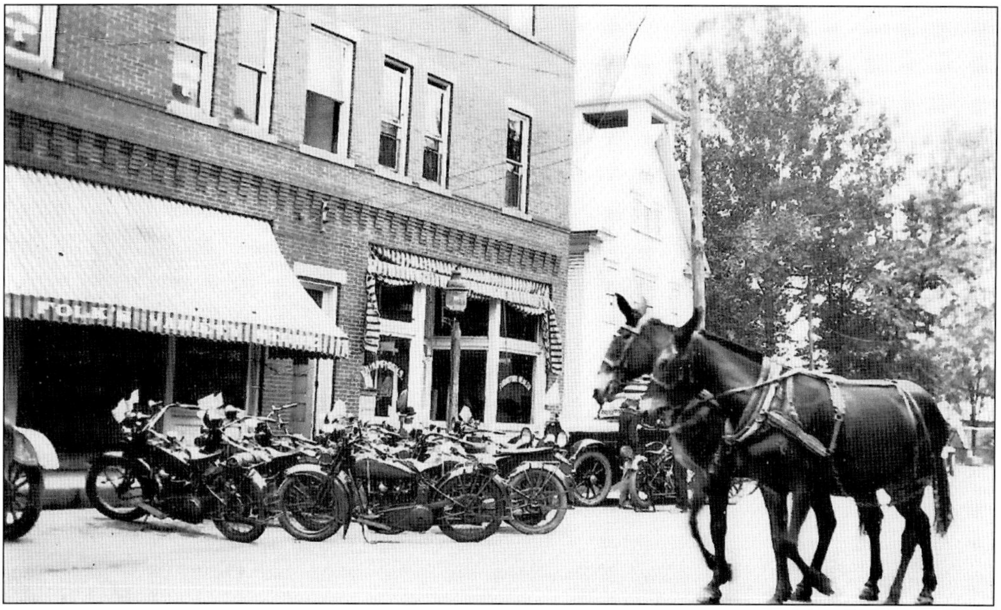

These state police motorcycles are seen parked in front of Folk's Variety Store in 1925 during a celebration marking completion of a concrete highway from Grafton to Bridgeport. (Courtesy of Paul Whiteman family.)

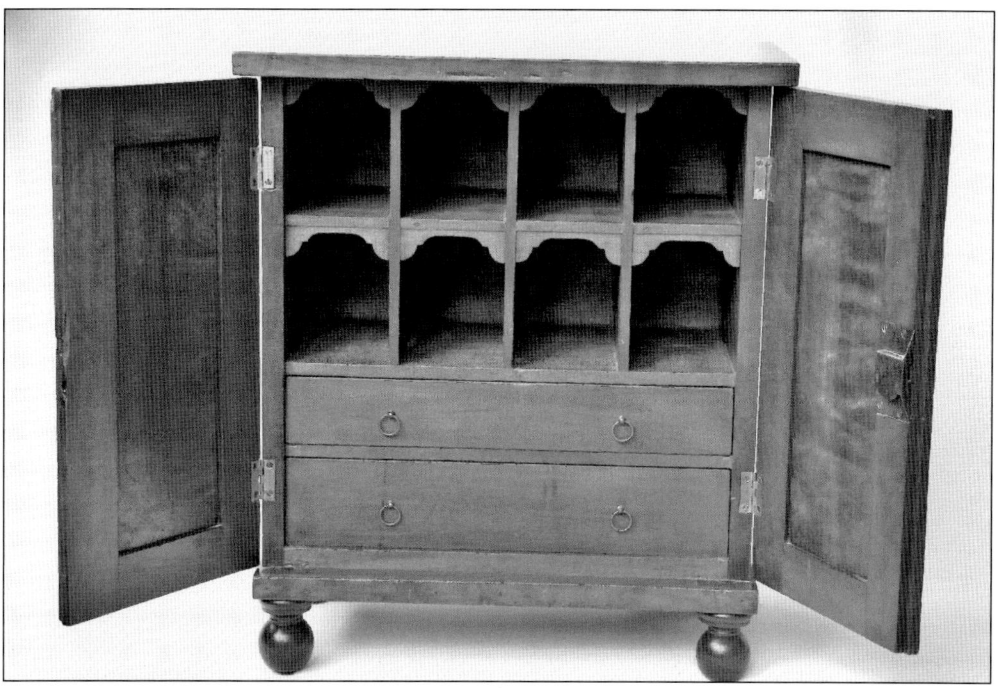

Emanuel Benedum built this small cherry cabinet. He completed it October 1, 1851, in Bridgeport, Harrison County, Virginia. (Courtesy of Dick Duez.)

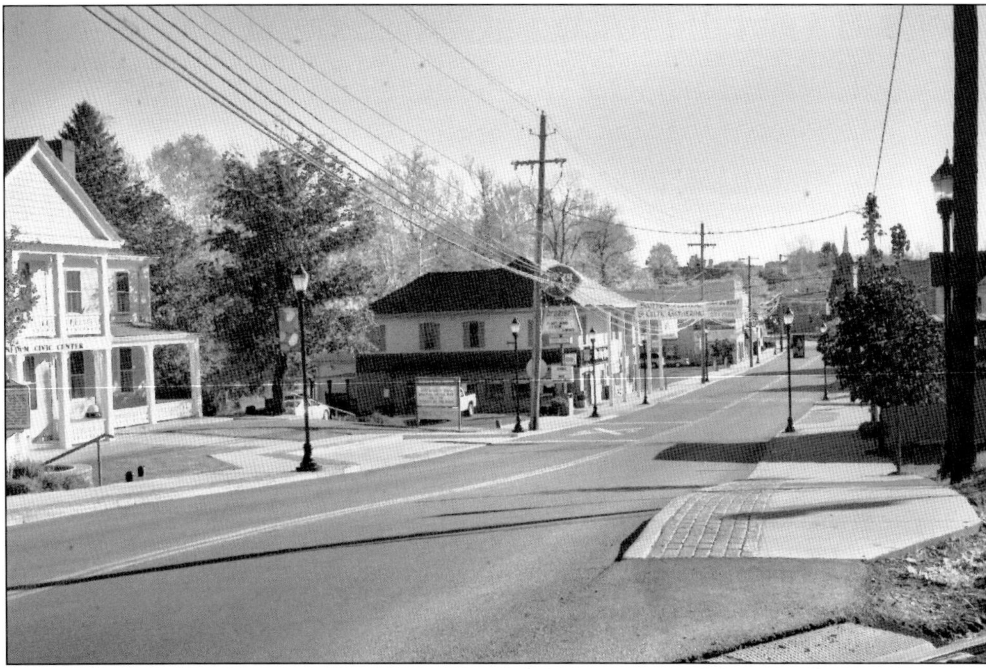

Here's a recent look down West Main Street in Bridgeport. Part of the Benedum Civic Center can be seen at far left. The next building is the Dairy Queen. The picture was taken on a quiet Sunday morning. (Courtesy of Dick Duez.)

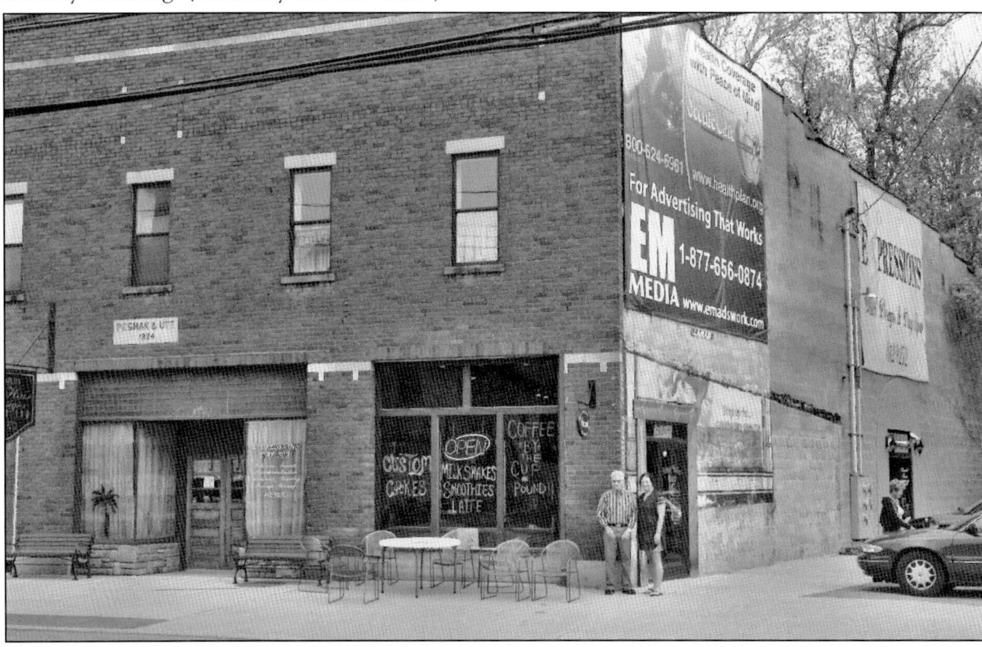

The Peshak and Utt Building, at the corner of West Main and Center Streets in Bridgeport, was built in 1924. It is now owned by Mark Bonamico. His daughter and father-in-law can be seen to the right of the Heavenly Delight shop. Also on the ground floor was the Expressions Dry Spa, at left. The Bridgeport Pottery had an outlet at one time at the right of the building. (Courtesy of Dick Duez.)

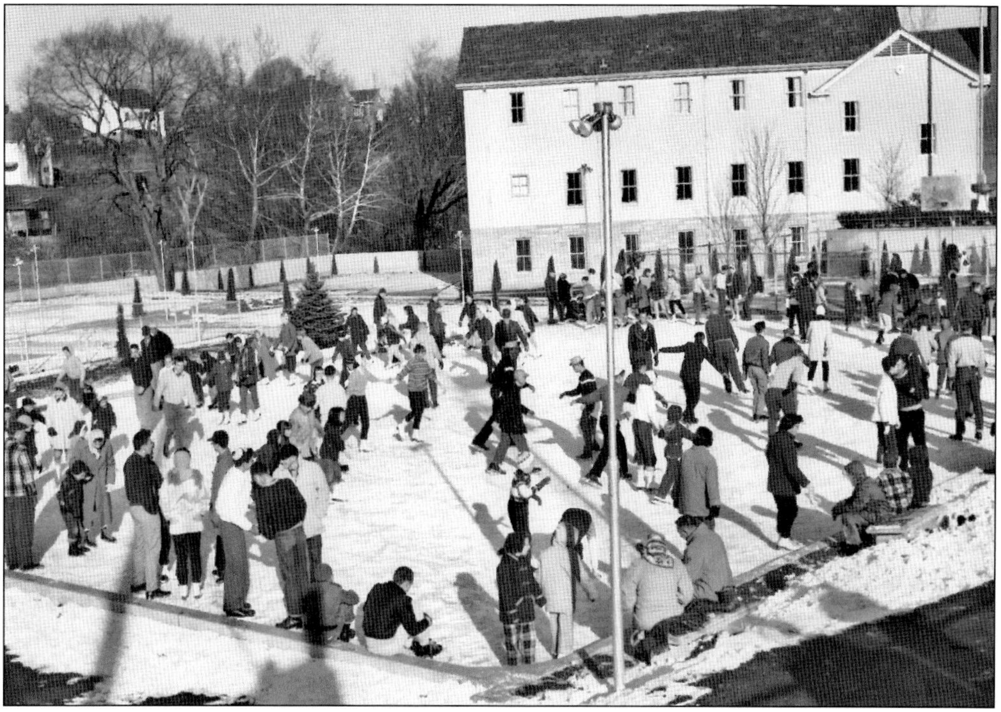

What could be more exciting on a winter day in 1958 than outdoor ice-skating? The newly built Benedum Civic Center is seen in the background. It appears from the photograph that it had snowed shortly before it was taken. (Courtesy of Benedum Civic Center.)

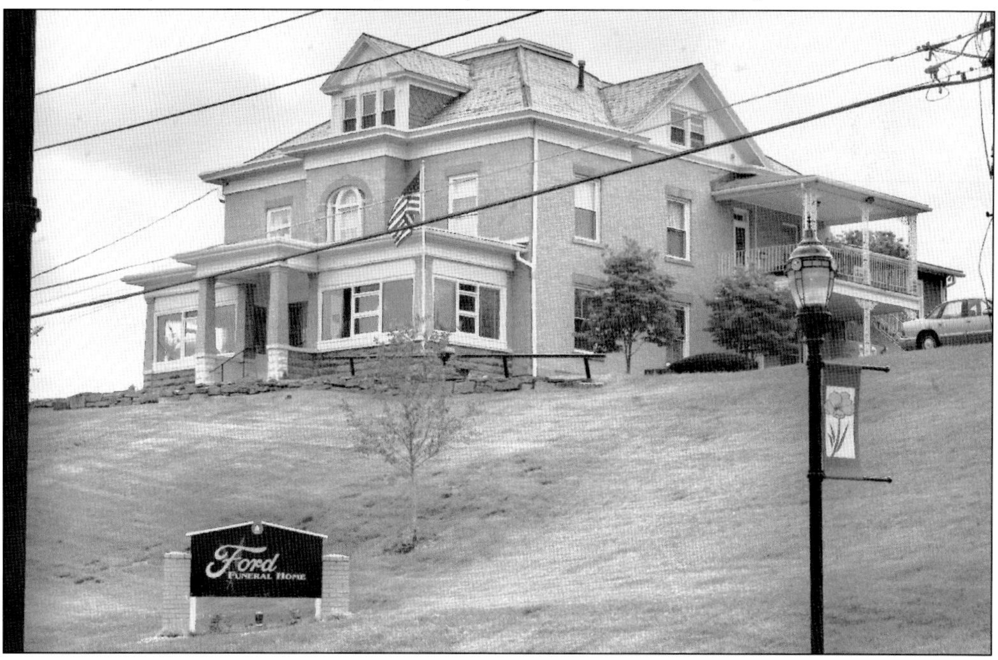

At the top of the hill is the Ford Funeral Home's Allen Chapel. It was once the Bartlett-Tucker Funeral Home and then Tucker-Allen Funeral Home. Bridgeport now has a second mortuary, the Burnside Funeral Home on South Virginia Avenue (State Route 58). (Courtesy of Dick Duez.)

Consistent with our mission to preserve history on a local level, this book was printed in South Carolina on American-made paper and manufactured entirely in the United States. Products carrying the accredited Forest Stewardship Council (FSC) label are printed on 100 percent FSC-certified paper.

MADE IN THE USA